ILLINOIS CENTRAL COLLEGE
PN1995.9.R4
STACKS
Religion in film /
A12900 828139

W9-AQY-249
A12900 828139

The Seventh Seal. Directed by Ingmar Bergman.

Religion in Film

EDITED BY JOHN R. MAY
AND MICHAEL BIRD

THE UNIVERSITY OF TENNESSEE PRESS
KNOXVILLE

Special Consultant for Film Studies
for The University of Tennessee Press : NEIL D. ISAACS

Manufactured in the United States of America
First edition

Clothbound editions of University of Tennessee Press books are printed on paper designed for an effective life of at least 300 years, and binding materials are chosen for strength and durability.

Library of Congress Cataloging in Publication Data

Main entry under title:

Religion in film.

Bibliography: p.
Includes index.
1. Religion in motion pictures—Addresses, essays, lectures. I. May, John R., 1931– II. Bird, Michael S., 1941– . III. Title.
PN1995.9.R4R4 791.43'09'09382 81-23983
ISBN 0-87049-352-3 AACR2

IN MEMORY OF *Arthur Gibson* 1922–1981

are made to world religions or divisions thereof—and there are necessarily many, especially to Christianity—the proper designation is used. Just as the overall structure of the book leads from the universal to the particular, from theory to individual directors and films, so too our concern with religious interpretation flows naturally from the universally religious to the particular religious sensibility. And if among world religions Christianity seems to claim a disproportionate amount of attention, the reader must keep in mind that the writers have acknowledged Christian roots and, more significantly, that Judaeo-Christianity has been the dominant religious influence in the West where film has more obviously flourished, if not excelled.

A word about our usage in quoting film dialogue is in order. Inasmuch as it is still a minority of films whose screenplays are published, we have had more often than not to count, as do most reviewers of film, upon notes taken during actual film screenings. Where the screenplay was available and used, the quotation is acknowledged in the customary fashion. If no source documentation for a quotation is signaled in the text, the authors are indebted to their own notes, which they trust are nonetheless accurate.

To end where I began, it is our conviction that no single interpretation can exhaust the richness of meaning in a film and that whatever remains faithful to the language of cinema preserves its integrity as a work of art, regardless of what depths are plumbed. Perhaps I should simply have said, "Especially if the depths *are* plumbed."

John R. May
March 2, 1981
Louisiana State University

Acknowledgments

GRATEFUL acknowledgment is made to the editors of *Horizons, America, The Christian Century,* and *Journal of Popular Culture* for permission to reuse, sometimes in quite different form, the following material that appeared in their journals: John R. May, "Con Men and Conned Society: Religion in Contemporary American Cinema," *Horizons* 4 (1977), 15–26; Michael Bird, "Film as Hierophany," *Horizons* 6 (1979), 81–97; May, "Visual Story and the Religious Interpretation of Film," *Horizons* 7 (1980), 249–64; Neil P. Hurley, "Inside the Hitchcock Vision," *America,* 12 June 1976, pp. 512–14; Hurley, "Lina Wertmüller as Political Visionary," *The Christian Century,* 17 August 1977, pp. 726–28; and Hurley, "Christ-Transfigurations in Film: Notes on a Meta-Genre," *Journal of Popular Culture,* 13, No. 3 (1980), 427–33. The note on Sam Peckinpah is a shortened version of Chapter One of William Parrill's *Heroes' Twilight: The Films of Sam Peckinpah* (Hammond, La.: Bay-Wulf Books, 1980) and is used with permission.

We are also deeply indebted to Martha Haley for her assistance in preparing the manuscript, especially in its earlier stages, to Mavis Bryant for her interest and encouragement, and to Neil D. Isaacs, special consultant for film books published by the University of Tennessee Press.

Contents

Illustrations

PART I

Approaches to the Religious Interpretation of Film

MICHAEL BIRD

Film as Hierophany

In his classic study of the mythic and ritualistic dimension of religion, Mircea Eliade introduces a concept that serves well the purposes of theological explorations of culture and art. This is the term *hierophany,* utilized by Eliade "to designate the *act of manifestation* of the sacred."[1] This concept is particularly valuable for those explorations that begin with the everyday raw material of existence, for a hierophany is a disclosure of the transcendent or sacred precisely through the material of reality, "the manifestation of something of a wholly different order, a reality that does not belong to our world, in objects that are an integral part of our natural 'profane' world."[2]

The paradoxical nature of reality seen in this light consists in the fact that it discloses not only itself but also another dimension underlying it. "By manifesting the sacred, any object becomes *something else,* yet it continues to remain *itself.*" While particular objects and places have traditionally been set aside in religious cultures as holy objects or spaces, a hierophanous manifestation can occur anywhere. "All nature is capable of revealing itself as cosmic sacrality. The cosmos in its entirety can become a hierophany."[3]

In proceeding from a general theological analysis of culture to a specific consideration of artistic expression—in our case, the film—it becomes necessary to clarify the special relation that film possesses to culture or reality. The popular reference to film as a "window" on culture does not of itself indicate the film–culture relationship, for the open window of Coventry Cathedral with its view of the surrounding urban-industrial setting is surely not attuned to culture in the same manner as the translucent apertures of Chartres or the sensual windows of the Art Nouveau Age. If film is to be considered as the locus of a hierophanous manifestation, it becomes imperative first to consider in what way culture itself can be said to point beyond itself toward the transcendental dimension, and then to specify the unique position among the arts that cinema holds in the realistic representation of the world. In any cinematic theology one is required to delineate the objects of study; in the case at hand, they are culture, art, and film.

CULTURE AND TRANSCENDENCE

In the theological analysis of artistic experience, account must be taken of a fundamental problem: how does the artist render visible that which is inherently invisible? The gravity of this problem goes unrecognized when we restrict our investigation to works of art whose subject matter is the tangible manifestation of a particular religious cultus. Such works do not of themselves point toward the religious depth underlying particular religions and all of culture itself.

If art cannot give a direct representation of the dimension of the holy, it can nonetheless perform an alternative religious function: art can disclose those spaces and those moments in culture where the experience of finitude and the encounter with the transcendent dimension are felt and expressed within culture itself. Where art is unable to portray the face of God, it can on the other hand show man's struggle to discern the divine presence. While lacking the capacity to represent infinity, art can locate, emphasize, and intensify those strivings in culture for the transcendent that occur at the boundary of finitude. In this way, the theological function of art is that of bringing before the viewer a picture of culture's own striving for the infinite.

In what sense does culture "point" toward the transcendent dimension? Among theologians who take up this theme, Paul Tillich has perhaps developed the most succinct and comprehensive analysis. This "striving" toward the holy is expressed in various ways by Tillich, notably in his idea that "reason asks for revelation," seeking an ultimate unity of its conflicting and unresolved polarities. "The quest for a reunion of what is always split in time and space arises *out* of reason and not in opposition to reason. This quest is the quest for revelation."[4]

If the possibility of a religious art is predicated upon the representation of culture itself in search of its spiritual depth, it is useful to consider briefly Tillich's investigation of "culture pointing beyond itself."

Tillich understands reality in such a way that it tends simultaneously toward self-sufficiency and toward self-transcendence. In culture it is possible to behold a vacillating movement to and fro between these extremes, "between the desire to be a mere vessel and the desire to be the content."[5] In the twentieth century this pointing-beyond is particularly well expressed in existentialist language. For Tillich, it is the "age of anxiety" that most movingly presents us with the limits of finitude and the awareness of nonbeing. Yet it is just this emptiness that places us in a condition of "openness" to the Unconditioned, as for Luther the discovery of one's radical sinfulness is the starting point of redemption by grace. This paradoxical discovery of finitude and openness to the transcendent is, according to Tillich, the moment at which culture inevitably is driven beyond itself to an awareness of its "depth," the dimension of the holy:

> A present theology of culture is, above all, a theology of the end of culture, not in general terms but in a concrete analysis of the inner void of most of our cultural expressions. . . . Often one gets the impression that only those cultural creations have greatness in which the experience of the void is expressed: for it can be expressed powerfully only on the basis of a foundation which is deeper than culture, which is ultimate concern, even if it accepts the void, even in respect to religious culture.[6]

CULTURE AND "REALISM"

The specific manner in which Tillich conceives the self-transcending tendency of reality is by means of the idea of "belief-ful realism." This concept seems paradoxical (faith transcends every reality, but realism questions every transcending of the real). Yet for any theology that seeks to articulate religious experience "from below," it is realism rather than idealism that provides an orientation and a starting point. For Tillich, idealism fails to attain the fullness of a genuinely religious understanding because it idealizes the real rather than transcends it by looking within it. "Hence we are led to the result that faith and idealism, just because of their radical tension, belong together."[7]

Realism is an ambiguous term and has frequently been used to express a world view within which the religious proposition is unnecessary or untenable (it describes, for example, Marx as well as the proponents of mechanical realism that he dismissed in *The German Ideology* and elsewhere). Therefore, Tillich distinguishes his "belief-ful realism" from either a "technological realism" (which recognizes only the immediately visible world) or a "mystical realism" (which eliminates the material world as an obstacle to the ascending mind). "Belief-ful realism" seeks paradoxically the power of being in a concrete situation in time and place: "The power of a thing is, at the same time, affirmed and negated when it becomes transparent for the ground of its power, the ultimately real. It is as in a thunderstorm at night, when the lightning throws a blinding clarity over all things, leaving them in complete darkness the next moment. When reality is seen in this way with the eye of self-transcending realism, it has become something new."[8]

In such moments and places, reality is no longer self-sufficient, but is rather experienced as opening itself to its ground or depth. It is "transparent" as we feel ourselves to be grasped by ultimate power. Tillich describes this experience as one of "simultaneous crisis and grace." The present situation in culture is always characterized by "critical elements," that is, by forces of disintegration and self-destruction. Such moments become crisis in the religious sense (i.e., judgment) by uniting with the experience of grace. "Belief-ful realism" expresses the fundamental ambiguity in which discernment of the transcendent is made possible by turning in the direction of the real. Indeed, the problem of religious language itself is rooted in the necessary task of designating this paradoxical relationship of realism and self-transcendence: "Religious terms are the more adequate, the more they express this paradox in its depth and power."[9] "Belief-ful realism" represents, then, a religion-and-culture typology which is at once "realistic" and "self-transcending," which in its seeking of the Unconditioned focuses upon the concretely finite, which perceives culture both as surface and as transparent to its religious depth.

Tillich's "cultural theology" is, in a sense, a theology "from below," juxtaposed to the Barthian school and its emphasis upon the Word as starting point. Indeed, Tillich's understanding is consciously attuned not only to reflections by fellow theologians but also to the speculations of artists, poets, and philosophers. The theme of artistic expression as an indication of the "soul of culture" appears repeatedly throughout both the systematic and the occasional writings.

Corresponding to Tillich's theological analysis of culture (belief-ful realism) is the fascinating contribution of the French philosopher Mikel Dufrenne, whose *The Phenomenology of Aesthetic Experience* and related works set forth the notion of a "sensuous realism" as a means by which the viewer is brought into an encounter with a "depth" in the world.

It would be worthwhile to sketch briefly the highlights of Dufrenne's analysis, particularly his treatment of aesthetic experience, as a last preliminary stage before taking up the question of how cinema may be said to possess the capacity for enabling the spectator to discern strivings in culture toward its sacred dimension.

A distinctive feature of Dufrenne's examination of aesthetic experience is his rejection of the heavily subjectivist orientation of most twentieth-century philosophies of art. Unlike the views of many art historians and philosophers (Collingwood and others), in which art in its extreme form may be equated with the most random utterances of the artist or responses of the spectator, Dufrenne places the subjectivity within the reality of the art object itself. It is true for Dufrenne as with other writers that the aesthetic object must, in a sense, be "completed" by the spectator. Yet, his understanding is at odds with those views that examine aesthetic experience principally in terms of perception. Dufrenne claims rather that, "in opposition to every subjectivism, we must state that man brings nothing to the work except its consecration."[10]

Dufrenne's emphasis upon the concrete and the real, echoed also in the philosophies of Sartre and Merleau-Ponty, is expressed repeatedly by the term *sensuous.*[11] Aesthetic experience means that a work of art is encountered at the level of the sensuous, which for Dufrenne implies not only the material of the object but also the mode of the subject, a "bodily reception." According to this view, "meaning is not primarily something that I think with detachment but something that concerns and determines me, resonating in me and moving me. . . . Meaning is a demand to which I respond with my body."[12]

A convergence between Tillich's idea of a "belief-ful realism" and Dufrenne's concept of "the sensuous" occurs at the point at which each of these writers speaks of an implicit transcendence or depth underlying reality. Dufrenne refers to a *Real* that underlies the *real.* This *Real* "seems to solicit disclosure,"[13] by which art serves as expressive agent. How is this dimension of the *Real* encountered in aesthetic experience? According to Dufrenne, the encounter of the world through art is always an experience that leads the spectator beyond the level of reflection to the level of feeling. It is feeling that enables an encounter with *depth,* rather than merely the surface of reality. "Feeling is that in me which relates to a certain quality of the object through which the object manifests its intimacy. . . . Feeling reveals being not only as reality but also as depth."[14]

The idea of depth as a personal hiddenness of spectator and also of the art work, expressed in feeling, is finally the point at which the phenomenological analysis of aesthetic experience opens itself to an ontological or transcendent analysis: "Feeling distinguishes itself from presence in implying a new attitude on the part of the subject. I must make myself conform to what feeling reveals to me and thus match its depth with my own. For it is not a question of extending my having (étendre mon avoir) but rather of listening in on a message (attendre un message). That is why, through feeling, I myself am put into question. . . . To feel is in a sense to transcend."[15]

Dufrenne's imagery frequently likens "reality" or "the real" to a person, an other, who has already spoken and who awaits my response. The *real* is not a passive dimension, but rather has its own subjectivity, anticipating my reply after discerning, through the agency of art, an articulation of its meaning. "The real expects its meaning to be spoken."[16] Through art I gain access to the real (and being). Dufrenne's most striking description of the relationship between art and reality is provided in the statement, "Since art's mission is to express this meaning—we must say that reality or nature wills art."[17]

The theologian and the phenomenologist share in their analyses of culture and transcendence an emphasis upon the real (Tillich) or the sensuous (Dufrenne). Both stress the importance of the concrete, of tangible reality, as the focal point of ontological analysis, opposing the views of idealism or supranaturalism, which lead away from the everyday real. For both Tillich and Dufrenne, the object perceived turns out in fact to possess a subjectivity (Tillich conceives a work of art that "speaks" or "moves" toward the spectator; Dufrenne refers to the ability of the aesthetic object to "take the initiative" and of the real that "expects its meaning to be spoken").

FROM ART-AND-REALITY TO FILM-AND-REALITY

In the foregoing discussion, drawing from the writings of the theologian Paul Tillich and the philosopher Mikel Dufrenne, attention has been focused upon the search for the transcendent dimension by means of a "realist" analysis which takes as starting point the "here-and-now" of existence. The question of the relationship between perceiving subject and encountered reality must take into account the further question of the relationship between art and reality. For the purposes of developing a theology of film, this means a consideration of *cinematic* art and reality.

A principal difficulty, if not the primary obstacle, in the development of a theology of film is the problem of how to place cinema within the category of "art" at all. Although film long ago won its battle for respectability within the arts, the early arguments for its prestige frequently had the unfortunate consequence of denying its essential qualities in order to fashion it after other art forms (especially painting) whose relationship to reality is generically at odds with that of cinema.

Much of the early defense of "film as art," argued in the 1920s by Paul Rotha, Ernest Lindgren, Rudolf Arnheim, the Russian theorists Eisenstein and Pudovkin, and others, sought to establish the aesthetic virtues of film by seeing in it a potential for transformation and abstraction comparable to that of painting. Indeed, the emergence of cinema coincides historically with the appearance in painting of non-objective approaches—Surrealism, Dada, Metaphysical Art, Cubism, and Futurism. It is noteworthy that the chief defender of the artistic potential of the "newest art," Rudolf Arnheim, resorted to the subjectivist canon of theories of painting of the time, which emphasized the almost God-like role of the artist as shaper and transformer of reality: "In practice, there has always been the artistic urge not simply to copy, but to originate, to interpret, to mold."[18] For Arnheim, art is distinct from "mere" imitation or representation—art is a creative transformation rather than "mechanical reproduction."[19] Arguing that film art follows the same age-old principles of every other art, Arnheim actually expresses horror at the prospect that film makers might give in to the easy temptation to use their medium for photographic-recording purposes, rather than to exploit its artistic-creative potential: "Reproduction that is true to nature provides the thrill that by the hand of man an image has been created which is astoundingly like some natural object. . . . Apart from rare exceptions, only our modern age has succeeded in approaching this dangerous goal. We know that the very powerful and widespread rejection of modern art is almost entirely supported by the argument that it is not true to nature. The development of film shows clearly how all-powerful this ideal is."[20]

It is interesting to note Arnheim's caution against the hazard of permitting film to merely represent, rather than artistically transform, the raw material of nature: "There is a serious danger that the film-maker will rest content with shapeless reproduction."[21]

This understanding of film as interpreter of reality was echoed by most other critics as well. Ernest Lindgren phrases the art-as-transformation theory still more sharply: "Only if the film itself can be utilized to *mould and shape the event* (italics mine), to express an attitude toward it, has it any claim to be an art form."[22] This formula was perhaps most evident in the theory and work of the major Russian film makers, exemplified in Pudovkin's comment: "Between the natural event and its transformation on the screen there is a marked difference. *It is exactly this difference that makes film an art.*"[23]

The consequence of these "formative" theories is that film becomes art only when it moves beyond its recording potential and makes use of its manipulative devices, particularly editing and montage. It is no wonder that these early critics had little to say on behalf of the documentary, and that they reserved their highest praises for films such as Eisenstein's *Battleship Potemkin* with its meticulous editing and its array of montage sequences and images.

The two principal tendencies of film theory—formative and realist—came to establish themselves from the first days of cinema. These alternatives were already evident in the work of two of the earliest figures in film making, Lumière and Méliès. Lumière's first films recorded seemingly mundane events, signified by such simple titles as *Baby's Breakfast, The Card Players, Lunch Hour at the Lumière Factory,* and *Arrival of a Train.* They are portrayals of "nature caught in the act."[24]

At the opposite pole from Lumière was Georges Méliès, who created extravagant and surrealistic sets, substituting staged illusion for everyday events, and who augmented perception with fantastic adventures of the imagination. His films are excursions into inaccessible fantasy worlds, represented by such productions as *An Impossible Voyage, The Haunted Castle,* and *A Trip to the Moon.*

THE AESTHETIC REALISM OF FILM

The aesthetic defense of cinematic realism, a dramatic rejection of the formative theory of Arnheim and others, did not surface in a noticeable manner until the 1950s. Its chief spokesmen were André Bazin, Henri Agel, Alain Bandelier, Amédée Ayfre, and others in France, and, almost simultaneously, Siegfried Kracauer in Germany.

Bazin began his reformulation of classical film theory by revising the art-reality formula that had been dominant in the 1920s. Where it is the function of "art" to transform nature (referring particularly to painting), it is the "virtue" of photography, according to Bazin, to record nature as objectively as possible. Photography and cinema possess an *inherent* realism in that their relationship to nature is chemical. The consequence of this ontogenetic link between medium and nature is that the role of human subject is drastically minimized: "For the first time, between the originating object and its reproduction, there intervenes only the instrumentality of a nonliving agent. For the first time an image of the world is formed automatically, without the creative intervention of man."[25] In an even more vivid distinction, Bazin argues, "All the arts are based on the presence of man, only photography derives an advantage from his absence."[26]

This defense of the unique aesthetic realism of film is echoed in the writings of Bazin's German counterpart Siegfried Kracauer, in the latter's criticism of films that seek to be "artistic": "These films organize the raw material to which they resort into some self-sufficient composition instead of accepting it as an element in its own right. In other words, their underlying formative impulses are so strong that they defeat the cinematic approach with its concern for camera-reality. . . . All in all, films of this type are not only intended as autonomous wholes but frequently ignore physical reality or exploit it for purposes alien to photographic veracity."[27]

For Bazin, as well as for Kracauer, the unique opportunity available to film is the proper disclosure of reality, not its reinterpretation. The film maker's eternal temptation is to follow the cause of *art,* which "overwhelms reality."[28] This special potential of film is expressed by Bazin as one of opening the doors of the world to the attentive spectator. "The aesthetic qualities of photography are to be sought in its power to lay bare the realities."[29] Film does not "add" anything to reality, as is required by the art-as-transformation theory. Rather, it uses the raw materials of reality to disclose reality.

To be certain, the film maker's subjectivity is never totally absent from even a documentary film, particularly at the level of *selecting* the reality to be recorded; nevertheless, in the arguments of Bazin, Kracauer, and other "realist" spokesmen, reality awaits the opening of a door, and it is the physical relationship of film to reality that permits the greatest access to re-

in effect, one places them in aesthetic structures which have not been well thought out to receive them, or if one arrives at them with an insufficient sense of their incarnation and transcendence, their normal 'load' of mystery and the supernatural dissolves, leaving only traces of moral reminiscences, a few manufactured 'miracles' or some artificial 'idealizations.'"[35]

In these realist statements, one finds something of a *creed* in which cinema's technical properties become the vehicle of meditation. This creed requires a particular spiritual sensitivity in which the sacred is sought as the depth in reality itself. This understanding of reality has been expressed by film makers who adhere to this realist manifesto. A notable spokesman is the French director Robert Bresson, who said with respect to his 1956 film *A Man Escaped*: "I was hoping to make a film about objects which would at the same time have a soul. That is to say, to reach the latter through the former."[36] This understanding of reality pointing toward its depth is determinative of Carl Dreyer's realism in his film *The Passion of Joan of Arc,* as that realism is described by Henri Agel: "Thus Dreyer remains in love with the epidermic surface of things and beings. It is because Dreyer is concerned with this 'physicality' of his characters (Joan of Arc), because 'each pore of the skin is made familiar to us,' that the transfiguration of a tormented human substance can become a Christ-substance."[37]

This assessment of Dreyer's work suggests its affinity with Dufrenne's maxim, "To feel is, in a sense, to transcend." Indeed, paralleling Dufrenne's view that "the real solicits disclosure" or that "the real expects its meaning to be spoken" is Agel's lively description of nature as the "mother of images" (borrowed from Gaston Bachelard): "Nature is poetic in some of the images it offers because it is itself a poet in its own way, because it is not the Mother Earth, the Lucretian Venus, but is rather the mother of images. . . . These images are pregnant with their own world—their unveiling goes beyond the given data."[38]

The linking of images with nature, and of beauty with meaning, both ideas that are to be found in Dufrenne's phenomenology of aesthetic experience, means that a realism which is poetic (sensitive to beauty) is simultaneously a realism which is spiritual (sensitive to meaning). Cinema can heighten our perception of things pointing beyond themselves by means of a realism which is sensitive to the paradoxical character of reality, to be aware of a "distance within the heart of things," to see a thing "present in its very absence, graspable in its ungraspability, appearing in its disappearing."[39]

The critique of "contrived religious films" expressed variously by Bazin, Ayfre, Agel, and others brings to mind in a most pointed fashion the ancient debate over the religious function of Christian icons. Those who wished to save (or later reinstate) the tradition of icon-veneration were compelled to demonstrate that popular piety could comprehend the distinction between image and ultimate reality. Is this not the theological dilemma posed by the very idea of a "religious film"? The most dreaded consequences of misguided icon-veneration (giving way to worship of the image itself) are surely not lost in Agel's criticism of Eisenstein, for example. Eisenstein's films, for all their majestic drama and technical beauty, are works that seek to create experience rather than engender it. The spectator's encounter with reality or its ground is undermined by an art that overwhelms nature, as in the case of so many of the supposedly religious films in which an arsenal of cinematic devices is called upon to "create" supernatural happenings. Like Agel, Bandelier warns, "the image is not reality, it only gives the illusion. . . . It is necessary to recognize that this is the road paved by so many good intentions, from the great biblical 'machines' to the small hagiographic 'tricks.'"[40]

Common to all of these writers in defense of the inherent realism of cinema is the recognition of a spiritual orientation necessitated by the medium itself. This is cinema's "openness" to the cosmos which it seeks to represent. According to Kracauer, the film possesses, along with the novel, a capacity for the "rendering of life in its fullness" and a "tendency toward endlessness."[41] This openness allows the film to begin with reality and advance toward its spiritual depth. "The cinema is materialistically-minded: it proceeds from 'below' to 'above.'"[42] The encounter with the sacred cannot bypass the material world to which the film medium is so closely wedded. As Kracauer puts it, "we cannot hope to embrace reality unless we penetrate to its lowest layers. . . . But how can we gain access to these lower depths? One thing is sure, the task of contacting them is greatly facilitated by photography and film, both of which not only isolate physical data but reach their climax in representing."[43]

Of the films frequently emphasized by proponents of realist cinema when drawing attention to film's sacred or hierophanous possibilities, one work particularly worthy of consideration is Robert Bresson's *The Diary of a Country Priest.* Bresson repeatedly intensifies moments and events so as to create a paradoxical realism, in which the humblest subjects reveal within them certain stirrings of the sacred: "Yet, without obviously changing anything in this mediocrity and apparent filthiness, without expressionistic lighting or musical effects, simply through the precision of directing and acting, everything is turned inwards and takes on a different meaning. Beyond this surface, which is still and sordid as ever, one can glimpse another dimension: that of the soul."[44]

Bresson is one of few directors who has managed in his cinematic realism to focus simultaneously upon the familiar and the mysterious. Some writers (Ayfre, for one) have called attention to both the realism and the strangeness of Bresson's films. This is especially the case with Bresson's actors, who according to his dictates concerning realist cinema refrain from acting at all. Instead they pose as transparent figures through or behind whom a spiritual significance is discerned. "They open up a literally endless perspective on themselves, on the universe, even on the whole of existence. In fact there is always something fundamental and mysterious in them which escapes us."[45] This mysterious and discomforting quality is later described by Ayfre as the surface indicator of the depth of experience that each character possesses. Indeed, the significance of the mystery of characters for Bresson's style may be precisely that his style suggests his self-understanding as an artist, who is "not a god, but a mediator" (Agel), who lets his own experience of the awesome distance from the Absolute become that of the spectator. Concerning Bresson's characters, it is suggested that "they are people whose ultimate secret is beyond them, too."[46] The mystery of negation and affirma-

STILL 2: *The Diary of a Country Priest*
Directed by Robert Bresson.
The Curé of Ambricourt (Claude Laydu) pauses for a moment in writing the diary of his journey through doubt, suffering, and anguish toward death. The very emptiness of his stare is paradoxically filled with mystery as the viewer is drawn into the abyss of his loneliness. The simplicity of Bresson's style signals the sacred.

tion, of absence and presence, is expressed by Bresson by means of a realism that is "charged" – Raymond Durgnat calls it an "intense realism."[47] Durgnat argues that the power of feeling of such a physical work is what enables *The Diary of a Country Priest* to express the spiritual: "This intense 'physicality' and 'materialism' explain how the film feels so intense even though, dramatically, there is so little emphasis and so many omissions."[48] This description of Bresson's style echoes Dufrenne's understanding of "the sensuous" in aesthetic experience and its power of expression through feeling.

In Bresson's films, the human boundary-situation is reached through his frequent intensification of the physical world, accompanied by a dissolution of that very world. In *The Diary of a Country Priest,* for example, the conclusion of the film is marked by an absence of the foregoing world of "physicality" and "materiality" in favor of a sustained photograph of a plain cross accompanied by the voice of the Curé de Torcy which describes the death of the priest. Bazin says of this conclusion, "At the point which Bresson has reached, the image can become more eloquent only by disappearing altogether."[49] In this view, the final scene gains its power from the realism of the film, by which the spectator experiences simultaneously an interrelatedness of affirmation and negation: "For the final shot of the cross acquires its meaning by its relationship to the drama, by the way in which it 'supplants' the physical world by the venerable cinematic principle of montage. Bresson's film is firmly rooted in the physical – in the reflection of cancer in the priest's face – and the cross is an image of its total sacrifice. The spiritual has devoured the flesh."[50]

Bresson's realism is manifest in the almost non-expressive acting which he imposes upon his cast, a minimization which seems to produce that transcendence of which Ayfre speaks – a translucence to another world underlying surface appearances. Speaking of a man's countenance as the "imprint of his soul," Bazin says of Bresson's portrayal of faces: "What we are asked to look for in their faces is not for some fleeting reflection of the words but for an uninterrupted condition of soul, the outward revelation of an interior destiny."[51]

The simultaneous recording of absence and presence is itself reflective of the function performed by the aesthetic work upon the spectator in the representation of the holy. Bresson's cinematic representation would appear to fulfill that conception of the paradoxical possibilities with respect to the aesthetic expression of transcendence: "Because the image is always a fragile victory over the void or silence, it teaches us the fragility of the visible, of the sensible, and finally, the fragility of existence. . . . The image itself is at the crossroads of happy plenitude and tragic emptiness, of being and of being born."[52]

The fragility of existence—this continual discovery in the reality of the void, the silence, the boundary situation, becomes the point at which we are brought face to face with the reality of negation, behind which lies its ground, the affirmation within which it resides (for Tillich, the experience of nonbeing enclosed within being). While for Luther man is accused by the law and driven to the realm of grace, so for Agel, Ayfre, and Bazin, cinema offers a self-reflection indicating the limits of the film maker as artist, yet attests to his potential role in pointing to an initiating presence which comes from the "other side" of reality, and which is met in an open encounter. Speaking of the inner horizon of perceived objects, Agel describes the capacity of cinema to "allow nature to speak" precisely by recognizing the limits of film and by "not forcing nature, but rather on the contrary, respecting the given reality."[53] In this capacity, cinema becomes not so much a voice of the artist but rather a diaphragm which is sensitive to the speech of the cosmos waiting to be heard. In Eric Rohmer's words, "a film does not give a translation. . . . The cinema is an instrument of discovery."[54]

In their descriptions of the revealing power of film's realistic properties, these varied writers offer what is in effect a theological manner of speech. This is particularly the case in the frequent acknowledgments of a depth-dimension in reality that is discernible through the transparency of the celluloid medium as it attends to its proper function of "laying bare the realities," rather than remaking the world in the name of art.

The ontological significance of cinematic style is given expression in terms of the subjectivity that resides in the object to be represented aesthetically, for man stands in the presence not of a thing, but rather of an encountered subjectivity in the real. The aesthetic act becomes not a controlling gesture, but rather a participation, in the form of a response to an initiating otherness. Man is not dismissed in his artistic role, but neither is he the ultimate creator of meaning—he is subordinate to being, to whose initiative he makes his reply. Man becomes a listener to the speech of the sacred; cinema, in its inherent realism, allows for the possibility of a hearing and a re-presenting that need not be lost in the temptation of contrivance. This is the mysterious dimension, the "real world which he has been trying to forget" in his ephemeral creations,[55] but which from beyond the boundary-situation continually offers itself to the open eye and the attentive ear.

At this point we are brought back to Tillich's theological analysis of culture pointing beyond itself. In the outlook of these cinematic realists, a "depth of being" is encountered by the long, steady stare at reality. In this view we have a cinematic equivalent to Tillich's description of finite existence as "restless autonomy." Tillich's claim that "the here-and-now is the place where our existence must find an interpretation if it is to find one at all"[56] is expressed aesthetically by Dufrenne's concept of the sensuous: "The aesthetic object is above all the apotheosis of the sensuous, and all its meaning is given in the sensuous,"[57] and cinematically in Agel's view that film by nature does not "translate" so much as it "discovers" reality.[58] Insofar as culture possesses the quality of leading out of itself and toward the religious dimension as the realm of self-transcendence, cinema as a representational art, by remaining true to its realistic properties, is invested with the power for the disclosure of that continual striving within culture toward the holy, by bringing us into the presence of the real as it "calls up" meaning from its inner depths. While "the subject is necessary to open a path for the flow of meaning, the object is necessary to propose it."[59] Cinema, because of its ontogenetic relationship to reality, enables the possibility of listening to "something deep which blossoms out, where the world is a depth which the object calls up whose meaning resonates in increasingly distant echoes."[60]

In its intensification of those movements and spaces where

reality is seen to be straining in its anguish, its void, its divisions, toward its boundary-situation, at which the dimension of depth breaks in, cinema becomes at least the witness for and frequently the agent of "the manifestation of something of a wholly different order, a reality that does not belong to our world."[61] At such points film becomes hierophany.

JOHN R. MAY

Visual Story and the Religious Interpretation of Film

THERE is that playfully mystical moment toward the end of George Lucas's *Star Wars* when Ben/Obi-Wan Kenobi assures Luke Skywalker that the Force will be with him. Now it is only in the most tenuous of senses that a scene such as this has anything to do with "religion *in* film," and there would seem to be even less consolation here for those whose concern is "religion *and* film," except as an instance of the metaphor of tradition. The scene appeals explicitly to the belief of religious man that the power sustaining him comes from beyond and endures and that somehow he must have the possibility of religious experience opened up for him: in this sense religion is *in* the film. What is of far greater interest for my purpose here is the way in which the scene symbolizes the "handing on" of knowledge or insight: and in this sense it is a metaphor that speaks directly to our contemporary concern about the interrelationship of religion *and* film.

The academic study of religion and film needs the reassurance that the force of interdisciplinary tradition is behind it, along with the respectability that comes from tradition. Such a statement, of course, presupposes the legitimacy of the union of religion and film, but that presupposition is surely secure today despite the early assumptions that with the emergence of cinema as an art form modern culture was at last dealing with a purely secular form, the child of technology. The source of cinematic art like any art is still the human psyche, and the physical reality of man and nature will surely remain the substance shaped by the director in celluloid. It is inconceivable, moreover, that either the human psyche or nature will ever be drained of at least the vestiges of the sacred. Archetypal image and sacred object remain irrepressible. There are, however, theoretical assumptions buried here that must indeed be exhumed, and acknowledged, but to do so now is to advance our investigation beyond the point of reasonable development.

The interdisciplinary tradition mentioned above is, obviously, that of literature and religion. Film and literature are not, of course, synonymous. Those who have reduced the interpretation of film to an analysis of its literary components – its plot, characterization, and most specifically its dialogue – have done it a disservice. There is no denying that these literary elements are part of the total fabric of our culturally typical films. However, the academic discipline of Literature and Religion has much more to offer the religious critic of cinema. In fact, if the religious interpretation of film is to be built on rock rather than sand, it is imperative that critics of the religious dimensions of film take advantage of the rich quarry of insights that have resulted from more than thirty years of interdisciplinary studies in literature and religion.

The debate over literature and religion has yielded three readily discernible theoretical approaches to their interrelationship that correspond roughly to historical stages. The interdisciplinary dialogue that I refer to here was grounded both on the recognition that literature and religion shared a common element – language – and on dissatisfaction with the prevailing moralistic approach to their relationship – censorship. *Heteronomy* ("the law is outside") aptly describes the position taken by T.S. Eliot in his famous essay "Literature and Religion" in *Essays Ancient and Modern* (1936).[1] Since Christian faith is superior to literature, Eliot argues, the norm for judging the *greatness* of literature can only be found outside of literature; namely, in theology. Eliot agreed that one should determine "what is literature" on the basis of literary norms alone; in the evaluation of greatness, though, he insisted that faith must intervene. This stand is also called "Christian Discrimination"; it assumes that one will, in the final analysis, distinguish clearly between works that are Christian and religious and those that are not.

A second position was advanced by Paul Tillich in his essay "Religion and Secular Culture," published in *The Protestant*

Era (1948).[2] Working from his view of faith as an expression of man's ultimate concern and of God as the ground of man's being, Tillich proposed *theonomy* ("the law is God") as the surest synthesis of literature and religion. Neither literature nor religion, he proposed, can sit in judgment of the other because neither is an absolute. God is the law, the root of religion's purpose and literature's meaning. This approach, also called "Christian Amiability," is inclined to consider religious most if not all literature worthy of the name inasmuch as it inevitably deals with the concerns of man. Even the most destructive urges can be considered expressions, however negative, of man's deepest need, which is to locate the ground of his being.

The most recent contribution to an understanding of the relationship between religion and literature is too broadly based in a variety of theorists to be credited to any one critic of culture, yet there is an essay by R.W.B. Lewis entitled "Hold on Hard to the Huckleberry Bushes" that describes *autonomy* ("the law is within") as clearly and pointedly as any.[3] The norms for judging the achievement of a discipline must come from within that discipline; thus, literature cannot be subjected to an alien norm any more than theology and religion can. Critics respecting the autonomy of literature would not shrink from the responsibility of investigating the religious dimensions of literature; they would not, on the other hand, expect to find religious or theological terms as such in a work of literature. Any discussion of the religious tone of a work would have to be done in the language of the text itself. Lewis' title, taken from Emerson's metaphor for the reputed quality of early Puritan perseverance in faith, says it all: any estimate of a work's openness to a particular religious vision will be successful only if the critic "holds on hard" to the concrete details and specific images of the text in question. In effect, the critic must be content with the literary analogues of religious or theological concepts; for example, mythic structures and archetypal images and symbols.

Paul Schrader's *Transcendental Style in Film* was the first book-length essay on religion and film to attempt a demonstration of the cinematic *style* that he perceived to be most akin to high religious art.[4] Acknowledging the various levels of meaning attached to "the transcendent," Schrader—whose screenplay for Scorsese's *Taxi Driver* is ample refutation of the biographical assumption[5]—draws exciting parallels between the cinema of Yasujiro Ozu and Zen painting, of Robert Bresson and Byzantine iconography, and of Carl Dreyer and Gothic architecture. In the films of these three directors, Schrader discovers that "disparity of abundant and sparse means" (transcendental style) which triggers awareness of the Transcendent or Wholly Other. Transcendental cinema transfers empathy to the viewer inasmuch as the image stops at the moment of maximum conflict, permitting the viewer to keep going *into* the image. Although Schrader deals with directors out of particular religious traditions, he limits himself to an analysis of that cinematic style which is universally religious and, in the final analysis, denies the possibility of sectarian criticism.

Building on insights from the theory of literature's relation to religion, one would have to admit that it is not only possible but also desirable (if not necessary in some instances) to interpret film from both a religious and a sectarian point of view. The critic, however, is least susceptible to that ever-present subjectivist tendency in criticism—and this is my main contention here—when he respects the autonomy of cinema as an artistic form. Any discussion of the religious or sectarian dimensions of cinema ought to be confined, as far as possible, to the language of film itself. The critic's task is to discover the cinematic analogue of the religious or sectarian question.

A brief survey of some of the problems related to interpretation based on heteronomous and theonomous assumptions is perhaps the best introduction to my proposal here of another way of viewing films from a religious perspective that respects their autonomy. I am indebted to Charles Moeller's "Religion and Literature: An Essay on Ways of Reading"[6]; variations on Moeller's ways of reading literature are clearly discernible in the body of recent film criticism from a religious perspective.

To approach the assessment of a film's religious dimension from the viewpoint of *biography* is the most obvious instance of heteronomy in film criticism. It is a more general application of the type of evaluation that frequently springs from references to a director's avowed intentions in making a particular film. Such criticism is heteronomous because it measures the film not on its merits as cinematic art but against the scale of "religious background" or "expressed intention." Religious critics of this sort will acknowledge that this director is "an avowed atheist," another "a confessing Christian," and that yet another was dedicated "to translating the essence of Eastern mysticism into moving images." The assumption is that intention or belief—or lack of it—inevitably governs artistic achievement. One need think only of Pier Paolo Pasolini's *The Gospel According to St. Matthew* to know how stunningly the personality of Jesus can be portrayed by a communist, in a film that must rank with the very few successful lives of Christ that have been made. On the other hand, for the discerning eye, even expressed intention yields "good fruit" occasionally, as Franco Zeffirelli's *Jesus of Nazareth,* produced for television, proves. If one keeps in mind that no single Gospel attempts to give us the whole picture of Jesus—even the four taken together leave many tantalizing questions unanswered—the carefully understated Nazarene of Zeffirelli's "good news" and even the dynamic urgency of Pasolini's more limited Marxist Jesus cannot fail to bear genuine theological meaning.

Pauline Kael in a talk to the Arts Club of Chicago in 1975 was treading dangerously close to the rigid line of heteronomous interpretation when she observed that some of the most exciting films being made in America in the 1970s were being made by Catholic directors. What saved her assessment of the works of Robert Altman, Francis Ford Coppola, and Martin Scorsese from being simplistically "biographical" was the fact that she was relating evidence of their "sensuous style" to a certain shared richness of ethnic religious background—not to religious belief or practice or intention. In asserting that they were "dealing truthfully with the American experience for the first time," she was, once again, tracing film style to psychic heritage.

One can also call those films religious that treat explicit religious material, and many critics still do—though less so now than a few decades ago. The explicit material of religion ranges all the way from full-length religious epics—lives of the saints and founders of religions as well as sacred narratives of a mythic nature—to the passing acknowledgment of religious persons, places, and things. Hollywood has made the biblical epic a household word for the western world, but the alert viewer knows instinctively that the cause of art—and religion—usually remains unadvanced. Adaptations of the literal level of biblical stories may help to popularize sacred names and events—more often only stars and studios—but they do little or nothing for Christianity except confirm a fundamentalist mentality. The truth of the matter is that if the critic takes explicit religious narrative, situations, or images to be a sure indication of a religious film, he is in deep trouble.

Cecil B. DeMille's *The Ten Commandments,* for all of its literal fidelity to the Book of Exodus, does little more than create the impression that God is the Divine Impressario. The Catholic rite of exorcism is elevated to the level of the parting of the Red Sea in William Friedkin's *The Exorcist,* but when all the swelling subsides and the blood and vomit dry it is a simplistic view of Satan rather than a hint of the genuine experience of evil that has been served. Despite all apparent good intentions, it is horrifying peripheral images of the abuse of religion that linger—a young girl tortured in the name of healing and a crucifix used as a vibrator. Just how confusing the appeal to explicit material can be is clearest in some rare, but happy instances in recent cinema where the explicit appears to be ridiculed. Lina Wertmüller, with a sympathetic eye for the details of human inconsistency, carefully notes the presence of images of Madonna and Child as the patron saints of the bordello in *The Seduction of Mini* and again in *Seven Beauties.* These latter films, I have tried to show elsewhere, *are* nonetheless open to a religious interpretation.[7]

A third form of heteronomous interpretation dwells on the thematic element in films, specifically on those themes that are traditionally related to religious belief or moral conduct: mystery, transcendence, evil, brotherly love, freedom, grace, conscience, sex, and so on. At a certain level of interpretation it is usually impossible to avoid discussing theme; any work of art with the literary basis that film has will invariably reflect the sensibility of historical periods and the history of ideas. Heteronomy is most obviously the basis of criticism, however, when particular themes are isolated, discussed, and judged apart from their total context in the film. Such was the case in the religious press at the appearance of Bernardo Bertolucci's *Last Tango in Paris*; his treatment of human sexuality was discussed without consideration of the film's evident apocalyptic ambience. I am not concerned here, therefore, with scholarly efforts at assessing the thematic tone of a period—for example, the treatment of sex in the cinema of the 60s—but with the sort of heteronomous treatment of religious themes in a particular film that imposes categories from without or judges the effectiveness of a theme according to doctrinal presuppositions. Discussions of "Spirit" theology based on references to the Force in *Star Wars* or of the appearance of "angels" at the end of *Close Encounters of the Third Kind* typify the imposition of extraneous categories, whereas the rejection of Peter Brook's adaptation of William Golding's *Lord of the Flies* because it is too Calvinistic reveals doctrinal assumptions not shared by all.

Religious interpretation of film that focuses exclusively on the development of characterization is very often based on theonomous assumptions. The experience of the cinematic hero—today, almost invariably, an un-hero—in relation to the world of the film offers us our clearest insight into the film's feeling for existence; it is the surest way a director has of elaborating a world view. Eric Rohmer's *My Night at Maud's* portrays a world in which the principal character rejects a liaison with Maud because he perceives design, not chance, at the heart of existence. Such a basic feeling for life is not always as evident, however, as it is in Rohmer's film.

What makes the discovery of a character's deep motivations theonomous is the presumption on the part of the critic that fundamental concern, however articulated, is at the core a quest for the ground of our being, namely God. Where this presumption in favor of religion makes its most sophisticated appearance is in the analysis of certain films of the acknowledged European masters, like Bergman, Fellini, and Buñuel.

STILL 3: *Close Encounters of the Third Kind*
Directed by Steven Spielberg.
The descending alien spaceship transmits a sense of harmonious acceptance in proportion to its celestial radiance. That the earthlings who sought an actual encounter with extraterrestrials are finally rewarded is a mythic expression of hope that is far more fundamentally religious than the possibility that the visitors may be angelic messengers.

Is the acknowledgment of the "silence of God" equivalently an act of faith? If one answers the question affirmatively, as is so often the case with the "religious" interpretation of the films of these directors, then one has skirted the shores of theonomy if not landed.

What seems more reasonable, to me at least, is the discovery of grounds for claiming in *cinematic* terms that certain films are open or not to a religious world view, regardless of the auteur's reputation or of a presumption in favor of ultimate concern. An approach to the religious interpretation of film that respects its autonomy as an art form will, by definition, have to explore those dimensions of the formal structure of film that represent the visual analogue of religious or sectarian questions. As the debate over the relationship between literature and religion has so clearly demonstrated, one need not demand that the language of religion or theology be present in a work for the work to be considered religious. In fact, one cannot demand it if the autonomy of a work of art is being respected.

What are the religious questions or the basic areas of religious concern that we must seek the cinematic counterpart of? Huston Smith in his immensely popular *The Religions of Man* speaks of three questions that have divided religious man, and it is significant to note that they are all expressed—as Jesus' parables about the kingdom are—in the idiom of everyday discourse.[8] Concerning our relationship with the world, we ask: "Are we on our own or can we count on support for our endeavors?" Is the universe, in other words, radically indifferent or is it friendly? With a view to others, we inquire: "Are we isolated from others or is it our fate to be linked with them?" Are human beings independent or interdependent? Finally, about ourselves, we wonder: "Is our purpose ultimately a matter of the head or of the heart?" Does human liberation consist in wisdom or in compassion? In religious terminology, we are inquiring about the nature of God, the problem of evil, and the possibility of salvation. Each question poses a dichotomy; the answers sketch roughly the religious differences between East and West. In each instance the first alternative suggests the oriental vision—an impersonal universe, the isolated individual, and release from self through exercises of the mind; the second, the religions of the West—a personal force, social involvement, and liberating love. Within western tradition, Christianity distinguishes itself from Judaism and Islam on each count: Ultimate reality shows itself benevolent in mercy rather than justice; we are impotent of ourselves to dissolve the bonds of our involvement in the sin of the world; and, finally, the release of liberating love comes through the image and power of the self-sacrificing Jesus.

How then does the critic of the religious dimension of film discover a work's openness to the religious or sectarian question? On the level of visual continuity, all of our culturally typical films are stories. Story in film, moreover, is discerned in the formal elements of film—composition, movement, and editing. The autonomy of film is preserved, then, if theological critics view film as *visual story.*

John Dominic Crossan, in *The Dark Interval: Towards a Theology of Story,* develops a convincing case for considering myth and parable as the extremes of story. Myth, he says, establishes world, whereas parable subverts it. "What myth does is not just to attempt the mediation in story of what is sensed as irreconcilable, but in, by, and through this attempt it establishes the possibility of reconciliation."[9] The advantage of myth, then, its basic function, is to establish the very possibility of solution; it is more important, Crossan claims, to believe that solution is possible than ever actually to experience it. Parables on the other hand are meant to change us, not reassure us. Parable like myth has a double function. Crossan explains: "The surface function of parable is to create contradiction within a given situation of complacent security but, even more unnervingly, to challenge the fundamental principle of reconciliation by making us aware of the fact that *we made up* the reconciliation. . . . You have built a lovely home, myth assures us; but, whispers parable, you are right above an earthquake fault."[10]

Between myth and parable, as the extremes of story, there is a spectrum of types that includes satire, apologue, and action. They are worth noting here inasmuch as each of the types is applicable to visual continuity, although myth and parable are more closely related to religious meaning. Sheldon Sacks in *Fiction and the Shape of Belief* provides the intermediate typology of story (based on his reading of eighteenth-century novelists) that Crossan delineates in terms of world.[11] If at one extreme myth establishes world and at the other parable subverts it, apologue defends world, action investigates or describes it, and satire attacks it. The scale of types and their interrelationship can be illustrated as follows:

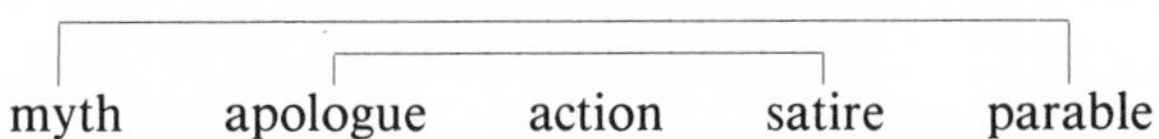

myth apologue action satire parable

Both myth and parable as forms of story are inextricably interwoven into the fabric of religion. They are indeed the principal types of story that most clearly express religious self-understanding the world over; they are the substance of religious heritage. What is most curious about these forms of story—which are as a matter of fact religious in their origins—is that they invariably present themselves as narratives of human conflict, of man with himself, of man with man, and of men among themselves. If we turn to the Judaeo-Christian scriptures for familiar examples, we discover that myth and parable have one further distinguishing characteristic. Yahweh is almost invariably among the cast of mythic characters, especially in the most ancient layers of narrative in Genesis (the garden of Eden, Cain and Abel, the tower of Babel), whereas he is almost never explicitly a part of a parabolic narrative (the Book of Ruth, Ezekiel's parable of the whore, Hosea's wife). This is specifically true of the parables of Jesus in the strict sense—those self-contained narratives that possess microscopically all of the formal structures of normative short fiction. In fact, with the exception of the parable of the Sower, which was consciously interpreted, within the traditions of the synoptic evangelists, as an allegory concerning God, his Word, and man as hearer, the parables of Jesus are not allegories at all but simple narratives that dramatize human conflicts. If they speak of ultimate reality, they do so in the mode of fiction—indirectly, figuratively, symbolically.[12]

There are, moreover, typical structures of myth and parable

that relate to the basic religious questions. Herbert W. Richardson in *Transcendence* speaks of three myths of transcendence in successive historical stages, roughly corresponding to the age of primitive religion, to the Christian era, and to the modern period.[13] They are respectively the myths of separation-and-return, conflict-and-vindication, and integrity-and-transformation. The first two are built obviously on the contrast-resolution structure that Crossan describes; the third fits Crossan's pattern if we understand the presumption of integrity to be antithetical to the actuality of evolving self-awareness. Richardson's historical survey of myths of transcendence serves with only slight modification our present concern for the perennial religious questions—man's relation to the universe (the God question), to other men (the problem of evil), and to himself (the nature of salvation). The myth of separation-and-return speaks as well to the western concept of man's linear origin and destiny as it does to the cyclic pattern of illusory change in the eastern world view. For our purposes here, however, the mythic pattern of Babel-Pentecost is certainly a more appropriate representation of the problem of evil as posed by western religions. Division-and-unity as a narrative structure, therefore, will support the discrimination between the oriental and occidental emphases on independence and interdependence if division is conceived of as "within" and "among," respectively. Conflict-and-vindication, Richardson's second mythic pattern of transcendence, is broad enough then to satisfy the question of salvation as posed by world religion.

The full story of the Christian faith is properly called its myth, too, and any *one* of these mythic patterns of transcendence could serve as its basic narrative structure. It begins with the story of Jesus of Nazareth, but as the fully elaborated understanding or explanation of the existence and action of a faith community it becomes the myth of the Christ. (I appeal here obviously to the nineteenth-century distinction between the Jesus of History and the Christ of Faith.) Viewed as self-understanding or world explained in narrative, the Christian faith is *myth*; but the sort of fully developed self-understanding that is the formula or creed of faith took centuries to develop. The earliest expression of self-understanding that followers of Jesus could appeal to (and I use "Jesus" advisedly) is found, if not exclusively in the *parables* of Jesus, just as clearly there as in his discourses. The point that I wish to make here is that the earliest stages of religious understanding appear in story as parable rather than as fully developed myth. It is imperative for the religious leader to set his teaching apart from the self-understanding that grips his hearers.

There is another irony here. Parable rather than myth accounts not only for the emergence of a new religious story in history, but also for the awakening of religious self-understanding in the individual believer. Historical genesis and personal religious experience share parable as the literary form that most closely approximates the stimulus to religious faith. Jesus' ministry and Christian proclamation through the centuries have depended quite simply, but understandably, upon parable.

Separation-and-return, division-and-unity, and conflict-and-vindication as structures of reconciliation, that is, of myth, are narrative patterns that establish world. Inasmuch as parable emphasizes the absence of resolution, it is endurance of mystery, absence of unity, and perseverance of conflict that typify the parabolic narratives corresponding to the fundamental religious questions. The parables of transcendence like their respective myths would be expressed in terms of the tension of story—without discrimination between East and West—as risk-not-security, weakness-not-strength, and death-not-life. More specifically, Christian parables subvert world by challenging the listener to attend to mercy's unpredictability, to our impotence due to the demon within, and to the anguish of unrequited love. The diagram that follows demonstrates the extremes of parable and myth in relation to the three basic religious questions distinguished according to eastern/western responses; the subheadings under the mythic patterns suggest once again the polarities between East and West whereas the concrete applications of the parabolic structures emphasize specifically Christian responses.

Religious Questions

UNIVERSE	OTHERS	SELF
(ultimate reality)	(evil)	(salvation)
indifferent/ friendly	independent/ dependent	wisdom/com- passion

Extremes of Story

MYTH (establishes world)

separation-and return	division-and- unity	conflict-and- vindication
(closed/open design)	(wholeness/ communion)	(illumination/ saving love)

PARABLE (subverts world)

risk-not-security	weakness-not- strength	death-not-life
(mystery)	(demon within)	(unrequited love)

To simplify story in this way, however necessary for the sake of typology, is of course a distortion; form and meaning are aesthetically inseparable even if analysis and understanding may demand that we distinguish between them. The parables of Jesus of necessity address the principal religious questions. An appeal to them at this point may help to counteract the effect of our unavoidable distinction between structure and meaning. The Workers in the Vineyard (Matt. 20:1–16) and the Talents (Matt. 25:14–30) speak, in the mode of story, to the issue of our relationship to the universe; there is indeed a design that supports our actions, but it is not the way of justice or merit. Unexpected reward awaits the wholehearted laborer, no matter how late he accepts his task; failure to risk losing one's talents is reprehensible. The Unforgiving Servant (Matt. 18:23–35) and the Rich Man and Lazarus (Luke 16:19–31) show indirectly and symbolically how dependent we are upon others and, sadly enough, how often the last to forgive are those who have been forgiven first. Lastly, the Wicked Tenants (Mark 12:1–11; Matt. 21:33–44; Luke 20:9–18) and the Prodigal Son (Luke 15:11–32), if one considers the fate of the elder brother, demonstrate the redemptive value of unrequited love by urging us not to expect to be loved in return.

Doubtlessly an appeal to films in the mythic and parabolic modes would also help both to illuminate principles that have tended toward the abstract and, I would hope, to provide further demonstration of the validity of visual story as a religious/sectarian hermeneutic for film. The examples that follow will include works both open and closed to religious interpretation; moreover, I have made a deliberate effort to avoid examples from the standard canon of "religious" directors. The world Roman Polanski's *Chinatown* (1974) establishes, as it resolves the mystery surrounding Noah Cross's family, is not just indifferent to man's plight, it is cohesively malignant. Evelyn Mulray instinctively claims the impossibility of liberating her daughter from the clutches of her own father, who sired the girl by incestuous rape, when she shouts at Detective Gittes, "He owns the police!" Evelyn nevertheless tries to flee, is shot by the police with her father's consent, and dies slumped over the wheel of her car as Noah soothes his screaming granddaughter-daughter. The stunned Gittes mutters, "It still is possible." The established officers of the law are the servants of organized crime. Inasmuch as the master-steward relationship of the Gospel stories is emblematic of God's relationship with man, *Chinatown*'s world resists appropriation to religious sensibility altogether. It is no doubt a special irony that Los Angeles' Chinatown—an oriental sector—is the setting of the film's despairing climax. The Taoist world view, though closed in design like the Hindu and Buddhist, seems more benign even than the latter; in no one of the three, however, is the universe positively malevolent, as Polanski sees it.

A film in the mythic mode whose pattern like *Chinatown*'s is separation-and-return, but that remains faithful to the cyclic pattern of eastern religious sensibility, is Terrence Malick's *Days of Heaven* (1978). It begins in Chicago after the turn of the century and ends there, or some equivalent midwestern urban setting. Within this narrative frame, the film follows a young fugitive from the law, his mistress, and his younger sister as they survive and even thrive by guileful ingenuity as migrant farm workers in the Texas Panhandle, through a completed cycle of seasons, harvest to harvest. The girls survive to drift again into seasonal opportunity; the men—the fugitive and the Texas farmer—die violently, with nature's fading cycle, as payment apparently for the mixture of good and evil that is in people as well as nature. The fugitive's unlettered young sister, who provides the appropriately distant narration, comments: "Nobody's perfect—you got one-half devil and one-half angel in you." The story, however, is secondary to the opulence and scourge of nature; not even the farmer's wrathful destruction of the crop by fire can match nature's apocalyptic plague of crickets. Nestor Almendros' stunning cinematography emphasizes the insignificant passage of man against the awesome panoply of nature's death and rebirth. Nature's persistent return is highlighted by the beauty of time-lapse photography of the vigorous growth of the wheat seedling. An extraordinarily beautiful shot, showing a wine glass fall to the bottom of a stream, balances the shot-from-below of the fugitive falling dead into the water. Both man and the man-made return to nature.

Moshe Mizrahi's *I Love You Rosa* (1972), as brilliantly realistic as the Hebrew tradition it is faithful to and that Christianity at its best has sustained, plays out its historical pattern of separation-and-return on several levels. Rosa's anticipated reunion with Nessim in death, which forms a frame for the story of their earlier growth in love that overcomes temporal and spatial separation, demonstrates faith in love's power to transcend history in the very act of embracing its trials. This important Israeli film, which North American audiences have unfortunately had little exposure to—at least prior to Mizrahi's more recent acclaim for *Madame Rosa* (1977)—is mythic to the core; its world is one open to historical possibility. On the other hand, the filmic world of Stanley Kubrick, similar to Alfred Hitchcock's, thrives on the unexpected, and most of his major films, like *2001: A Space Odyssey, A Clockwork Orange,* and *Barry Lyndon,* are perfect instances of cinematic parables. Whereas Hitchcock's characters must discover that appearances are inevitably deceptive (see Part III), Kubrick's world is one that in genuine parabolic tradition subverts man's best, that is, his most presumptuous, efforts to begin again, to absolve himself from the often regrettable consequences of his actions.

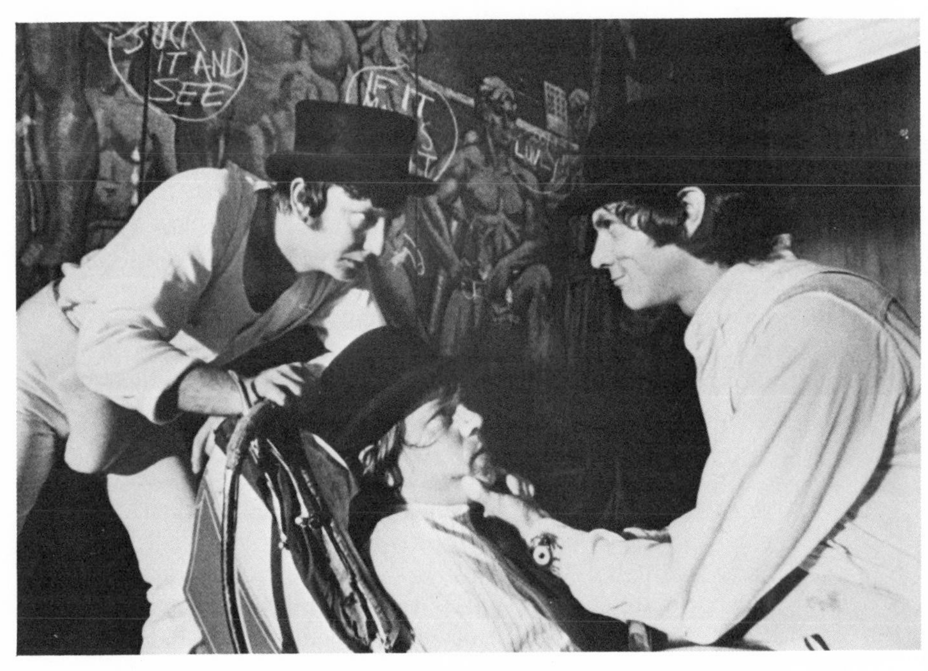

STILL 4: *A Clockwork Orange*
Directed by Stanley Kubrick.
The violent tension between Alex (Malcolm McDowell) and his "droogs" (James Marcus, left, and Warren Clarke, center) is typical of the unresolved tensions within the human personality—and of the apparently irresolvable conflict between the individual and society. One of Kubrick's recurring themes is that humans unwittingly subvert their own best efforts.

The theological critic of film will find that the second major religious concern—the question of our independence or mutual interdependence—often provides the kind of perspective on story that readily aids understanding of the presence or absence of a religious dimension in film. John Schlesinger's *Marathon Man* (1976), probably because of its fidelity to William Goldman's novel, fails to yield a religious reading. The hostile world of espionage and double agents into which Babe Levy is unwillingly drawn in an attempt to satisfy his curiosity about his father's death is one of thinly disguised racism and sanctioned vengeance. The title image, focusing as it does on the individual, suggests both the isolation of the human condition as well as the positive alienation of one who must be perpetually on the run *from* society.

Among the films in the mythic mode, there is no better recent example of the stoic dignity of the isolated self than Michael Cimino's *The Deer Hunter* (1978). This film, like its literary forerunner *The Deerslayer,* celebrates the American as Adamic hero, even if Cimino's variation on James Fenimore Cooper's character is more obviously a victim of the fall. D.H. Lawrence, in his classic essay on Cooper's novel, calls Deerslayer "the very intrinsic-most American, . . . an isolate, almost selfless, stoic, enduring man."[14] What must be inferred from (perhaps imposed upon) *The Deerslayer* is patent—though artistically stated—in Cimino's film. Michael, Cimino's Vietnam deerslayer, prides himself on dispatching a deer with a single shot. With the same coldblooded precision, he survives Russian roulette with the Viet Cong and returns intact, unlike his less fortunate comrades, to begin a new—self-sufficient—life amid the appearances of communion, as he joins the mourners for his friend Nick in singing "God Bless America" at a meal following Nick's funeral. The irony of the film is that both division and unity are attributed to the wholeness of self-reliance.

A film whose world like its title suggests the mythos of interdependence is Joshua Logan's *Picnic* (1956), an adaptation of William Inge's play that transcends the original material. Whereas the play seems obsessed with the oppression of proximity—in a small town—and of the mother-daughter relationship—in the closeness of the family—the film stresses the importance of connections and how self-love grows out of acceptance by others. Hal is a stranger to the midwestern town the film is set in; Madge is a victim of (s)mother-love that alienates her from her family. They share a common problem: they are both attractive young people with low self-esteem. The film *Picnic* resolves the conflict through the love of mutual acceptance that Hal and Madge seem to promise one another. Even though they leave the town separately—to be reunited, we assume, elsewhere—there is a sense of visual reconciliation in the film's final shot as the bus carrying Madge and the train Hal is on merge in the distant open prairie. The limited hope the film offers is unquestionably a mythic affirmation of interdependence.

Robert Altman's *A Wedding* (1978), like most of his films devoted to the importance of ritual in our society, is concerned with the paradox that is central to Christian parable: our very weakness is our strength. Another of Altman's virtuoso orchestrations of characters—forty-eight members, friends, and employees of the two families—*A Wedding* proceeds from the clumsy High Episcopal ceremony conducted by a bishop in his dotage all the way through to the departure of the last guest from the reception. In brilliantly edited, fleeting vignettes, the characters are drawn together, interact, and disclose their secrets—none horrifying, yet all typical of the inside of the American whited sepulcher. When finally we see the black angel peering out from the shrubbery in front of the groom's family mansion, we know that we are taking a look at the darkness in our own hearts. The ability to survive revelation of the worst about ourselves may indeed be our greatest strength.

A film that clearly asks the last of our three fundamental religious questions—where salvation lies—is Woody Allen's *Interiors* (1978). Perhaps because of the later Bergman, whom Allen seeks to emulate, he presents a world that is ultimately cool, if not inimical, to religious sensibility. A marriage of thirty-odd years is broken by the husband's abrupt announcement that he is leaving; the wife disintegrates psychologically as she has apparently done before—but this time completely. Eve is an interior decorator, with a passion for beige and cold, open spaces. "She was always designing interiors for us to live in," one of the three daughters comments. It is a remark that works perfectly on two levels: the physical space has a chilling beauty; the isolation of the characters, concerned only with their inner selves, is appalling. Having abandoned love, if they were ever strong enough to embrace another, they seek within themselves some kind of psychic wholeness, and all that their narcissistic gaze discovers is emptiness.

A highly sophisticated screenplay by Penelope Gilliatt became, in the hands of John Schlesinger, mythic gold. *Sunday Bloody Sunday* (1971) is perhaps the first film to have presented a love triangle with a sexual twist—a male physician and a female employment counselor love the same confused young sculptor, Bob Elkin. They also share the same telephone answering service. The film's added twist is pure irony: the only solution to their entangled love, symbolized by crossed telephone lines and mixed messages, is through the head rather than the heart. When Dr. Hirsh and Alex Greville are faced with the prospect of their lover's extended and perhaps permanent absence—Elkin announces a business trip to America—they discover that they can survive because they *were* something for a time and, more importantly, as Alex comments, because "there are times when nothing *has* to be better than anything." The acceptance of limitation—"there is no whole thing"—is salvation through illumination.

The mythic pattern of conflict and vindication is present too in Milôs Forman's superb adaptation of Ken Kesey's novel, *One Flew Over the Cuckoo's Nest* (1975). The conflict is with the institution, here portrayed as an asylum's staff that is clearly more deranged than the inmates. For leading a rebellion against the establishment, McMurphy is lobotomized, a deliberate attempt to destroy his spirit. Chief Broom, a massive, silent Indian, mercifully ends his friend's life, which is clearly worse than death; the killing, however irrational, is an act of love intended to liberate McMurphy's spirit. The final scene is one of cinema's most extraordinary evocations of resurrection: Chief Broom leaping to freedom through the barred window he has just shattered in a superhuman eruption of strength. If McMurphy suggests the mythic Christ, *Serpico* (1973) is pure parable, a contemporary tale of the unrequited love typified by Jesus' passion. Sidney Lumet's film dramatizes the true story of Frank Serpico, the New York policeman who "blew the whistle" on corruption within the force (leading to the Knapp Commission investigations) and had to flee the country, after attempts were made on his life. He is still a fugitive from "official" reprisal.

In proposing that films be viewed as visual story in order to discern religious potential, I have emphasized the structure of story. I have presumed that the elements of film themselves and their aesthetic effects—the visual and aural medium for story—have been adequately treated elsewhere inasmuch as continuity is fundamental to cinema. The filmic techniques that normally contribute to continuity will support these and other particular structures of story. It is noteworthy, nonetheless, that certain cinematic elements seem more suitable than others for the visual representation of our basic concerns about the universe, others, and self. For instance, composition of frame, camera movement, and editing are most pertinent to shaping a film's world, whereas choice of physical reality, type of shot (camera distance), and mise-en-scène in general are typically more suggestive of human interrelationships or the lack of it. Finally, camera angle and cutting are usually aimed at giving the viewer a feeling for the human subject.

In the last analysis, a way of reading films from a religious viewpoint that respects the autonomy of cinematic art need never describe a film as specifically "religious" or sectarian, for example, "Christian." Although a word is obviously shorter than a phrase and the tendency to abbreviate appealing, it is more precise to speak of a film's world view as being *open* to a religious or sectarian interpretation or to appropriation for the faith experience. Nor need one, on the other hand, hesitate to say when it is not.

ERNEST FERLITA

The Analogy of Action in Film

In the fall of 1976, a few days after an interview with Lina Wertmüller in Rome, I received a phone call from her secretary. Wertmüller was in the process of writing a new screenplay and she wanted to know the old formula, in English, of the Catholic "Act of Contrition." After more than a dozen tries I finally got it out; the trick was to say it without thinking. The obvious humor in the situation—at my expense—was the repetition into a phone in an open hallway, as people passed, of the words: "O my God, I am heartily sorry for having offended Thee."

Whether or not Wertmüller actually uses the prayer in any of her films, the incident illumines the Wertmüller I am primarily interested in here, and that is Wertmüller the scriptwriter.[1] The scriptwriter is an identical twin of the playwright, when the arts of both the one and the other meet. They meet, of course, at the origin of their work, for both are concerned at that point with the imitation of an action. The scriptwriter like the playwright, after choosing the action to be imitated, will often use an old dramatic device—the analogy of action—in order to deepen the meaning of his work. It is by analogy of action that the possibility of religious meaning is often effectively realized.

The analogy of action is a dramatic device of considerable antiquity. It is at least as old as the Greeks, but is perhaps best understood in the use that the Elizabethans made of it, beginning with the so-called double plot. Aristotle apparently knew of plays with a double plot, one of which ends happily, the other tragically; but in his *Poetics* he considered them less perfect than pure tragedy. It is significant that none of these double-plot plays of the Greeks has come down to us whereas with the Elizabethans it is quite the opposite: we have not only double-plot but also multiple-plot plays, and with a craftsman like Shakespeare these plots have a wonderful interdependence. Shakespeare's artistry lies not in his talent for inventing plots but rather in his remarkable ability to adapt old stories or weave two or more of them into an artistic whole. The unity of his plays is precisely there, not in unity of action understood as that single plot line which Aristotle preferred and the neo-classicists canonized, but in analogy of action, in the interdependence of several stories so juxtaposed one to another that each elucidates the central action, first by its similarity but finally by its difference.

King Lear is double plot executed to its most powerful effect. There is the story of Lear, who divides his kingdom between two of his three daughters, having exiled Cordelia, the daughter he most loves, because he willfully misinterprets her words. There is also the story of Gloucester, who makes his illegitimate son his heir, having banished from his sight Edgar, his legitimate son, because he all too willingly believes that Edgar has been plotting against him. In both stories the father is in turn exiled by the progeny he has entrusted himself to. The question arises: Will fathers be reconciled to their own flesh and blood? Will Lear be reconciled to Cordelia? Gloucester to Edgar? To be reconciled to the alienated (including the alienated self): this is the action of the play. As the characters move not only within their own story but also in and out of the other, the action moves toward reconciliation through all the forms of alienation until it comes at last to the final alienation of death. Edgar is reconciled with his father Gloucester at the very moment of death: the old man's heart, "too weak the conflict to support! / 'Twixt two extremes of passion, joy and grief, / Burst smilingly" (V.iii). Gloucester's death, first by its similarity but finally by its difference, deepens our perception of death in the story of Lear. In that story the action passes into the alienation of death, first Cordelia's, then Lear's, *after* his reconciliation with her. Her death, for him and us, becomes for that reason all the more insupportable: "Why should a dog, a horse, a rat, have life, / And thou no breath at all?" (V.iii).

In Peter Brook's film version of the play (1971), however, a film that reflects the theories of the Polish critic Jan Kott,[2] the modes of reconciliation are so muted that the alienation of death strikes, ironically, with lesser impact.

When we speak of the action of a play, what exactly do we mean? What Aristotle says of tragedy can be said of every play and film: it is an imitation of an action. Certainly he means by action all those things that the characters say and do, structured in such a way as to form a plot with beginning, middle, and end. But Francis Fergusson thinks Aristotle means more.[3] Plot is only the surface level of action; on a deeper level is the underlying movement of spirit. William F. Lynch reminds us, however, that the distinction is not all that clear-cut. "It is true enough that 'plot' is *only* the literal level of the drama, and that it may be looked upon as a mere external level of movement, to be deepened by the insights proceeding from other and deeper levels of action. Yet it is also necessary to remember that, when all these other levels have been gained and added, it is the literal level itself, that is to say, the plot, which has been deepened and illuminated for the content it always had, at least in potency."[4] The distinction between the two levels is nonetheless useful, not only with reference to the same play, but also with reference to *kinds* of plays. There is the kind that offers us escape from reality, and there is the kind that forces us to measure our own reality against it. The former operates mainly on the first level of action, the plot level; the latter, even as it moves horizontally on the first level of action, thickens vertically on the second level, as it traces the underlying movement of spirit. An example of the former would be Agatha Christie's *The Mousetrap,* a murder mystery that has been running in London for over twenty years now. This is not to disparage it, for it is quite entertaining: but once you know the "plot," as they say, you've exhausted it. In fact, the murderer steps forward at the curtain call and says, "Please —don't tell anybody I did it." As an example of the other kind of play, we can do no better than to cite the play from which Agatha Christie took her title, namely, *Hamlet.* It is probably the most challenging play in the whole of dramatic literature, constantly fascinating to actors and audience, constantly forcing both actor and audience to measure their own reality against it. What makes it so inexhaustible is its underlying movement of spirit.

Fergusson's splendid analysis of the play in *The Idea of a Theater* begins by citing those critics who, for all their praise of particulars, consider *Hamlet* to be an artistic failure. Among them, surprisingly, is T.S. Eliot. Eliot finds it formless, lacking a principle of unity, and filled with unexplained scenes, the Polonius-Laertes and the Polonius-Reynaldo scene, for which, he says, there is little excuse. "There is no explanation and no excuse for them," Fergusson argues, "if Shakespeare was merely trying to convey the feeling of a son toward a guilty mother. If he was also picturing the relation of a son to his father, then the whole Polonius-Laertes-Reynaldo sequence makes sense as a comic-pathetic sub-plot, with many ironic parallels to the story of Hamlet and his father's Ghost."[5] The trouble, he adds, is that Eliot and others are looking for the wrong principle of unity; the right principle is precisely the analogy of action.

The analogy of action is akin to Henry James' technical concept of the "reflector," of those "peripheral intelligences" that James used to mirror the central action of his story, revealing it "from various (ironically different) angles." The action as a whole is grasped "only as each character in turn actualizes it in his story and according to his lights."[6] In other words, the various stories with their own characters are analogous; the unity of the work as a whole is to be found in the analogy of action.

The main action of *Hamlet,* as Fergusson sees it, is the attempt to find and destroy the hidden "imposthume" which is poisoning the life of Denmark, and all the characters realize this action "in comic, or evil, or inspired ways." If one describes the main action of a play or film in terms of the relationship of characters—an approach I prefer—situating it more clearly on the first level of action, the plot level, the action not only expands horizontally by analogy but also thickens vertically (again by analogy) as it moves through deeper levels. The main action of *Hamlet* in terms of relationships, then, is to avenge the death of a father.

Once Hamlet determines that his uncle Claudius, the present king of Denmark, is his father's murderer, he feels himself called upon to avenge the murder. As he moves toward the execution of that vengeance, he sees his action in several mirrors, as does the audience. There is Fortinbras, threatening invasion of Denmark, because Hamlet's father had killed in battle Fortinbras' father, the king of Norway. "How all occasions do inform against me," Hamlet cries, "and spur my dull revenge" (IV.iv). There is Laertes, threatening vengeance on Hamlet for killing his father, Polonius. And, of course, there is the play within the play, designed to catch the conscience of the king, which Hamlet calls "the mousetrap," dramatizing the murder of one Gonzago in Vienna. Earlier, a player, at Hamlet's request, had told about the death of Priam, "father" of the Trojans, moving Hamlet to one of his great soliloquies: "O, what a rogue and peasant slave am I!" (II.ii). All these serve as mirrors for Hamlet's action, on one level advancing the plot, on a deeper level clarifying his sense of mission. In the words of Henry James, they serve as "so many distinct lamps," the function of each being to light up the deep design of his life: "There's a divinity that shapes our ends, / Rough-hew them how we will" (V.ii). The action of the drama as a whole, unified by analogy, is seen only as each character moves through it within his own story and in and out of Hamlet's story.

It is interesting to note that in Olivier's film version (1948) two of the mirrors in which Hamlet sees his action are removed: the entire Fortinbras sequence and the player's speech about Priam. Restrictions of time, no doubt, necessitated certain cuts, but Olivier's Freudian interpretation of the play also dictated other cuts; that interpretation, as expounded by Ernest Jones,[7] is a reduction of the play's complexity. It reduces the dynamic interplay of characters to the psychological mechanisms of the Oedipus complex.

Two films with original screenplays in which the analogy of action is effectively used are Ingmar Bergman's *Wild Strawberries* (1957) and Lina Wertmüller's *Seven Beauties* (1975). While the overall structure of *Wild Strawberries* is a literal journey, the inner journey proceeds by analogy of action.[8] Or, to call again upon Henry James, we are constantly shifting

STILL 5: *Wild Strawberries*
Directed by Ingmar Bergman.
Isak Borg (Victor Sjostrom), reliving an episode from his youth in one of the film's dream sequences, eavesdrops on preparations for his uncle's birthday party. Analogy of action proceeds through the union of sight and sound as Isak hears his aloofness described by his cousin Sara (Bibi Andersson), to whom he was secretly engaged at the time.

"from reflector to reflector" throughout the film, each reflector mirroring the central action, revealing it from various, ironically different angles. The central action is, of course, Dr. Isak Borg's; enroute to the city of Lund, he retraces the steps of his life. It is an attempt to face the frozen misery of generations, to feel the ice in the heart and then to move against it. Marianne, Isak's daughter-in-law, expresses and reflects this action when, after accompanying Isak on a visit to his mother, she says: "I thought, here is his mother. A very ancient woman, completely ice-cold, in some ways more frightening than death itself. And here is her son, and there are light-years of distance between them. And he himself says that he is a living death. And Evald [her husband, Isak's son] is on the verge of becoming just as lonely and cold—and dead. And then I thought there is only coldness and death, and death and loneliness, all the way. Somewhere it must end."[9]

Three other encounters serve as reflectors in the film. Isak, in his youth, had loved a girl named Sara and had lost her to his brother. Now, on his journey to Lund to receive an award for his life as a doctor, Isak picks up three hitchhikers: a young girl named Sara and her two male companions. Like his own Sara, she is engaged to one man but is also attracted to the other. Once, in a dream, Isak had said to his Sara: "It wasn't always like this. If only you had stayed with me. If only you could have had a little patience" (222). The second encounter is a near collision with a reckless driver. A man and a woman crawl out of the other car unhurt. "I was just going to hit my husband," the woman says, "when that curve appeared" (195). Isak gives them a lift in his already crowded car, but they continue to tear at each other with such malice that Marianne insists they get out and walk. Later, Isak will say: "It reminded me of my own marriage" (228). The third encounter is brief but deserves mention because it shows us a man and woman apparently content in their marriage and gives us a glimpse of Isak as he might have been. The man, a gas station attendant, recognizes him and says to his wife: "Here you see Dr. Borg himself in person. This is the man that Ma and Pa . . . still talk about. The world's best doctor" (200). Almost to himself, Isak says: "Perhaps I should have remained here" (202). It may be that in service of others the ice would never have formed.

Still another episode brings to the action the lens of a wistful eye. When Isak and Marianne and the three hitchhikers stop to rest at a roadside inn, Isak dreamily begins to recite a poem:

> ISAK: "Where is the friend I seek everywhere? Dawn is the time of loneliness and care. When twilight comes . . ." What comes after that?
>
> MARIANNE: "When twilight comes I am still yearning."

Isak, in the twilight of his life, is still yearning. Is there fire enough to thaw the ice in his heart?

> ISAK: "I see His trace of glory and power, In an ear of grain and the fragrance of flower . . ."
>
> MARIANNE: "In every sign and breath of air. His love is there" (204).

At journey's end the honorary degree is conferred upon him: at journey's end the ice begins to thaw. To be spiritually dead, as Isak sees it in reflector after reflector, is to be buried in the frozen self; to be spiritually alive is to go out to others.

In Lina Wertmüller's *Seven Beauties,* her most ambitious film to date, the central action is survival. The film opens with two men attempting to survive through desertion from the Italian Army. One man, Francesco, had been found guilty by a military tribunal of a previous attempt at desertion and was to be shot the next morning; the other, Pasqualino, had been on assignment to Stalingrad. All too soon they are captured and taken to a Nazi concentration camp. "Not even Dante," Wertmüller says in her script, "could have envisioned a 'hell' like this one."[10] The idea of survival in such a place seems preposterous; nevertheless, it flares up in Pasqualino's fevered brain. His present predicament reminds him, at intervals, of an earlier predicament before the war when he was known in Naples as Pasqualino Settebellezze, or "Seven Beauties," so called because in spite of his ugliness women would lose their heads over him; people said it must have been because he was charmed, he had the "seven beauties." It so happens that he also has seven sisters, beauties none of them, and as the only

STILL 6: *Seven Beauties*
Directed by Lina Wertmüller.
The mirror as literal reflector is only one technique Wertmüller uses in this film to allow Pasqualino (Giancarlo Giannini) to see within himself. He discovers finally what we suspect from the beginning—that he is only the shell of a man. His determination to survive the Holocaust at any price has cost him his soul.

man in the family it is up to him to defend the family honor. When that defense involves him in murder, he shows he will do anything to survive, even if it means giving up his "honor" in order to enter a plea of insanity. After a hectic period in the insane asylum, he is drafted into the insanity of war.

In the concentration camp, Pasqualino tells his fellow prisoner: "Francesco, I don't want to die! I'm young, I have to live, I haven't had a chance to live yet . . . I can't die like this, I've got to get out of here . . . I've got to find a way out . . ." (291). The way he chooses is an act of sheer desperation: he imagines that he still has power to make any woman lose her head over him, even the Commandant of the camp, whom Wertmüller calls Hilde, the Great Beast. For her own purposes, the Commandant strings him along: "Make love to me," she says, "and then I will kill you" (323). But afterwards she makes *him* play the butcher: as block-elder of his barracks, he is ordered to hand over six prisoners for immediate extermination. When the moment of truth arrives, with the entire camp gathered to witness, two men react with vehemence: one is Francesco, Pasqualino's friend; the other is Pedro, an anarchist who has failed in assassination attempts on Hitler, Mussolini, and Salazar. (Earlier this anarchist had proclaimed his hope in "man in disorder," a new type of man, not that "intelligent" type which has destroyed the harmony of nature up to now, but a civilized man, "a man who would be able to find peace and harmony within himself," 295.) Shouting "Man in disorder," Pedro dashes into the latrine and hurls himself into a vat of excrement, and there the guards open fire on him. Francesco goes wild; he shouts abuses at the Commandant and the other officers. Once he is subdued, the Commandant orders Pasqualino to shoot him then and there. "No," Pasqualino cries, "I can't!" "Shoot!" Francesco pleads. "It'll be my freedom. Be brave and shoot. If you don't somebody else will, and I'd rather it was a friend. Shoot!" (332). Finally, after further pleading, Pasqualino pulls the trigger—and survives.

Back home after the war, his mother cries out exuberantly: "You're alive, Pasqualino! Alive!" (334). At this point an actual mirror, through the art of the camera, becomes a reflector of meaning. As Pasqualino stares into the three-panelled mirror, his face is split down the middle by the frame between two of the panels. "There is at first neither Pasqualino nor his full reflection, only a split image shouting duplicity."[11] Finally, when the camera brings his face, undivided, into view, we hear him say: "Yeah . . . I'm alive" (334). In my interview with Lina Wertmüller, I remarked that Pasqualino's salvation was merely to survive; to which she answered: "But of course that kind of salvation is a death."[12] There are different kinds of salvation. When we reflect on Pedro's and Francisco's actions, we can even argue the converse of Wertmüller's statement: "Death is a kind of salvation." Central to the meaning of the film, lit by analogy of action, is that paradox so integral to Jesus' teaching: "Whoever seeks to save his life will lose it" (Luke 17:33).[13]

I am suggesting here that the analogy of action has its own dynamic, and if its progress is not deliberately thwarted it will enter the realm of religious meaning. Its progress is first a *descent* into reality and then an *ascent*. "With every plunge through, or down into, the real contours of being," says William F. Lynch, "the imagination also shoots up into insight, but in such a way that the plunge down causally generates the plunge up."[14] Unfortunately, the imagination does not always make this descent into the real. It may exploit the real or only touch it lightly or recoil from it or face it as something opaque and unyielding, as Lynch shows; but it is a reasonable certainty, he insists, "that an art which really follows the lines of human experience will be following the lines of light and the Holy Spirit, and will willy-nilly get to God."[15]

Following the lines of human experience implies, for Lynch, an exercise of the analogical imagination. Insofar as there are both sameness and difference everywhere in our lives and in our literary images, the *univocal* imagination tends "to reduce everything, every difference and particularity in images, to the unity of a sameness which destroys or eliminates the variety and detail of existence" (113). The *equivocal* imagination, on the other hand, "opts always for difference alone" (114). But "the *analogical* imagination insists on keeping the same and the different, the idea and the detail, tightly interlocked in the same imaginative act" (133). In its passage through the finite on its way to insight, it makes everything radiate the same light and yet its own proper light. Robert Bresson, in an interview about his film *The Trial of Joan of Arc,* said this of his subject: "I see her with the eyes of a believer. I believe in the mysterious world upon which she opens a door and closes it."[16] Whether a writer/director believes in God or not, it seems that he must believe in the possibility of that "mysterious world." He must believe that in his passage through the finite he may indeed come up against the door; otherwise he is not imagining analogically.

But what if a writer/director explicitly denies that belief? If his images had been going one way, must they not now inevitably go the other way? Or will they continue to intimate the possibility of mystery, of transcendence, *in spite of* that explicit denial? In 1976, Bergman declared in an interview that he and God parted company many years ago. "We have nothing to do with each other now. We are on this earth, here, this is the only life, from beginning to end, and when the end comes the light is switched off. You exist and you don't exist. That's the whole thing, the remarkable thing. Life is just as cruel and beautiful as it is, and no God, nobody except yourself and other human beings on this earth, has anything to do with it."[17] For Bergman, if we take him at his word, there is no true passage through the finite; there is no door either at the beginning or at the end. So much for what he says; what he imagines may be something else again. He made *Wild Strawberries* in 1957; it is not clear if at that time he already considered himself an unbeliever, but he has one of his characters (the young girl Sara) say: "How *can* one believe in God!" (211). Still, when we consider the movement begun in Isak, such a statement belongs to the character who utters it and not to the meaning of the film. Isak's icy heart is turned into a heart of flesh: he reaches out to others. Why not to the Other? To that "friend" whose love is "In every sign and breath of air?" The most we can say is that the final images remain open to mystery. That is quite enough.

Lina Wertmüller has also argued against a belief in God, certainly against any institutionalized belief. She told me in an interview:

> I had a conflict with the Church when I was young, a great conflict, which may sound rather silly if I try to explain how it came about in me. I was thirteen years old when I reflected on the first principles of the catechism. I reasoned on this equation that was proposed to me: God is omniscient, omnipresent, omnipotent. Therefore he knows all, he wills all. Then he decided to create humanity *the way it is,* with free will, knowing (because he is omniscient) all that would happen, with man placed within the confines of good and evil and with his great facility for slipping into evil. And so if at the end of all this you propose to me a heaven and a hell, I have to think that this omniscient God knows from the beginning that he will construct a series of eternal miseries. He has himself constructed the whole mechanism, and therefore he is bad! You laugh, but this is what brought a revolution in me. I refuted every concept of faith, didn't I? This was no way to teach me catechism; you ought to tell me rather that God is a mystery.[18]

Her unbelief does not preclude mystery; in her passage through the finite she leaves open the possibility of coming up against that door. What she hopes to express in her films, she says, is her "great faith in the possibility of man becoming human."[19] Pasqualino at the end of *Seven Beauties* is something less than human. Merely to survive is no kind of salvation. Wertmüller equates it with death. We are forced to ask: If that kind is death, what kind of salvation is life? If Wertmüller's art truly follows the lines of human experience, must it not follow the lines of light?

What then is required of the scriptwriter? The scriptwriter must first perceive an action. He perceives the rhythm of it, its beginning, middle, and end. First, the rhythm of its surface level, then its deeper levels of meaning: at any point on that surface level he is prepared to descend. He perceives the action flowing through his characters—through this or that character more clearly than through others—and rising from their depths.

This he imitates, by all the art at his command: he creates situations, words and images, metaphors and music. He moves with his characters on the surface level (the plot) but not only on the surface; he descends whenever he can and creates depth as he goes. As the plot thickens, so does reality. The way in and down is actually the way up and out. Following the line of action is following a line of light. He is moving toward insight. But this coming to insight, in and through his central characters, is paralleled, sometimes ironically, by the analogous progress of his other characters. By following their similar but different ways, he creates other lines of light. He does not distort, he does not deflect them. He trusts that by their dynamic interplay with the central line of light he will come at last to insight, even if, paradoxically, that insight opens on mystery.

PART II

Cinematic Genres and Cultural Trends

NEIL P. HURLEY

Cinematic Transfigurations of Jesus

WITHIN the genres of motion pictures is a hidden but nevertheless identifiable meta-genre comprising those films which have transfigurations of the Jesus portrayed in the Gospels. Theodore Ziolkowski in *Fictional Transfigurations of Jesus* indicates that, in the nineteenth century, Protestant and agnostic/atheistic biblical scholarship succeeded in breaking the monopolistic grip that the Christian Church had maintained for centuries in its presentation of the Christ of Faith. This led to secular, at times irreverent, interpretations of Jesus in literature and drama.[1] The Gospel narratives became part of the public domain. The Church's patent had run out, so to speak. Thus there emerged through the artist's imagination an array of secular portraits, ranging from Christomaniacs to socialist variations of the Jesus material. In short, the Gospels influenced the literary imagination not by faith but through fascination with a person who, though admittedly historical, remained mysteriously and irresistibly contemporary—independent of faith in him as God and as the savior of mankind.

Ziolkowski identifies some thirty important Christomorphic novels, that is, fictional pieces that though not written from the perspective of faith would be inconceivable without the Gospels and the oral and written traditions regarding Jesus. In my research over the past decade, I have identified over sixty instances of cinematic transfigurations of Jesus, including adaptations from literature treated by Ziolkowski (for example, *Nazarin, The Grapes of Wrath,* and *The Greek Passion,* retitled *Celui Qui Doit Mourir* or *He Who Must Die*).

I do not refer, of course, to the silent celluloid costume dramas that re-created the Gospel narratives, such as Thomas Ince's *Civilization* (1915), D.W. Griffith's *Intolerance* (1917), Fred Nibo's *Ben Hur* (1925), and Cecil B. DeMille's *King of Kings* (1926). These films were the forerunners of extravagant biblical epics such as *The Robe, The Greatest Story Ever Told,* and *The Ten Commandments.* These Hollywood films have stressed the popular human qualities of Jesus and his miracles. The transfigurations of the Gospel messiah I am concerned with here leave more for the imagination and do not try not to offend religious pressure groups. John Ford's *The Fugitive,* based on Graham Greene's *The Power and the Glory,* is an excellent example. Henry Fonda stars as the Mexican "whisky priest" who heroically stays behind to serve his flock even though it means capture, arrest, and execution by the authorities of an anti-clerical police state. He carries his sacred treasure in a vessel of clay, this minister of the Gospel who at one level exhibits all the classic marks of *homo peccator,* the sinful species, and yet serves as an ironic instrumentality of divine mercy. Graham Greene is fascinated by signs that turn out to be countersigns and countersigns that conceal in their essence a sign of transcendence, of true spiritual power. It is sufficient to note at the outset that any discussion of this genre must look at formal patterns of resemblance and not at the theological substance of the life of Jesus as we find it in its exemplary expression in the Gospels.

In modern German philosophy there is a distinction between *das existenziell* and *das existenzial. Das existenzial* refers to the external determination of human life through the cumulative past decisions of others, while *das existenziell* embraces the concrete choices that affect primarily personal lives and secondarily those of others, thus becoming for these persons *das existenzial.* We condition others' lives as we are also influenced by them. The nuance is one pregnant with meaning, especially when applied to the person of Jesus, for he has changed the course of history as no other historical figure. We can appropriate him as Christ in a personal act of faith, but even if we do not our lives are influenced by Christianity and its impact on world history, especially western civilization.

Ziolkowski distinguishes between pseudonyms of Christ as mere extrinsic substitutes for the Jesus of history and faith—the hero as "christlike"—and genuine transfigurations which are imaginative reworkings of that material. Robert Detweiler, in his illuminating essay "Christ and the Christ Figure in

STILL 7: *The Fugitive*
Directed by John Ford.
The total composition of this extraordinary frame is ultimately more significant for the film's transfiguration of the Jesus story than the mere presence of the crosses. The "whiskey priest" (Henry Fonda), despite his weakness for women, refuses to save his life by fleeing his Mexican persecutors; instead, he risks his life for the good of others in the hope of saving his soul.

American Fiction," points out that "the Christ of faith and the traditional Christ story supply the best known, most viable body of material for the expression of meaning in Western culture."[2] The question, however, arises: where is the dividing line between the Christ of a faith community and the Jesus of culture—the capitalist Jesus, the socialist or "comrade" Jesus, the rebel-liberator Jesus of the Third World, the pain-hero Jesus who can be exemplified by any suffering prisoner, victim, worker, or "uncommon" common man?

To speak of cinematic variations on the Gospel material is to recognize both the faith-inspired representations of Christ and the more humanistic, even atheistic, projections of the Jesus persona. Examples of the former would include Carl Dreyer's *Ordet,* Robert Bresson's *The Diary of a Country Priest,* Curzio Malaparte's *Strange Deception,* and Vittorio De Sica's *Brief Vacation;* instances of the latter would be Luis Buñuel's *Nazarin,* John Sturges' *Old Man and the Sea,* Ken Russell's *Tommy,* and Gillo Pontecorvo's *Burn!.* There is, nonetheless, a significant difference between Jesus transfigurations in the narrow sense (where the secular literary and historical traditions serve as a subtext for the film) and Christ figures (where the notions of messiahship, divinity, or resurrection are demonstrably at work). Henceforth, we will consider these the major divisions of the meta-genre of cinematic transfigurations of Jesus.

A clear instance of an explicit Christ figure appears in Alfred Hitchcock's *I Confess.* Fr. Michael Logan (Montgomery Clift) learns that Inspector Larrue (Karl Malden) has a motive for proving he killed a lawyer who blackmailed Ruth Grandfort (Anne Baxter), the priest's sweetheart from pre-seminary days. It is clear that Logan's walk through the streets and along the heights of Montreal is a *via crucis,* a passage from Gethsemane to Golgotha. First he espies a photo on a newsstand of a man being arrested, then he sees a male mannikin with no head, a reminder of his possible fate; then he walks uphill in front of a basilica. The camera tilts down at an angle, framing the priest in the background, while the foreground is dominated by an alabaster statue of Christ laboring under his cross. Father Logan makes his resolve: instead of fleeing he

STILL 8: *Tommy*
Directed by Ken Russell.
Tommy (Roger Daltrey), like Jesus, must be crucified in order to live for others. Crowned with poppies (an ambivalent symbol at best) and pierced like St. Sebastian, but with syringes not arrows (from each wound a poppy blooms), Tommy is both the victim of the acid-age and its savior.

goes to the office of Inspector Larrue and surrenders, knowing full well that he cannot defend himself since he is bound by the seal of confession. These narrative signals are critical both semantically and stylistically. Later in the courtroom we see the Special Prosecutor (Brian Aherne) ask whether Logan can further explain the circumstances of his meeting the sacristan murderer on the night of the crime. At this moment Hitchcock's camera tilts upward to catch the crucifix on the wall in the background while Father Logan in the foreground firmly replies "No," thus protecting the secrecy of the confessional and, ironically, the penitent. Again we have a christomorphic signal.

The setting of *I Confess* is Catholic Montreal, which adds force to the power that faith and its convictions exert in the life of Father Logan. As for Hitchcock, he himself had a Catholic upbringing. This personal faith, however, is not relevant to determining whether Logan is a Christ figure or a Jesus transfiguration. Father Logan's own *via crucis* is spelled out in unmistakable images within the Catholic culture of the film's world. We trust the images, not external evidence. When, however, we have repeated instances of Jesus and/or Christ references in the filmography of certain directors whose own personal religious leanings are known, as in the cases of Carl Dreyer, Robert Bresson, Frank Capra, and John Ford, we must allow for a religious bias, it seems to me, even if only at the subconscious level.

Christ figures and Jesus transfigurations in cinema are differentiated, we have noted, on the basis of whether one affirms, at least implicitly, faith in Christ (an existentiell) or whether one draws on the universal cultural symbolic value of the Jesus persona (an existential). Although Theodore Ziolkowski apparently rejects this crucial distinction, it is clearly implied in Robert Detweiler's seminal study of literary form in relation to religious meaning.

The distinction is especially important for the study of cinematic variations of the Gospel materials inasmuch as the visual image heightens the appeal of charismatic personalities. Students of literary figures of Jesus must look largely to "narrative signals": symbols of the cross, the presence of a Judas, a

Peter, or a Magdalene, a final meal, an allusion to Gethsemane or Golgotha, a descent from the cross or a Pietà scene. In cinema studies, however, one must look more deeply into the visual-aural experience itself to see why, for example, audiences in the 30s and 40s began to like rebels and pain-heroes such as James Cagney, Paul Muni, John Garfield, Humphrey Bogart, and Alan Ladd, even though they were on the other side of the law or died for violating society's code. How often we identified with gangsters, criminals, gun molls, and prostitutes in Hollywood films: Paul Muni in *I Was a Fugitive from a Chain Gang,* Clark Gable in *Manhattan Melodrama,* James Cagney in *Angels with Dirty Faces,* Bette Davis in *Marked Woman,* and Gloria Grahame in *The Big Heat.* The nature of Jesus' death as a criminal, uncontrovertible as a historical datum, makes the persecution or death of certain rebels take on a mystical aura. This is especially true of films dealing with political rebellions: the Marxist martyr and the executed priest in *Open City,* Che Guevara in the Argentinian film *Hours of the Furnaces,* the black insurgent Jose Dolores in *Burn!,* and Kirk Douglas' title role in *Spartacus.*

Equally noteworthy is the "wrong man" theme in Hitchcock, who often treats the imprisonment, suffering, or death of innocent persons. In *I Confess, The Wrong Man, Psycho,* and *The Birds,* there are scenes that are veritable passion plays. *Psycho* and *The Birds* with the shower scene and the final attack of the birds respectively are more secular, while in *I Confess* and *The Wrong Man* the metaphorical crucifixion scenes have explicit religious signification.

Transfigurations of Jesus play a central role in the films of several world-class directors who return again and again to Gospel signals, even if subconsciously. In John Ford, we note the cross-bearing chaplain (Boris Karloff) in *The Last Patrol,* the wronged Dr. Samuel Mudd (Warner Baxter) in *The Prisoner of Shark Island,* Katharine Hepburn's lead role in *Mary Queen of Scots,* and the roles of Henry Fonda in *The Grapes of Wrath, Young Abe Lincoln,* and *The Fugitive.* In Frank Capra, there are the roles of Gary Cooper in *Mr. Deeds Goes to Town* and *Meet John Doe* and those of James Stewart in *Mr. Smith Goes to Washington* and *It's a Wonderful Life* (despair, psychic agony, a ministering angel, and a metaphorical resurrection). Luis Buñuel's Jesus transfigurations in the narrow sense are found in *Viridiana, Nazarin,* and *Simon of the Desert;* Carl Dreyer offers us *The Passion of Joan of Arc, The Day of Wrath,* and *Ordet* (Dreyer never did film his projected life of Jesus); Robert Bresson, *The Diary of a Country Priest, A Man Escaped, The Trial of Joan of Arc,* and Jesus as the tramp in *Au Hasard, Balthazar.* In this last film, Arnold the tramp is an ambivalent figure: he receives a Judas kiss before dying; he rides on an ass; he even, as Jean Luc Godard put it to Bresson in an interview, has something of the look of Jesus.

To study the internal criteria for analyzing Christ figures in cinema, no more illuminating instance exists, I believe, than Paul Newman's title role in Stuart Rosenberg's *Cool Hand Luke.* For the purpose of analysis I have appropriated Northrop Frye's five modes of fiction: (1) the legendary or mythic mode whereby the hero is immortalized as in the tales of the gods, (2) the romantic mode in which the protagonist is seen as superior to the run of humanity and to the environment, (3) the high mimetic where the hero is accepted as a leader but with real limitations, (4) the low mimetic in which the protagonist is seen as equal to us; and (5) the ironic where the principal character is our inferior and we look down on his absurd plight.[3] Paul Newman's Luke follows a curve of rising action just as the Jesus of the Gospels does. In other words, both exemplify Frye's modes, but in reverse order. Jesus is born in a cave and then leads a hidden life as a carpenter, becomes a itinerant preacher, then a wonder-worker whose growing popularity finally threatens both the religious and the secular establishments. They plot his downfall. Though he dies alone, his disciples find strength in his example. The parallel in *Cool Hand Luke* is clear.

Luke is shown in the opening scene as a drunken vagrant who shears off the tops of parking meters. His situation is decidedly ironic—an absurd appearance inviting pity and wonderment. Having been arrested and sentenced to a Florida chain gang, Luke engages the prison's prize boxer (George Kennedy) in a match and is badly beaten, though he displays

STILL 9: *Cool Hand Luke*
Directed by Stuart Rosenberg.
The character of Luke (Paul Newman) is a Jesus transfiguration fully integrated into the narrative continuity of the film. Luke is the archetypal figure of the captive who transcends his captivity, at least in spirit, and leads others to the same victory. The sadistic efforts of Captain (Strother Martin) to humiliate him are paradoxically the seeds of his survival in the memory of his mates.

great fortitude. Luke thus takes on a more dignified aura as fully human.

The bulk of *Cool Hand Luke* deals with the growing hero worship accorded Luke under the leadership of the gruff inmate who defeated him in the fight. First, Luke spurs his fellow prisoners on to finish tarring a country road in record time to the embarrassment of the guards, who sense the presence of an independent spirit, a potential leader. Secondly, Luke gains the admiration of the prison population by betting he can devour fifty hard-boiled eggs—and succeeding. Luke is the natural leader of the camp, but there is also an official leader—the warden. The confrontation with the establishment is inevitable, something Luke cannot master. He meets the limits of his endurance when he is handcuffed and publicly struck down by Captain, the warden, who remarks sardonically: "What we have here is a failure to communicate!" Moreover, the guards humiliate Luke by forcing him to dig, fill, and re-empty a deep pit until he grovels at their feet and admits that his mind is "right." Luke then becomes a submissive trustee, carrying water to the road crews and guards. Thus the mimetic modes of fiction are present in Luke's potential for leadership being abated by the will of those in authority.

The romantic mode of fiction expresses itself when Luke reverts to his former rebelliousness. He makes a dash for freedom with the police dogs in hot pursuit. Eventually he becomes entrapped in a lonely, rural, wooden-frame chapel. The allusion to Jesus is unmistakable in this scene. Rather than surrender and be further degraded before the men, Luke chooses the posture of total liberation by resisting. He appears in the doorway and defiantly shouts at the warden and his officials: "What we have here is a failure to communicate!" The response is infallible and immediate. The captain of the guards with his dark glasses (often a cinematic symbol of spiritual obtuseness) shoulders his rifle and puts a bullet into Luke. With cynical calculation the warden orders the gravely wounded Luke taken to the distant prison hospital rather than a nearby civilian facility where he might be saved.

The mythic fiction mode is apparent in the closing scene of the film as the prisoners gather in the recreation yard and with nostalgic fondness recall—through imaginative embroidering, of course—the feats Luke performed and how he, the captive, was always ahead of his captors. A kind of resurrection is implicit in this scene. As the Christ of Faith lives on in his followers and, for many Christians, in a glorified state, so too Luke has a timeless place in the hearts and minds of those who know him and would keep his memory alive.

This reversal of fate, the loss that is not a loss, recurs in many prisoner movies where the hero, though abused and even killed, is regenerated through the faith of others or by his victory over the will of his antagonists: Peter Glenville's *The Prisoner,* John Frankenheimer's *The Fixer,* Miguel Littin's *The Jackal of Nahueltoro.* Northrop Frye's fictional modes have illuminating relevance for other films such as *La Strada, The Fugitive, The Man in the Glass Booth,* and Chaplin's *Limelight.*

In this latter film, an autobiographical rendering of an aging vaudevillian's rejection by the audience, Chaplin plays Calvero, a wise, caring person who finds strength in drink, old music-hall troupers, and a suicide-prone ballerina, Thereza (Claire Bloom), for whom he has become guardian. The growth follows a steady line of ascent similar to that in *Cool Hand Luke.* Just as we met Newman's Luke, so are we introduced to Calvero as he staggers drunkenly down the street and enters his apartment. The hero is inferior to us, but suddenly he assumes a more somber roll, rescuing the desperate ballerina from a gas-filled room (low mimetic). He allows the recuperating woman to share his room, overcoming the objections and suspicions of the landlady: the arrangement is indeed platonic. His leadership (high mimetic) is shown by his inspiriting her with hope and purpose, while he himself—a once famous comedian—is suffering the embarrassment of bored audiences and the loss of reputation. The romantic mode, a poetic highlight in the history of cinema, occurs during a benefit show in honor of Calvero when he and another "silent clown" (Buster Keaton) mime to musical accompaniment, earning a standing ovation from a grateful audience.

The mythic dimension follows during Thereza's opening-night ballet performance. When she loses confidence, Calvero slaps her and commands her to go on stage. The strenuous efforts of his own act plus the strain of worrying about Thereza bring on a heart attack. As Thereza, renewed in hope, pirouettes on the stage, Calvero dies with a peaceful look on his face. Could one see in this the satisfaction of Jesus' "*Consummatum est*—My mission is finished"? In any event, the way Calvero is carried out is reminiscent of paintings of the descent from the cross. Moreover, Calvero lives on in Thereza—an artistic reincarnation and, I would maintain, a resurrection image. One should notice, too, the affinity of the name Calvero to Calvary.

Plot, action, and character in film often resonate with the discernible allusions to that other story that is the basis of our genre. Three very different examples illustrate the breadth of possibilities for transfigurations of Jesus: *The Old Man and the Sea,* based on Ernest Hemingway's famous novel; *The Poseidon Adventure,* a box-office "disaster" hit; and a rollicking British comedy, *Heavens Above!*.

In John Sturges' *The Old Man and the Sea,* Spencer Tracy plays the aged Cuban fisherman whose luck at sea has been failing. A boy, Manuel, takes care of him in a loving, dutiful way, holding out hope for him, bringing him food and coffee laced with rum. The old man carries his mast to his thatched hut when he returns from fishing trips and in the rosy dawn carries it back down to the sea.

The underlying theme of the film as well as of Hemingway's fiction piece is endurance. Such a theme must be tested in character. How far can a man go to prove himself? The monologue of the old man, alone at sea, highlights the alternating cooperation and hostility of nature—now sun, now rain, now wind, now calm, now an evasive marlin, now a proud catch which must be kept from the voracious jaws of the relentless sharks. The struggle between the weather-worn fisherman and the marlin lasts for three days as the embattled fish, larger than the skiff, pulls it out deeper into the ocean.

The marlin typifies the object of a love–hate relationship—something that is confronted and conquered even though it is sought and needed. The giant fish is the "cross"—resisted, reluctantly engaged, yet finally accepted in death. The two—marlin and man—become one. The old man fights off the predatory sharks, first with a harpoon which he loses, then with a knife tied to an oar, and finally, when the gaff and a marlin spike are also gone, with the tiller. The flesh of the marlin is stripped away, and the trail of blood attracts other sharks. The marlin is his cross: he identifies with it, calling it brother. It has given him life—new life in death. His raw, bleeding hands, cut by the coarse drop-line through days of fitful struggle, are stigmata. His strength ebbs, but his spirit is renewed. Sighting the lights of the village harbor, the old man brings in the skiff with the mutilated marlin. Burdened with the mast he carries, he stumbles in front of a church. A light streams forth; the old man doffs his hat. The way of the cross is clearly symbolized. The novel is clearer; the old man cries out "Ay!!!" which, Hemingway interpolates, is the sound a man makes when a nail is driven into his hand. The film's voice-over informs us that he had to sit down five times before he arrived home. The way home is an ascent to the bed he longs for. Manuel, the admiring disciple, goes for coffee with rum. Other fishermen cut off the head of the marlin. The skeleton floats, bobbing near the shore. A plump, overdressed American tourist mistakenly tells her male companion that it is a shark: "I never knew that sharks had such beautiful tails!" The cut to the fish reveals a tau cross, the intact tail supported by the lengthy skeleton backbone. Allegory turns to irony: the cross symbol of agony and death is seen from a distance as a thing of beauty. Discipleship, agony, the way of the cross, the stigmatized hands, and the tau cross are the descriptive and narrative signals here of transfiguration. The absence of strong images of survival or new life places Sturges' film more within our sub-category of Jesus transfigurations in the narrow sense.

In Irwin Allen's *The Poseidon Adventure,* the Reverend Scott (Gene Hackman) is a passenger on an old luxury liner making its last voyage. An enormous tidal wave strikes; the boat capsizes and many lives are lost. When the disaster occurs, Scott is eating in the first-class dining room at the Captain's table. The room goes topsy-turvy; people scream and struggle. Chaos and panic ensue. Scott along with a handful of survivors must make the arduous journey to the surface through the twisted hulk of the overturned ship: Under Scott's leadership, two couples, a waiter, a singer, a haberdasher, a young woman, and her brother move toward the stern and up into the suspended bulkheads of the ship. Trials mount; discouragement increases. However, Reverend Scott shows perseverance, witnessing to the lesson he had preached in a sermon earlier that day: God's work is everyone's work and God helps those who help themselves and others.

As the group approaches the stern, only seven of the original ten are left alive. Rosen (Jack Albertson), an early doubter in strong opposition to Scott, now appears convinced of the latter's ability and purpose. No sooner has this happened than Mrs. Kago (Stella Stevens) falls to her death in a flaming pool of fuel. Kago (Ernest Borgnine) harshly denounces Reverend Scott: "Preacher, I just started to believe in you but you took the only thing I loved in this world." Almost immediately another impasse is reached; a valve suspended out of reach over the burning fuel is emitting steam directly in the path of the survivors. No one can move on and only one solution is possible; Scott exclaims, "Haven't we suffered enough? If you want another life then take mine." He leaps to the gate valve to cut off the flow of steam and thus saves the lives of all the others. He succeeds in closing the valve, but falls to his death in the flaming pool. Kago assumes Scott's position and leads the five remaining survivors to safety. Scott had stated in his sermon that "there is a little part of God in each of us which will strive forward if we strive with it." The film bears testimony to that. Scott is a secular transfiguration of Jesus, a model of perseverance in a world apparently devoid of an effective God.

In Roy and John Boulting's *Heavens Above!* Peter Sellers plays an Anglican minister. Through confusion at the Chancery, he is assigned as pastor to a comfortable rural congregation. He is, in an odd way, the "wrong man," a holy, zealous cleric filled with the spirit of the Gospel, but inadvertently assigned to a parish that expects a more predictable spiritual guide. The humor lies in the threat that this detached man of God represents by his fiery sermons on justice and judgment, in his conversion of the parish into a welfare center (shades of

Buñuel's *Viridiana*), and in his providing free bread to the poor (thus reducing the market for the local baker). The bishop is appraised of the disorder occasioned by this priest against whom no one can bring any real charges, for he lives like St. Francis of Assisi or Christ come back to earth.

The Bishop hits on a strategic solution by consecrating the holy man of innocence as a bishop and assigning him to Ultima Thule, the northernmost diocese of the United Kingdom. There he discovers a missile base where rockets are tested for explorations of outer space. With some unexplained craving to travel, he substitutes for an astronaut and is lofted by means of a booster-rocket-propelled space capsule into extraterrestrial orbit. The last scene is English humor carried to ultimate absurdity. It is clear narrative signal for an ascension into heaven (mark the title—*Heavens Above!*). It is as if the earth cannot really accommodate such a man of intense spiritual integrity. The benign banishment to Ultima Thule after the protests and pressures of the townspeople was a veritable burial alive. The ascent into the heavens is the voluntary deliverance from a human condition that is hypocritical and basically hostile to the pure applications of the Scriptures. There are elements of Luis Buñuel's film signature in *Heavens Above!* Produced and directed by the same Boulting Brothers who made *The Man in the White Suit,* the comic allegory is clearly laid out as a tale of the Christ, a story of hypothetical hilarity—"What would happen if Christ came to earth again?" The answers provided by the Boulting Brothers in *Heavens Above!* and *The Man in the White Suit* are identical—he would be rejected; he would be "wronged" but he would exercise an irrepressible force for good and as a victim would establish an ironic victory—comic but convincing.

I submit that there is a compelling mysterious force within the creative human imagination that shapes fictional characters and dramatic plots in the image and likeness of the central personage and events of the four Gospels of Matthew, Mark, Luke, and John. The history of motion pictures reflects both the existential and existentiell influence of the historical figure of Jesus as represented in religious and secular chronicles, whether literary or oral. No more compelling recent example exists than the box-office success *Star Wars,* a film with multiple levels of meanings.

George Lucas' immensely popular film is as simple in its portrayal of the forces for good and evil as D.W. Griffith's *Birth of a Nation* and *Intolerance.* The heroine (Carrie Fisher) is a classic Victorian woman—demure, easily frightened, and in need of rescue by a valiant male. We meet a simple farmboy, Luke Skywalker (notice the biblical name). He becomes a disciple of Obi-Wan Kenobi (Alec Guinness), last of the Jedi Knights who fought to defend the Force, a mysterious fount of universal good. Obi-Wan Kenobi is a Jesus figure—a man who lives simply, imparting wisdom and giving good example to people like Luke, whose father was killed in a vast interplanetary conflict against those who had perverted the Force. The leader of these cosmic rebels is a former Jedi himself—Darth Vader, Dark Lord of Sith. Not only is Obi-Wan Kenobi a gentle, detached man with a single-minded mission, his one weapon is a light saber that he uses against the heavily armed, faceless black knight Darth Vader. The death of Obi-Wan Kenobi completes the allegorical link to Christ. In fact, Obi-Wan Kenobi even physically resembles that Jesus which the religious and western cultural traditions have handed down in art and literature. The final scene of apocalyptic confrontation between Darth Vader and Luke Skywalker implies that the battle will be waged not by the Jesus figure himself but by his disciples and converts such as Han Solo, the opportunistic loner and mercenary who wears both black and white as a sign of ambiguous allegiance. In the last scene, however, he aids Luke and enlists on the side of the Force. "The Force be with you!," the blessing of Obi-Wan Kenobi, is realized after his death. It recalls the greeting of the Risen Lord to his disciples after his passion and death: "Peace be with you!" *Star Wars* fuses eastern religious symbolism with Christian signs, providing an unusual cosmic Jesus transfiguration.

In short, cinema bears the imprint of Christ's countenance in an uncanny way similar to the way in which the Shroud of Turin bears a remarkable resemblance to a crucified man fitting both the faith and historical criteria of that Jesus whom

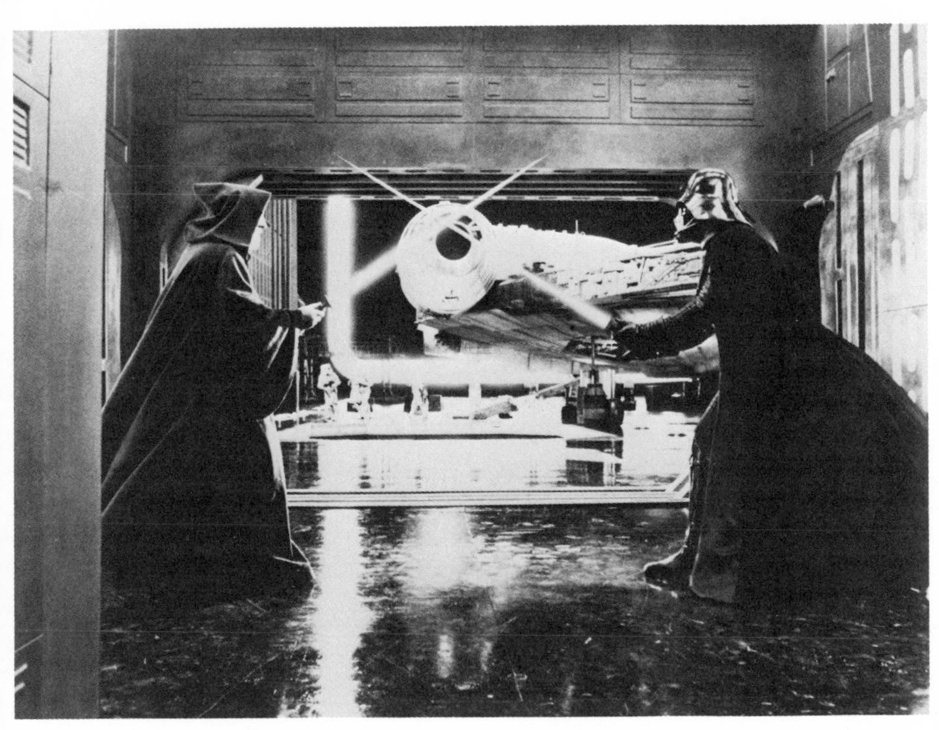

STILL 10: *Star Wars*
Directed by George Lucas.
Ben Obi-Wan Kenobi (Alec Guinness) and Lord Darth Vader (David Prowse), representing good and evil respectively, with less subtlety of course than imaginative novelty, engage in a duel to the death. Kenobi is clearly a Jesus figure insofar as he works to preserve the Force, the galaxy's fount of power, from subversion by the enemies of goodness and order.

no one denies had suffered and died on the cross under Pontius Pilate, the Roman Procurator. True, it is not always easy to conclude whether we are dealing with a Christ figure inspired by faith (as is presumably the case in the films of Carl Dreyer and Robert Bresson) or a Jesus transfiguration, a cultural event in the lives of people and nations (as in some movies of Luis Buñuel and Alfred Hitchcock). Nevertheless, there is a meta-genre of cinematic transfiguration of Jesus running throughout all the conventional genres such as the western, the comedy, the gangster, and horror films. Film research should begin to attend to the combined influences on cinema of faith in Christ and also of milieu Christianity.

JOHN R. MAY

The Demonic in American Cinema

WHEN Andrew Greeley presumed in *The New York Times* (January 18, 1976) to tell us "Why Hollywood Never Asks the God Question," he was really begging the question. Greeley is not precisely a theologian of culture and the *Times* is hardly a standard vehicle for academic debate, yet the audience that the *Times* reaches is undoubtedly awesome and Greeley has a reputation for serious cultural comment. Without any apparent awareness of the analogy between his assumption concerning American films—that they never ask the God question—and the battle that has raged in academe for the past two decades over the relationship between religion and literature, Greeley gives the nod to the European directors whose works seem to hold a hypnotic attraction for the American intellectual turned film buff.

Greeley is not so monolithic in his assumption about films that he could be accused of saying that raising the God question is equivalent to professing belief; he is aware that at least two of his directors, Buñuel and Bergman, are unbelievers—the former is routinely, and with reason, characterized as an atheist. Fellini, though profoundly imaginative, is scarcely orthodox; and only one, Rohmer—by far the least of the four artistically—fits a traditional religious frame. They at least consider the question worth raising, he insists. But even this reservation calls for careful distinctions. Because they are all victims, to an extent, of varieties of religious dualism—an orthodox Northern European Protestant split in worlds (Bergman), an anti-clerical Southern European Roman Catholic schizophrenia (Buñuel, Fellini), or a confusion of semi-Jansenist piety and Pascal's gamble (Rohmer)—the God they can by a severe stretch of the imagination be said to raise the question of is one who is either dead or totally absent or perplexingly aloof. Greeley seems to know that he is skating on thin ice when he characterizes their movies as religious, yet he concludes that "European directors are not afraid to *speak directly* about the meaning of human life and the mystery of human death—which is what religion is supposed to be all about" (my emphasis). Even this minimal concern he refuses to acknowledge in the works of American directors, not apparently because he has failed to see the right films, but rather, we can suppose, because he refuses to investigate any other mode of treating these issues other than "direct speech."

"The good religious film has eluded the American industry," Greeley asserts. "American filmmakers have produced movies about religion, movies which use religion, movies which exploit religion to titillate or terrify, but no religious movies."[1] As evidence of European directors' "eagerness to come to grips with religion," Greeley repeats the usual examples: Buñuel's *Nazarin* and *Belle de Jour,* Bergman's *The Seventh Seal, Through a Glass Darkly,* and *Cries and Whispers,* Fellini's *La Dolce Vita,* and Eric Rohmer's *My Night at Maud's.* The American films that he lists as using religion or being "about" it are for the most part not even good films—from *The Ten Commandments* through *Going My Way* all the way to *The Exorcist.* Only Martin Scorsese seems to make the grade for Greeley inasmuch as he "is able to drag in the God question for a few moments in *Mean Streets.*"

The reason for this lamentable failure, according to Greeley, is that for the past half century America's cultural elite—"made up of first generation alienates from either pious Christian families . . . or strictly observant Jewish families"—has been "convinced that religion was not worth writing about." Even though Greeley is flexible when he suggests a workable paradigm for the "God question," there is a regrettable literary bias to his film interpretations that seems consistently to ignore the uniqueness of American cultural trends *and* the dimensions of the language of film. The reason why Hollywood (Greeley's synonym for "American directors") never asks the God question "in so many words" (and this seems to be the *literal* bias of his objection) the way some outstanding European directors like Fellini, Bergman, Buñuel, and Rohmer have is surely this: It is more in the American cultural tradition (formed by Hawthorne, Melville, and Twain) to raise the "demon" question,[2] and this is precisely what American cinema at its recent best has been doing—subverting the facile optimism of the American dream by revealing the evil within us and our institutions.

The most blatant presentations of the occult or demonic are neither the best films Americans have made on the subject nor the most faithful to geniune American cultural patterns. This is especially true of our recent overexposure to what I would call "the return of the demon as persona" through certain major studio releases, based on best-selling novels, like William Friedkin's *The Exorcist* (Warner Brothers, novel by William Peter Blatty), Roman Polanski's *Rosemary's Baby* (Paramount, novel by Ira Levin), and Robert Mulligan's *The Other* (20th Century Fox, novel by Thomas Tryon). No American director, for example, has matched the insight or, in my estimation, the artistic success in creating human analogues of the demon as persona that Joseph Losey achieved in *The Servant* (1963) or Pier Paolo Pasolini in *Teorema* (1968).

The question that perplexes the theologian of culture in the face of this mass exposure to imagined instances of demonic possession and incubus is whether we are experiencing a genuine recurrence of the figural[3] imagination in an age that has generally accepted its decline or at least witnessed the beginnings of such an acceptance.[4] Although the demon as persona is all but absent from normative American literature, there are at least two strands of American variations on the demonic that are worthy of note.[5] One, employing a retrospective analogue for the demon as persona, considers the demon in each man's heart; it sees man's present failure as a repetition of the Edenic covenant with presumption. The other, using a proleptic analogue, imagines the mythical end-time of the last loosing of Satan in terms of the protean presence of the secular confidence man; it projects man's continuing perversity into a catastrophic future of crisis. In our literary history, the former strain traces a line from Hawthorne's "Earth's Holocaust" through Nathanael West's *Miss Lonelyhearts* to Flannery O'Connor; the latter originates in Melville's *The Confidence-Man* and Twain's *The Mysterious Stranger* and moves through

STILL 11: *The Servant*
Directed by Joseph Losey.
In one of the masterfully composed shots in recent cinema, Barrett (Dirk Bogarde) polishes the frame of a mirror in which his master, Tony (James Fox), is shown as a mere moon in the orbit of his servant's dominant image. This demon comes as a "single spy," but his devastating effect upon his master's world is the work of "battalions."

West's *The Day of the Locust* into the present in O'Connor, Percy, Ellison, Barth, Pynchon, Heller, and Vonnegut. Both strands, it seems to me, are at least broadly figural inasmuch as they impart a sense of the mystery of evil that cannot be explained simply as the sum of man's offenses or be controlled through merely human effort.

However much the idea of an independent personal force for evil may seem consonant with certain developments in traditional Christianity, it has not been particularly successful as a literary phenomenon in the American tradition; it is evil in the individual heart or rampant in human society that has influenced our best literary efforts. The same distinctions seem to hold for the best of recent American cinema. Our most compelling directors have avoided the demon as persona in favor of the demon in men's hearts and the loosing of Satan as confidence man. The reason, I feel, is as simple as this: artistic sensibility has never been too far removed from genuine religious sensibility to fall for that most subtle of all "demonic" ploys that someone else is the source of the problem. The tendency to locate evil outside of man is a characteristic of primitive religions whereas the singular blessing of the world's great religions has been their persistent determination to interiorize evil. It is encouraging to recall that the earliest Judaeo-Christian evidence concerning belief in the origin of evil, the Jahwist tradition of the fall in Genesis, makes the unequivocal point that evil enters the world through man, and, regardless of how one interprets the role of the serpent, the narrative is equally clear that blaming the serpent is passing the buck.

The Exorcist epitomizes the theological dangers inherent in the presentation of a personalized demon. Warner Brothers provided background material in support of its 1973 release that had at least the ring of theological sophistication. "By charting the specific symptoms of a young girl presumed 'possessed' and detailing the methods by which the demon was exorcised from her," the studio claims of the novel, "Blatty hoped to frame the unending battle between good and evil in dramatically compelling and philosophically provocative narrative." Although the same high intentions are attributed to the movie adaptation, the promotional release inadvertently reveals the Achilles heel of the project. "Director William Friedkin's film version of *The Exorcist,*" it goes on to say, "has the same goal: to look realistically at the inexplicable events during a thoroughly documented, bizarre outbreak of evil in one contemporary American home."[6] The phrase "bizarre outbreak of evil in *one* contemporary American home" (my emphasis) is closer to the truth (read "falsity") of the film than anything else that has been said about it. Imagine a Washington, D.C., setting in the indeterminate present (the events that the novel and film are based on occurred supposedly in 1949), and ask any intelligent American audience to accept the assumption that we have to create an imaginary "contemporary American home" (singular) to "look realistically" at a "bizarre outbreak of evil." Even before Watergate that would have been sufficiently offensive to prevent our willing suspension of disbelief. The film strains credibility so severely that one need not be particularly attuned to religious sensibility to be offended, although Pauline Kael acknowledged that "religious people . . . should be most offended."[7] Vincent Canby was less kind in his choice of language; he called it "a chunk of elegant occultist claptrap" and suggested that its $10 million budget "could have been better spent subsidizing a couple of beds at the Paine-Whitney Clinic."[8]

The film's most reprehensible omission from a theological perspective, as I have implied above, is its failure to create a world in which there is *any* evil at all apart from the demon's possession of Regan. The child's mother, Chris MacNeil, curses like a sailor, and Father Karras doubts the existence of his faith. Yet neither qualifies as evil. The former we are asked to accept as reasonable lamentation (what did this poor woman do to deserve such a hyper child?), and the latter could obviously be taken in the world of the film as the understandable penalty for Jesuit addiction to fine Scotch. (Father Karras actually makes the ultimate Christian sacrifice; he gives his troubled life for Regan's freedom: the film's saddest expectation of credulity. Karras' doubt, even disbelief, is infinitely more deserving of life than Regan's insipid adolescence.) The film also makes the regrettable neo-Puritan assumption that sex is at least reductively demonic since practically all of Re-

STILL 12: *The Exorcist*
Directed by William Friedkin.
The exorcist, Father Merrin (Max von Sydow), approaches the MacNeil house, where the demon Pazuzu has taken possession of an actress's daughter. The motivation is shallow, the setting contrived. Despite apparent good intentions, this is more a horror film than one with any relevant religious meaning.

gan's symptoms are portrayed as sexual aberrations, spoken or otherwise.

In Richard Donner's *The Omen* (1976), the incarnate beast of the apocalypse appears as the adopted son of the soon-to-be-appointed American Ambassador to Great Britain. Less publicized than *The Exorcist* (except perhaps in the trade journals), but of sterner substance than any of its big-budget predecessors featuring the demon as persona, including *Rosemary's Baby,* which it resembles, *The Omen* links the Antichrist with politics. If it asks too much of us initially in accepting the mode of adoption, it quickly recovers a sensible, though frightening pace of discovery and reversal. And it carefully avoids the tragic omission of *The Exorcist* by having the demon infiltrate the political order, an assumption that has both biblical warranty and perennial plausibility.

Damien (1978), the second part of *The Omen* trilogy, suffers the fate of most sequels, but one proportionate to the difficulty of the material it treats. Whereas there is a certain chilling effect to the final shot of *The Omen,* showing the boy Damien accompanied by the President and First Lady at the burial of his foster parents, the political implications of the presence of the Antichrist are diluted as Damien moves toward control of Thorn Enterprises through another branch of his foster family. Yet, we know enough about "the powers that be" to continue to suspend disbelief, especially as efforts to kill Damien fail and darkness cloaks the economic order.

The Final Conflict (1981), the trilogy's conclusion, however, because it leaves literally nothing to the imagination, leaves everything to be desired. It makes even less sense than *The Exorcist* inasmuch as it portrays the devil as a fool, and this was never part of any received tradition. Damien Thorn uses his financial prestige to have himself appointed Ambassador to Great Britain just as the coincidence of three stars discloses the time of the second birth of the Messiah, and that of course is the heart of the film's absurdity. Seven inept Benedictines from Subiaco, each carrying one of the sacred daggers of Megiddo (any one of which, if driven into the heart, would suffice to dispatch the demon), converge upon England determined to kill Damien before he has succeeded in his systematic extermination—aided by the Disciples of the Watch—of all of the male innocents born on the day the stars converged. The film's almost comic conflict rests on the devil's (and apparently the monks') thinking that the second coming will be like the first! Damien without any apparent effort eliminates the monks, singly and in pairs—less effective special forces in the service of good could hardly be imagined. It is, curiously enough, a television newswoman, whose son has come under Damien's influence, who triumphs over evil incarnate, and, instantly, the space between the walls of a ruined abbey—where the final conflict takes place—is filled with a heroic-sized image of Christ in glory, as the appropriate passage from the canonical scriptures reminds us, if we were among those who had forgotten, that the second coming will *not* be like the first. Once again demon greed seems to have triumphed over good taste, turning an originally good idea, shrouded in suggestion, into a travesty of religious belief.

There are other major American releases that appeal to an externalized demon, yet the tendency is not the best our culture has had to offer, and their incidence, we can be thankful, is decidedly less frequent. *Jaws* (1975) makes a bid, at least in its advertisements, to a dimension deeper than the ocean haunts of its dreaded great white shark, yet neither novelist Peter Benchley nor director Steven Spielberg has the talent to create another *Moby-Dick*. Frighten us it may, or perhaps our children, but as a symbol of evil the film's great white is never more convincing than the $150,000 plastic machine it so obviously is. The fact that this particular shark seems so relentless in disrupting the peace of an otherwise serene and, we must remember, successful resort town seems less a question of the malignancy of nature than the fault of the tourist industry. If there is any villain in the piece it is certainly not the shark who reacts naturally when food happens to swim in his direction or when he is attacked by men, but rather the officials of Amity who are guilty of the regrettable American crime of sacrificing lives for dollars. What need is there for us, following the suggestion of one of the television spots advertising the film, to treat the matter "*as if* God created the devil and gave him jaws" when human stupidity suffices to explain the only evident evil the film discloses. By the time *Jaws* II (1978) was hauled in, there was no point in appealing either to contemporary instances of national crisis like Watergate or to the perennially notorious demon; it was hard to get intelligent audiences to accept the film even as a fish story.

Where demonic possession or the malignancy of nature is not the focus of the world's evil, there is evidence in American cinema of the more prevalent but equally superficial approach to evil that blames society or its institutions. Alan Parker's *Midnight Express* (1978) is a perfect example of this latter phenomenon. The maximum-security prison in Istanbul, where Billy Hayes is subjected to the tortures of the damned for attempting to smuggle hashish out of Turkey (in sequences of appalling realism designed, one guesses, to play upon American distrust of asiatics), makes Dante's hell look like purgatory at best. Parker strains so hard to make his point that Billy's punishment far exceeds his crime that he seems to want us to forget the crime altogether. There is even the paranoid suggestion that Billy is a pawn in Nixon administration attempts to get the Turks to crack down on the drug traffic out of their country. At the film's end when Billy escapes (adding murder —justifiable of course—to his own list of shortcomings), the perceptive viewer is annoyed at having been manipulated into thinking that the devil is a sadistic foreigner.

Michael Cimino's first two films have both dealt, though in vastly different degrees and with disparate success, with an external institutional demon. *The Deer Hunter* (1979) comes tantalizingly close to being an artistically perfect indictment of the killer instinct in everyone, but unfortunately leaves a stronger impression that the killer is just a macho man who inevitably hunts both deer and his fellow man with gusto; regardless, the film is masterful and a brilliant first effort for any directorial career. *Heaven's Gate* (1981), Cimino's long awaited but sadly disappointing (and ridiculously expensive) second film, reveals an inherited immigrant's instinct for the glorification of the oppressed. Set in Wyoming before the turn of the century during the infamous Johnson County wars between established cattlemen and immigrant farmers, the film never catches dramatic fire: it is a wasteful conjunction of visual beauty and black-and-white morality. Its vision of a demonic WASP alliance extending from local ranchers all the way up to the President of the United States is a facile neo-Marxist portrait of an American proletariat subjugating the poor.

One of the early examples of the demon as oppressive institution within society is in John Ford's *The Grapes of Wrath* (1940). Now a minor classic of American cinema, the film has much to its credit if not to its vision of evil: it is just slightly more sophisticated theologically than John Steinbeck's novel and only because it is less specific. Although the film faithfully dramatizes the plight of Oklahoma's migrant farmers who went to California in search of the promised land, it scrupulously avoids the novel's clear accusations precisely because big business threatened to withdraw its financial support from the film venture. Yet even if the politico-economic dynamite of the novel becomes, in the film, powder in search of a fuse, it is nonetheless characteristic of a revolutionary vision reappearing recently as a liberation theology that distinguishes good and evil as simplistically as white and black or oppressed and oppressor.

One Flew Over the Cuckoo's Nest, Milôs Forman's adaptation of Ken Kesey's novel—a film that garnered all of the major awards of the Motion Picture Academy for 1975, though apparently none of the American Academy of Religion's—raises the right question for our investigation, namely, who is to blame for society's ills, gives the same basic answer as does the novel—a wrong one—and once again tones down the source's demon, this time presumably for artistic reasons alone. The metaphor for society is obvious yet shocking—the asylum. In Kesey's novel the Combine is responsible for extinguishing the fire of our minds; he was anticipating if not setting the tone for the mid-to-later 60s preoccupation with the Establishment. Nurse Ratched is the front for the Combine in the novel; in the film she is merely the ward's head nurse. Yet so subtly sinister and brilliantly controlled is Louise Fletcher's performance under Forman's direction that we instinctively sense the presence of some externalized demon, if not the Establishment/Combine, at least the oppressive sexual mores of our Puritan heritage. This is particularly clear in the film's climactic confrontation when Nurse Ratched coolly turns the liberated Billy Bibbit back into a stuttering slave of the superego.

Although *The Grapes of Wrath, One Flew Over the Cuckoo's Nest,* and *The Deer Hunter* illustrate well what I consider to be a more subtle instance of the externalized demon, my theological reservations about these works are decidedly minor in comparison with my estimate of their general excellence as films. They are, finally, worlds apart from the sensationalism, mass exploitation, and overall inferior artistry of *The Exorcist, Jaws,* and even *The Omen.*

More substantial evidence in contemporary American cinema for the demon within man and human society is found generally, I propose, in the works of such directors as Arthur Penn, Francis Ford Coppola, Robert Altman, Martin Scorsese, Hal Ashby, Jerry Schatzberg, Terrence Malick, Dennis Hopper, John Schlesinger, and Stanley Kubrick. The latter two of course can be considered American only with qualification. John Schlesinger is a British director who has recently directed films of considerable importance for American studios. Stanley Kubrick on the other hand is an American who has made England his artistic home. Focus on the demon in the human heart is evident in Coppola's *The Rain People* and *The Conversation,* Penn's *Night Moves* and *Alice's Restaurant,* Ashby's *Shampoo,* and Schatzberg's *Scarecrow.* Here American cinema most closely parallels the retrospective strand in American fiction. The proleptic analogue of the demon within society as pervasive confidence man appears in Coppola's *The Godfather,* Scorsese's *Mean Streets,* Malick's *Badlands,* Hopper's *Easy Rider,* Schlesinger's *Midnight Cowboy* and *The Day of the Locust,* Kubrick's *Doctor Strangelove,* and Altman's *Nashville.*

In *The Rain People* (1969), Francis Ford Coppola traces a variation on the American mythic quest. A young Long Island housewife flees into the heartland of Nebraska to come to grips with an unwanted pregnancy. In fleeing one obligation, though, Vinny unwittingly embraces a greater one. She offers a ride to a brain-damaged ex-football player, a macho model whom society has abused and rejected, who is literally helpless without her and who quickly shows a capacity to love embarrassingly superior to her own. The attempt to abandon Killer Gannon leads to his death. Vinny's acceptance of unborn life in senseless death, however, implies the realization that the tragedy was a consequence of her own childish refusal to accept one of life's reasonable obligations.

Arthur Penn's *Night Moves* (1975) is more a metaphysical parable than a moral one. In telling the story of a private detective's determination to get to the bottom of a mystery surrounding the truancy of a movie heiress, it raises an epistemological question of such profundity that it resembles Melville's genius in *Benito Cereno;* yet the film works on the moral level as well. The havoc that Harry Moseby perpetrates stems precisely from his conviction that life's mystery and his own can be solved completely; the narrative is so structured that each time Harry forces a revelation he compounds his problem. The circle that his motorboat traces in the ocean off the Florida Keys is the film's final image for the vicious circle his presumption has created. The demon in Harry is at the center of the circle.

Scarecrow (1973) is a deceptively simple film about the liberating power of love in friendship. Jerry Schatzberg, dealing with thematic material strikingly similar to John Schlesinger's *Midnight Cowboy* (1969), does not, like the latter, hedge his bet. What needs to be exorcised here are the complementary demons in his two loners, not something in the society around them. Max is a burly, aggressive man who insulates himself from genuine human contact in layers of clothing; Lion is sheepish, withdrawn, and guilt-ridden for having abandoned his wife six years earlier. Lion explains how scarecrows work—they don't really scare, he says, they make the crows laugh and thus distract them from the crops; later, in a barroom scene, Max turns from aggression as a solution to life's problems and, deciding to make the crowd laugh, acts the scarecrow for Lion and strips the clothes that symbolize his alienation from others. At the film's end only Max has changed; yet, strengthened by love's transformation, he pledges himself to work for the freedom of his mentally disturbed liberator.

In both *The Conversation* (1974) and *Shampoo* (1975), the sin of the individual reflects the perversion of trust in America as a whole. The wire-tapping, bugging expert in Coppola's film is forced to realize that his competent handling of electronic devices cannot be viewed apart from the use that society makes of his gathered information. Media of communication become ironic instruments of paranoid isolation. One of our least conscionable offenses in a technological age is the presumption of good will: that our inventions will not be used against us. The recognition scene at the Republican dinner party in Hal Ashby's *Shampoo* is a subtly humorous and brilliantly understated re-presentation of that earliest embarrassing confrontation over sin in the garden. One couple becomes three in six previously hidden variations, and George's inane "Remember the follicle never dies," though proportionate to the emptiness of the sexual circus he heads, is as radically ineffectual a distraction from exposed duplicity as "The serpent beguiled me." The hairdresser George is abandoned finally by the women closest to him, and he knows the reason—his refusal to commit himself beyond the pleasure of the moment. His cultivated infidelity is nothing more than rampant animal appetite. Yet as we watch his comeuppance (the traditional fate of the Don Juan) against the cultural backdrop of the 1968 election, we realize that George's promiscuity is only materially different from the betrayal of trust in the highest office of the land; both together reflect man's recurring inability to keep even his reasonable promises.

Alice's Restaurant (1969), an earlier film of Arthur Penn's, portrays an abortive, subcultural effort to create the ideal community that, in Harvey Cox's words, "will provide us with the family's warmth without its constriction, the city's freedom without its terrifying impersonality."[9] It refrains modestly from any general statement about the impossibility of new forms of community; it is content to say that these particular and otherwise appealing people repeatedly ignore their psychological limitations: one must know his needs before he tries to share himself. The fault lies not in life's possibilities, but in our own doubts, uncertainties, and selfishnesses. Sin is presented as the absence of beauty, as when Ray explains to Alice their part in Shelly's death: "Maybe we haven't been too beautiful lately."

Some individual works by established directors and one by a star turned director are also notable for their portrayal of the demonic heart, and in each instance undoubtedly because of the literary work the film is adapted from. Elia Kazan's *East of Eden* (1955), the latter half of John Steinbeck's sprawling tale of American genesis, begins with the biblical premise running through the patriarchal accounts that evil and a father's curse are apparently as related as goodness and his blessing, yet finally discloses the more subtle scriptural assumption that everyone rejects his brother and thus bears the mark of Cain, that curious sign of God's mercy reserved for the fratricide. Mike Nichols' masterful adaptation of Edward Albee's *Who's Afraid of Virginia Woolf?* (1966) answers the title's question by showing that we all are. Virginia Woolf is Albee's stunningly clever image for the capacity—and need—we have to destroy the protective illusions others live by.

More recently, three films from 1980, all adaptations from skillful and perceptive novelists, reveal the varieties of the demonic heart. With a screenplay by Tom Stoppard and the direction of Otto Preminger, *The Human Factor* should have been far more successful than it was; the novel was certainly vintage Graham Greene. Agent Maurice Castle, safely back home processing reports for British intelligence, wants simply to retire with his African wife and her son. But security, particularly with love, is unattainable in Greene's fictional world. And although on one level this *is* the human factor or condition, there is also the specific factor that makes security unattainable—the consequence of one's past actions, the heart's treason, however petty. John Huston converted Flannery O'Connor's comic novel *Wise Blood* into a truly zestful film (as hard as that may be to imagine) about the radical need we all have to acknowledge our uncleanness. We are all, as O'Connor's bible-belt billboards proclaim, "whoremongers and blasphemers." The last of this trio of films is the least only in the sense that novelist Judith Guest has obviously not reached the stature of either Graham Greene or Flannery O'Connor, because the film *Ordinary People*, adapted by Robert Redford, is by far the best of the three and thoroughly deserving of the Academy Award it won as the year's best film. The Jarretts are ordinary people: in varying ways and with vastly different insights, they have fragmented their own family—and the human family. Ordinary people, wise blood, and the human factor are memorable images of the universal demonic heart.

Scorsese's *Mean Streets* (1973) and Coppola's *The Godfather* (1972) represent a smooth transition between the treatment of the demonic heart and the loosing of Satan, between everyman's sin and that general condition of sin that signals catastrophe. Each shows the divided heart against the background of destructive patterns of transcultural adjustment effected by the sins of our fathers. Scorsese's low-budget film features sub-Mafia punks in the obsessive Roman Catholic atmosphere of New York's Little Italy; Coppola shows the aristocracy of American crime as builders of our economic future and tenacious servants of a religious past.

In *Mean Streets,* Charlie is enlightened enough to know that he must discover his own meaningful acts of penance. "Ten Our Father's and ten Hail Mary's" yield to a bizarre combination of self-inflicted candle burns and frustrating attempts to shield his friend Johnny Boy from harm. The pains of hell, Charlie says, are of two kinds, "the kind you touch with your hand and the kind you feel with your heart." In one highly instructive far shot, Scorsese shows a decorated street as a thin band of light cutting through an ocean of darkness, with the Manhattan horizon barely visible at the top of the frame. The limits of Little Italy are literally mean streets. Sin here is viewed as a necessary prelude to penance that never liberates from guilt; instead of protecting Johnny Boy, Charlie seems in the resolution of the film to be drawn inexorably into the tragic consequences of his friend's amateurish crime. Although *The Godfather* takes dramatic shape against the same ethnic background, its appeal is ultimately more universal. In one of the most powerful sequences in contemporary cinema, the duplicity of everyman is apparent in the climactic intercutting of the baptismal ceremony and the Mafia vendetta. Michael Corleone, answering for his nephew, calmly, reverently renounces Satan and all his pomps as his lieutenants sys-

STILL 13: *The Godfather Part II*
Directed by Francis Coppola.
After succeeding to the petty throne of his father's underworld kingdom of criminal business connections and suppressing—for a time—the resistance of rival Mafiosi, Michael Corleone (Al Pacino) sits in solemn isolation. His uneasy mask of bourgeois self-complacency is the ironic measure of his achievement.

tematically exterminate the enemies whose death is a necessary condition for securing power.

Whereas depth of individual characterization makes *Mean Streets* and *The Godfather* balanced statements of individual and social sin, the demon within is somehow lost to that pervasive sense of evil that heralds the end-time in such films as *The Day of the Locust* (1975) and *Doctor Strangelove* (1964). Both films, of course, imagine the end, the former in microcosm, the latter literally. Schlesinger, in his second caustic view of the American scene, based on Nathanael West's slim though classic indictment of the American dream, portrays a Hollywood premiere-become-riot in terms of the European *Götterdämmerung* of the thirties. Schlesinger is a director of proven artistry: *The Day of the Locust* is a film that builds to its climax through the intricate variation of visual parallels. The collapse of the *Waterloo* set is completed by the riot touched off at the premiere of *The Buccaneer* (note the quiet allusions to violence in the very titles of the films) just as Faye Greener's narcissistic preening blends perfectly with the cock fight into a macabre image of the dance of death. The bored mass of "starers," who have come to Hollywood to die because it promises what it cannot fulfill, are the swarming locusts of apocalypse; a child's prank has sufficed to stir them to violence. If Tod Hackett seems to escape the doomed artificiality of Hollywood (a saving note that West's novel avoids), it is a minor victory in the face of the cataclysmic marriage of studio executives and fortune hunters.

Accidental riot becomes unavoidable holocaust in *Doctor Strangelove,* Stanley Kubrick's masterpiece of black humor. Even if General Jack D. Ripper's paranoia about Communist fluoridation of our waters is the actual finger at the trigger, it is quite clear that everyone has a hand in holding the gun to the world's head. Self-extermination is the final consequence of the sin of technologism compounded by mass stupidity and utter coincidence.

More typically American, though, are the cinematic presentations of rampant evil that employ some specific image of the confidence man or the conned society. Thus, more precise culturally than even *Mean Streets* and *The Godfather* is the folkloric world of *Midnight Cowboy, Easy Rider, Badlands,* and *Nashville.* Supporting these images of America is a sense of its people and its weakness. No impersonal institution or preternatural person is responsible for these often appalling visions of evil, but simply people themselves in their folksy, incomplete, even blatantly sinful ways. In Schlesinger's earlier view of American life, the cleverly satirical *Midnight Cowboy* (1969), Joe Buck and Ratso Rizzo, though willful servants of the American bitheon, sex and money, eventually break with the tradition of evil; their liberation—one to death, the other to new life—only serves to highlight the prevalent servitude. In *Easy Rider*[10] (1969), Dennis Hopper exposes the two faces of modern America, Wyatt and Billy, mind and body. Their mythic journey from west to east reverses the American pattern precisely because they are halves in search of a former self. Violence interrupts their journey and presumably the American dream—not because the enemy is straight Middle America but because, in Wyatt's words, "we blew it." *Badlands* (1973) is only superficially about the Charles Starkweather–Caril Ann Fugate Bonnie-and-Clyde escapade through the Dakotas in 1958. Its real subject is America's incredible propensity to make villains heroes. Once the literal badlands had been traversed there seemed to be nothing left but the badlands of the spirit where the desire for vicarious adventure becomes merely the canonization of criminals.

The most exciting perception of pervasive evil in contemporary America is undoubtedly Robert Altman's *Nashville* (1975) in which twenty-four mid-to-subcultural types twang their guitars and belt out "hymns" in quadriphonic sound to our mediocrity, indifference, and mindless vanity. Barbara Jean's homecoming to the Grand Ole Opry and the political rally for Hal Phillip Walker's Replacement Party are routine, but inescapably American. When Tom Wicker calls *Nashville* "a two-and-a-half hour cascade of minutely detailed vulgarity, greed, deceit, cruelty, barely contained hysteria, and the frantic lack of root and grace into which American life has been driven by its own heedless vitality," he is not criticizing the film, but praising its verisimilitude. He describes the film's world, not unlike ours, with matchless precision: "This is a

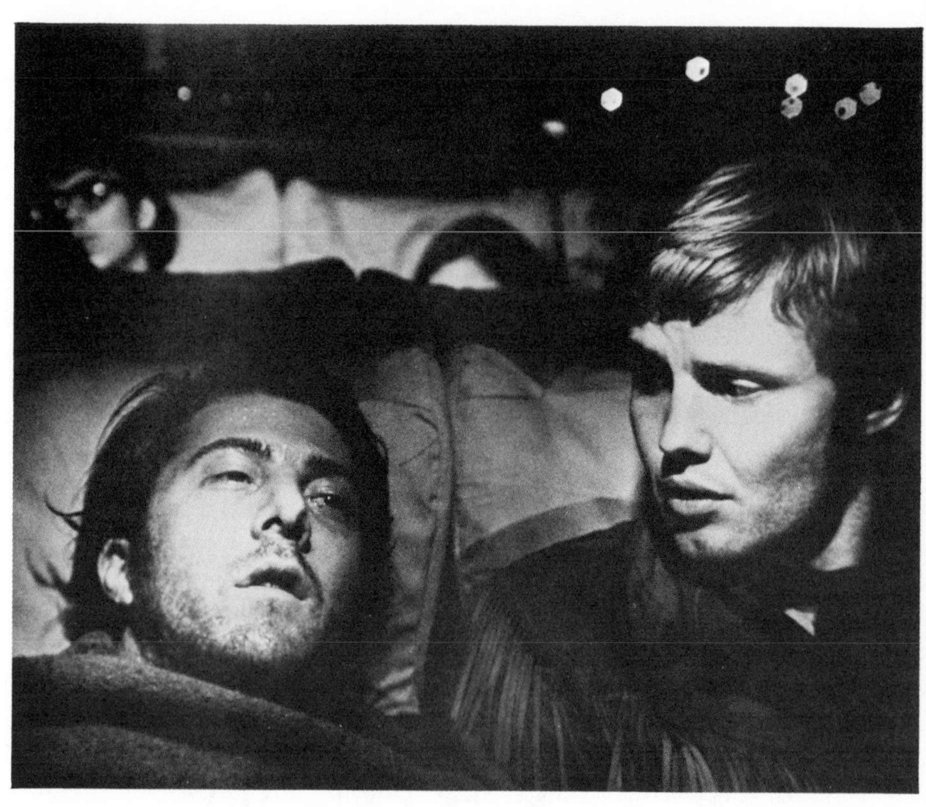

STILL 14: *Midnight Cowboy*
Directed by John Schlesinger.
Joe Buck (Jon Voight) struggles to assimilate the loss of his friend Ratso (Dustin Hoffman), who has just died en route from New York's frigid winter to the saving warmth of Miami Beach. Ratso's death will be Joe's invitation to a new life away from the midnight world of male hustlers—the film's image for America as a vicious network of con artists.

STILL 15: *Nashville*
Directed by Robert Altman.
In the chaotic aftermath of an abortive political assassination, Albequerque (Barbara Harris) seizes the microphone and realizes her ambition to perform in public in the country-and-western capital. In perhaps typical American fashion, an unknown but energetic presence reunifies the stunned crowd; her ironic refrain is "You may say that I ain't free, but it don't worry me."

culture in which old people are thrown aside as carelessly as Colonel Sanders chicken bones, patriotism and sentimentality salve the hideous wounds of progress, and madmen peer mildly from benign eyes just before they strike. The greatest reward in this world is prime time, the greatest achievement is visibility, the most profound corruption is not that of the con man but that of the conned, who march willingly into their delusions and falsities."[11] The country-and-western capital is the image of Bicentennial America. Like America it can apparently survive the senseless assassins it nurtures.

M. DARROL BRYANT

Cinema, Religion, and Popular Culture

GROWING up in a small North Dakota town in the 1950s, I regularly participated in the weekly Saturday ritual of going to the movies. This event was one I shared with a wide variety of folk: young and old, farmers and townspeople, men and women, Catholics, Protestants, and non-believers. For two hours the cares and demands of everyday were set aside as we entered the magical world of the cinema. Seated in the darkened theater we allowed our private fantasies, fears, and aspirations to meet the drama enacted on the screen. We gathered to watch the reenactment of the primordial conflict of good and evil, unmistakably attired in white and black hats, and the eventual but inevitable triumph of good. (In those days we watched a steady diet of westerns.) Filtered through our own particular feelings, the drama on the screen moved us, and shaped us.

Unlike some contemporary art forms, the cinema is distinguished by its mass appeal and accessibility. In this sense, film is a popular medium. From the very beginning, films were made to be distributed to and viewed by mass audiences; film was to be a *medium populi.* Thus film as a popular art shares an intention characteristic of the arts through the ages: to enhance, amuse, instruct, and serve the whole community. For example, the great artistic achievements of the Middle Ages, the cathedrals, were located at the center of the community for all the people to use. Images in stone and glass presented the Christian story for all to see. Shakespeare's plays were popular entertainment requiring from the audience nothing more than familiarity with the English language. Hence, to speak of cinema and popular culture does not demean our subject, but rather situates our subject within a context where we can best grasp the origins and dynamics of this popular art.

We must begin by recalling that cinema emerges within technological civilization.[1] The very materials on which this popular art depends are deeply situated within the technology of our age. The still camera (the technical antecedent of the movie camera), the motion-picture projector, and photographic film itself are the inventions of technological civilization. Hence, the very machines and materials that make cinema possible themselves grow out of an ethos shaped by technology. However, once the material elements of the film have emerged, they enter into a more complex and dynamic relationship with their environment since they can now re-present that environment to itself—in sight, sound, and motion. This is the first and most stunning feature of film, namely, that it can mechanically reproduce, in the filmic image, the very culture in which it originated.

It is crucial that this link between film and technology be noted. Otherwise, we could easily lose sight of the intimate connection between the aspiration of our technological culture and this popular art form. The popular art form does not float free above its cultural matrix, but is able to body forth the aspirations of technological civilization in sensible forms. The arts of primitive societies—the rituals of the hunt and planting—give visible form to the deep relationship that exists between the tribe and, for example, the sacral powers that dwell in the buffalo or the powers that transform a seed into a plant. Likewise, film as a popular art form must resonate in the deepest aspirations of the culture in which it emerges. Consequently, I propose that we approach film as a response to the ambition of a technological civilization to discover the alchemical formula that could wed the machine to the transmutation of nature and the deification of human culture. In a word, as we sit and watch a film, we are participating in a central ritual of our technological civilization.

While it is obvious that film could only emerge when a certain level of technological sophistication had been achieved, it is not obvious what aspirations of a technological civilization it embodies. Mircea Eliade has argued, in his study of the alchemical tradition *The Forge and the Crucible,* that technological civilization inherits the dreams of the alchemists. Eliade writes:

> We must not believe that the triumph of experimental science reduced to nought the dreams and ideals of the alchemist. On the contrary, the ideology of the new epoch crystallized around the myth of infinite progress and, boosted by the experimental sciences and the progress of industrialization which dominated and inspired the whole of the nineteenth century, takes up and carries forward—despite its radical secularization—the millenary dream of the alchemist. It is in the specific dogma of the nineteenth century, according to which man's true mission is to transform and improve upon nature and become her master, that we must look for the authentic continuation of the alchemist's dream.[2]

If, as Eliade contends, there is a connection, albeit camouflaged, between the alchemist's dream and the aspiration of technological civilization, then we may be able to glimpse an elemental connection between film and technological civilization. The alchemical dream, moreover, seeks to overcome time, to achieve immortality.

In this perspective the phenomenon of film is one means by which the technological civilization realizes its alchemical dream. Here in the cinema, the "stuff" of everyday life can be taken up and magically transformed; base metals are turned into gold. At the same time, the culture gains a certain immortality for itself by lifting its own contents—persons, objects, ideology—beyond the flux of every day to the permanence of the filmed image. In the cinema, then, we have confirmed the popular belief that the everyday world we endure, itself shaped by technological civilization, is capable of achieving its noble but hidden dream: the transmutation and deification of the world.

Due to the capacity of the camera to record, reproduce, and represent the natural, social, and human worlds—with a degree of realism unprecedented in the history of art—we, its audience, are vulnerable to being re-created by it. Unlike works of sculpture or even film's closest analogues, the theater and the novel, we immediately recognize and believe the figures on the screen. Consequently, the cinematic form can establish an immediate rapport with its audience; it can seduce us to set aside disbelief and enter with a high degree of identification into the lives of the characters on the screen and their story.

In many ways, this identification of the viewer with the thing viewed requires us to recall an older and more popular view of the link between art and culture. In his interesting study of the relationship between art and consciousness, *Icon and Idea,* Herbert Read argues for the vital role of the artistic image in the development of human consciousness. According to Read, "the image, which when projected into plastic form I call the icon, preceded the idea in the development of human consciousness."[3] The obvious implication of Read's thesis is that art plays a central rather than a peripheral role in the development of civilization. In the construction or articulation of an image, or icon, some veiled or hidden dimension of reality is rendered visible and thus open to contemplation. According to Read, this process of the creation of an image and its interaction with the viewer encourages and expands the range and depth of human consciousness. Although Read does not speak of film, his view is helpful to our understanding of the relationship between film and culture. Do we not in the cinema encounter significant images today? Is it not on the screen that we discover both new and familiar images of humanity that call forth in the viewer an expanded sense of what is possible? desirable? and worthy of emulating?

Moreover, Read's thesis reminds us that to separate art from the broader life of culture is a modern problem. The more common tradition—particularly with the popular artistic forms—is that art is centrally related to the whole life of culture. Such art forms interact with the cultural tradition in a twofold way: giving expression and visible form to cultural aspirations *and* reformulating and reshaping the aspirations of the culture. In primitive cultures, art was centered in the ritual life of the tribe and radiated out from that matrix to decorate, shape, and enhance the other activities of the tribe. In the medieval world, in spite of some serious theological reservations, artistic creativity found its expression in relation to the cultic activities of the church. The very origin of our term *culture* from the Latin *cultus,* meaning worship, is indicative of the awareness that a culture grows out of intimate life with the gods. But what happens when the *cultus* which sustains our life with the gods disappears?

An influential modern tradition, rooted in the Enlightenment's characterization of religion as superstition, has insisted that modern cultures have outgrown religion and, consequently, that cultic forms are unnecessary to the life of culture. This tradition, especially important to the modern intellectual, has obscured the deeply spiritual impulses and longings that are the matrix of culture, the relationship between cultus and culture. But have our cultic forms died? Or did they just undergo another metamorphosis? My point here is neither that religion still lives (though that is doubtlessly true) nor even that there is an irrational underside to the rational surface of modern technological civilization (though that is probably true too). My concern is to overcome a false dichotomy between "religious" and "secular" cultures. All cultures are dependent on cultic forms, even our technological culture. The difference between a "religious" and a "secular" culture is that a religious culture seeks to mediate a transcendent order, whereas a secular culture has no referent beyond itself and consequently worships itself. Thus, the basis of cultural life becomes power rather than the transcendent, and the cultic forms of secular culture become self-reflective.

When we understand, as suggested above, that modern technological culture has inherited the alchemical dreams of the past, then we can see the spiritual aspirations that have inspired technology. Moreover, I am suggesting that in film we can perceive *the marriage of the deepest aspirations of technology and the artistic impulse.* When that marriage issues in the popular medium of the cinema, which can imaginatively order and give vision to our culture while maintaining the illusion of reality, then a popular cultic form has been created that can sustain and nourish the aspirations of a technological culture. Why? Simply stated: cinema becomes a place where we can learn the myths of the culture, meet its heroes, and be instructed in its characteristic habits. In this perspective, then, films participate in the deepest longings of a technological civilization—the longing for a mechanical transmutation of things—and in the primordial longing of humanity to participate in the lives of the gods (the power-filled figures who overcome disorder).

The act of going to the movies is a participation in a central ritual of this culture's spiritual life. How we judge the quality of this culture's spiritual life as seen in the cinema I leave open here because it is the subject of other essays in this volume. I am more concerned to underscore my contention that cinema is a form of popular "religion." As a popular form of the religious life, movies do what we have always asked of popular religion, namely, they provide us with archetypal forms of humanity—heroic figures—and instruct us in the basic values and myths of our society. As we watch the characters and follow the drama on the screen, we are instructed in the values and myths of our culture and given models on which to pattern our lives.

When, however, we lose sight of the spiritual matrix of a culture's life, then we are apt to misconstrue the significance of the popular art forms that emerge within that culture. That the movies participate in this culture's primordial longing for intercourse with the gods is evidenced in the popular language that surrounds the cinema. We speak of "stars" and movie "idols." We insist that actors become something more than human. We allow them to operate, while all the time criticizing them, outside the boundaries of ordinary morality. Popular magazines abound that dwell on the details, more fantasy than real, of actors' and actresses' lives. Through the popular mind runs an ambivalence toward film personalities that characterizes a relationship between mere mortals and semi-gods. Popular movements emerge patterned on movie characters as we either recognize in them something we have felt in ourselves (James Dean in the late 1950s) or see something we desire to emulate. These evidences of the impact of the cinema upon popular culture suggest something of the significance film has in the people's mind.

As a popular medium, the film allows a culture to meet itself in a variety of ways: (1) by sheer reproduction in moving images of objects and persons in the culture; (2) by allowing us to view relationships of persons to the objects with which they live; (3) by presenting stories in which we recognize situations, events, attitudes, gestures, and habits characteristic of our culture; (4) by allowing us to explore relationships among people, between individuals and society, or between individuals and nature; (5) by examining ideas, beliefs, and ideologies current in culture; and (6) by dramatizing aspirations, fears, and desires that affect the life of culture. Projecting such elements onto the screen and employing cinematic techniques that affect our perception of these matters, films transform the cultural *ethos* in which we live into visual-aural objects of attention. The sheer fact of being able to *see* the familiar world in which human beings live and move is of profound importance. Moreover, the significance of this list of the cultural elements present in film does not lie either in its suggestion of exhaustiveness (it is not) or even in its accuracy (it may not be), but in the sheer fact that such a list can be made at all.

From an anthropological point of view, a culture is—in C. Kluckhohn's phrase—"the total life way of a people."[4] As a way of life that shapes *how* we do what we do as well as *what* we do, culture is largely invisible and unconscious. As members of a cultural tradition, we adopt its habits and ways over a long period of time, and they become so internalized that we are seldom aware of how profoundly we have been shaped. The culture becomes simply a part of the "way things are." Films, then, are a way of incorporating us, the viewers, into the dominant patterns of our culture by projecting images of that culture into our psyches.

At the same time—and this is film's paradox—the presence of film in our culture opens up the possibility of self-consciousness about the invisible milieu in which we live. By projecting our culture onto the screen so that we can *see* it, we are invited to a higher degree of self-consciousness about the way things really are. When we look at the screen, we can see our culture mirrored and writ large. This possibility of cultural self-awareness opened up to us distinguishes our cultural situation from that of preceding cultural epochs—at least in degree. Films, by raising to the level of visibility the ambience in which we live, invite us to become self-conscious about our own traditions.

However, the kind of consciousness of our culture that we can gain through the medium of the film is, in large measure, determined by the cinematic techniques employed in the making of a film. In spite of its apparent realism, film does not simply record but fashions its subject. In addition to the sheer re-presentation of the culture, films interact with that culture to shape our perceptions of it. Broadly considered, that interaction with our cultural milieu takes one of two basic forms: affirmation or critique. The director *both* presents a subject *and* instructs us as to how we are to regard it. In this respect, our response to the film is built into the film. The world we see presented in the film is a crafted world, crafted by the shape given to the subject.

There are, of course, many different stages in the making of a film where fundamental attitudes toward the subject matter are introduced. The script itself, the interpretation of the script by the director and the actors, the relationship that the story has to its filmic environment, the construction of sets or the selection of a location, the juxtaposition of images, and editing of the film are all subject to cinematic craftsmanship and artistic judgment. The way in which these moments in the film-making process are manipulated affects the perception the audience has of the world portrayed in the film. Through this complex process, the film both mirrors a larger world and interacts with that world to shape our perception.

How should we regard our culture? Is it worthy of our sacrifice? Is it noble or ignoble? Here film enters into the complex problematic that confronts all popular forms. The function of popular forms, including popular religion, is to affirm the culture, to criticize its failings, and, at its most creative level, to lead us beyond the culture to new visions that can renew our cultural life. These functions are readily apparent in the popular cinema. The bulk of the films produced affirm our cultural traditions, a much smaller number of them lead us to a more critical view of our culture, and the rare film incites us to new visions.

It is typical of art's indirect manner of expression, though, that the way in which film affirms, criticizes, or transforms our cultural situation remains largely hidden to us. The affirmation of our culture in film is achieved principally through the "narrative" form which offers us cultural heroes and myths; this form dominates American cinema from the western, through the musical, to more recent science fiction films. Film as narrative continuity simply *presents,* while hiding any awareness of discontinuity between the world of the cinema and the world of every day. The filmic illusion is maintained. The critique of culture is achieved through "ironic" modes of narrative, especially comedy, which juxtapose the cinematic world and the "real" world, thus clarifying the moral imperatives fundamental to our culture. The transcendence of culture —the achievement of new visions—is accomplished through "anti-illusionist" modes that seek to penetrate beneath the culture to a deeper reality.

However, unlike painting, sculpture, or theater, where the viewer suspends disbelief, the viewer of a film seldom, if ever, doubts the reality of what is presented on the screen. Indeed, it is even common to hear someone remark that a lived event is "just like the movies." This inversion of the cinematic illusion and lived reality is noteworthy because it points, on the one hand, to the seduction of the audience by the world of cinema and, on the other, to the hunger of human beings, in the midst of a technological civilization, to have their lives taken up into a more potent, magical realm.

We, the audience, hunger for a world in which we are more powerful than we are in the everyday world. The narrative film supplies this want by providing us with heroes who exercise control in the cinematic world which far exceeds our daily experience. The stranger who rides into town to restore peace and order meets our desire to live in a more ordered world. Consequently, the world of the cinema provides us, in the realm of popular culture, with a magically transformed and ordered world where the discontinuity between desire and reality is overcome. In the movies, boy gets girl, the lawman gets his man, the mistreated gets revenge. In film intimate and harmonious contact with the elemental powers that order things is reestablished: the human world is brought into line with the forces that rule our lives. We can thus see in the popular response to cinema a desire to reconnect the ordinary world with a more magical realm. This desire, as I have indicated, is reflected in our inadvertent, but revealing, comparison that our lived experience is "just like the movies." Rather than diminishing lived experience, this analogy suggests a desire to elevate everyday experience to participation in a more ordered reality—the magical world of the cinema.

The larger-than-life figures presented on the screen and the patterns of events become intermediaries between the confusing and piecemeal world of day-to-day existence and a realm of perfect order. The film presents a universe which, whether tragic, comic, trivial, or whatever, is orderly. Within a perfectly framed space and time where everything fits together to create a fictive whole, the viewer has an intimation of unity that is juxtaposed to his experience of the everyday world. It is reasonable, therefore, to speak of the cinema as escapist. But how are we to regard this escape? Perhaps it is true that we step out of ordinary time and space so that we may be reassured (in the dark) while watching a film that there *is* order somewhere. This movement outside the ordinary, jumbled world can be regarded in two ways. Some may argue that it serves as an opiate that leads us away from a proper encounter with the daily reality we live in. However, it may also be argued that it is precisely this excursion outside the ordinary world to the ordered world of the cinema that allows us to return renewed to the commonplace. Whatever one's judgment about this question, it is crucial that we recognize the central issue: the experience of order that film provides.

Moreover, we should be aware of the connection between the ordered world of cinema and the technological orientation of the dominant culture. The heroes of popular films are often technological adepts. The obvious suggestion is that the solutions to life's difficulties and disorders lie in the achievement of mastery through the techniques of order. The hero is the one who can manipulate the techniques of violence (Clint Eastwood), the tools of technology (Sean Connery), the techniques of love (from Clark Gable to Robert Redford), or who

STILL 16: *The Gold Rush*
Directed by Charles Chaplin.
Charlie Chaplin is not a hero of popular culture in any ordinary sense, but who can deny the enduring place his portrayal of "the tramp" has in the world of the spirit? His "clown of God" as American fortune hunter reminds us that there is no lasting order where human beings are concerned; in making us laugh at the absurdity of our pretensions, he is a hero of transcendence.

has other technical capacities that are the secrets to attaining mastery over the world. This very point has been made by Clint Eastwood: "A guy sits alone in a theater. He's young and he's scared. He doesn't know what he's going to do with his life. He wishes he could be self-sufficient, like the man he sees up there on the screen, somebody who can look out for himself, solve his own problems. I do the kinds of roles I'd like to see if I were still digging swimming pools and wanted to escape my problems."[5] Thus heroes are presented as those who have learned the secrets of technique which give power over the world in a way far beyond our ordinary abilities; we are implicitly led to affirm the orientation of our technological civilization and to grant to it the ability to overcome disorder and achieve the order we so desperately desire.

The experience of cinema allows the viewer access to an experience of unity that is seldom, if ever, achieved in everyday life. Visual, aural, and actional components are, in the cinematic world, orchestrated into a complete whole. That one steps out of the ordinary into the magical world of the cinema is not in itself a criticism of film. Rather, it is precisely this juxtaposition of the experience of unity in film and the discrete, jumbled experience of every day that sets in motion a dialectic within the discerning viewer. Moreover, the experience of seeing a familiar world imaginatively transformed in film may allow the viewer to hope that his often chaotic daily experience is not the last word. This element also accounts for the power of cinema. Indeed, we may now understand that the great film is the one that returns us to the world with a sense that we have seen, to use a liturgical formula, "in, with, and under" the recognizable and familiar in the film to a larger world of order and significance.

Thus, in the perspective outlined here, the profoundly spiritual significance of film lies not so much in content or subject matter as in our experience of the film itself—an experience of order and harmony that stands in counterpoint to our experience of the everyday world. The imaginative ordering of the substance of culture and the coming to visibility of the form of culture in cinema serve as grounds for the hope that the larger project of technological culture will succeed.

We are all aware that the quality of films varies greatly. But it may also be argued that the great film is the film that leads us to new awareness and vision concerning the world we daily suffer and that daily sustains us. This does not mean, as we have seen, that that film is best which is most "true to life," for the life we see in the film is not the life we experience in the world. Greatness is evident when a film discloses an order of being that lies behind it, yet manifests itself in the world of every day (see Michael Bird's essay in Part I). While film works with events, stories, characters, and situations that we recognize and find believable, it transforms them by giving them a new form that is thoroughly and exclusively cinematic. It is in that transformation of the familiar, as well as in the disclosure of the familiar, that we are led to see with greater insight. At the same time, the film like any popular medium must entertain as well as instruct, amuse as well as enhance. That cinema can do so many things simultaneously is its genius—and the reason for the public affection for it.

The popular religious character of the film—which provides the viewer with larger-than-life figures that he can emulate, while instructing him in the values and aspirations of his culture—raises important theological issues. The explicitly religious institutions of our society—the churches—have always had an uneasy mind concerning movies. If, as we have suggested, film is a form of popular religion deeply rooted in the spiritual aspirations of technological civilization, we can readily understand that uneasiness. The reason for it lies in the fact that the traditional religious institutions find themselves confronted with a new rival for people's loyalties: Their central role in determining the general direction of culture has eroded.

This question, though, is broad and complex and, fortunately, beyond the scope of this essay—though well within the scope of this collection. My point here is to suggest a reason for the ambivalence of traditional religious institutions to film. Moreover, it is important to underscore that ambivalence. Traditional religious institutions often find themselves *affirming* the content of one film and *criticizing* that of another. Such piecemeal criticism is seldom heeded and, more importantly, it misses the point. More crucial than any *ad hoc* criticism is the larger question of the theological assessment of the technological project of modern culture and, within that, the assessment of film itself in terms of the varieties of filmic styles and their implicit theological assumptions. Only when such an appropriation of film theory is undertaken can theologians enter into serious and significant conversation with this new popular art form—the cinema.

ERNEST FERLITA

Film and the Quest for Meaning

DRAMATIC art has always depicted the passions of the human soul. That is its power and its fascination, and that is why it is often regarded as dangerous. The following statement is a classic expression of this view:

> Few persons ever reflect, as I should imagine, that from evil of other men something of evil is communicated to themselves. And so the feeling of sorrow which has gathered strength at the sight of the misfortunes of others is with difficulty repressed in our own. . . . And the same may be said of lust and anger and all the other affections, of desire and pain and pleasure, which are held to be inseparable from every action—in all of them [poetic representation] feeds and waters the passions instead of drying them up; [it] lets them rule, although they ought to be controlled, if mankind are ever to increase in happiness and virtue.[1]

This is how Plato put it some twenty-five centuries ago in the tenth book of *The Republic.* His pupil Aristotle implicitly answered him in his famous definition of tragedy: dramatic art does not water the passions, it purges them "through pity and fear effecting the proper catharsis of these and similar emotions."[2] But the controversy did not end there, it has continued to our own day; and in the face of so much sex and violence on stage and screen, including recently the television screen, there are many who would readily side with Plato. And they are probably right—so long as the passions in these dramatic works are aroused for their own sakes, exploited and manipulated for other than aesthetic ends, without any regard for meaning. On the other hand, when our passions are aroused in the very act of our being moved to insight, then they are cleansed, and Aristotle is right. In other words, the passion for meaning—for meaning not only of one's personal life but also of existence as such—that passion, that drive, that quest must channel all the other passions and then prevail at the end.

There is a scene in Federico Fellini's *La Strada* in which the passion for meaning is poignantly expressed. It is the scene between Gelsomina (Giulietta Masina) and the Fool (Richard Basehart) that takes place at the close of the circus in Rome. Gelsomina, a simple-minded imp of a girl, has been brought to Rome by Zampano (Anthony Quinn), an itinerant stuntman who paid her mother ten thousand lira for her services. Callous and obtuse, he teaches her a few tricks to assist him in his act, which consists of breaking an iron chain with his pectoral muscles. Ordinarily, he performs alone on the road (*la strada*), but he decides to join the circus for the winter. There they meet the Fool, who makes fun of Zampano and provokes him into drawing a knife. Zampano is jailed for the night, and that night the Fool approaches Gelsomina. She is miserable. Zampano is a brute. He treats her like dirt. "Oh, why was I born?" she cries. And then the Fool tells her the parable of the stone, as a way of showing her that her purpose is to stay with Zampano.

THE FOOL. Of course . . . if *you* didn't stay with him, who would? Everything in this world is good for . . . for something. Take this stone, for instance.
GELSOMINA. Which one?
THE FOOL. Uh, this one—it doesn't matter which. This one, too, it has a purpose, even this little pebble.
GELSOMINA. What's it good for?
THE FOOL. If I knew that, I would be God. But if this stone is useless, then everything is, even the stars. You too, you have a purpose too. You with your artichoke head.[3]

We, too, also have a purpose. *La Strada* puts us on the road to discovery.

Film is a form of dramatic art ideally suited to the portrayal of the passion for meaning. Because of its unique power to imitate action in time and space, it can show man in search of meaning through every technique at its command: visual and aural imagery, composition of frame, movement of the camera and movement within the frame, visual continuity, and finally editing. Not surprisingly, the quest for meaning will often take the form of a journey; we should not be surprised, then, if the *motion* picture is of all the dramatic arts best able to depict man on the move. Nor should we be surprised if film appears to be the most suitable art for supporting our continued or renewed quest for meaning.

Our life moves on two levels, one exterior, the other interior. A film like Stanley Kubrick's *2001: A Space Odyssey* imitates action on both these levels. Exteriorly, David Bowman (Keir Dullea) goes on a mission that takes him to one of Jupiter's moons. Interiorly, he moves ever more deeply into the mystery of being. The first level is the level of plot; the second is the level of meaning; the first of visual-aural reality, the second of spiritual reality. They belong together like flesh and spirit. As Bowman plunges toward Jupiter, he continues a journey of the human spirit through time and space that began with the dawn of consciousness. The film raises once again the questions that surface in every age because the answers are never definitive: "Where do I come from? What am I? Where am I going?"[4]

There is a Nietzschean reach to David Bowman's journey; it is the journey of mankind. Gelsomina's journey in *La Strada* is more personal; the Fool's wisdom, encapsulated in the parable of the stone, is at the heart of one of the most significant recent developments in psychiatry—a type of existential analysis called logotherapy (from the Greek *logos,* which translates as "word" or "meaning"). For Viktor Frankl, the founder of logotherapy, a passion for meaning is not enough, there must be a *will* to meaning; and he proclaims this will against Freud's will to pleasure and Adler's will to power. In *Man's Search for Meaning,* Frankl tells of his own terrible ordeal at Auschwitz, of the challenge of survival, of the will to live that carried him "from death-camp to existentialism" (the original title of his book). He emerged after three years of unspeakable suffering and degradation to learn that his wife, his mother and father, and his brother had all perished in the camps; a sister alone survived. What he discovered during those three years he expresses in Nietzsche's words: "He who has a *why* to live can bear with almost any *how.*"[5]

Frankl insists that everyone has his own specific vocation in life; it is for him to answer and no one else, so much so that the question of the meaning of life may actually be reversed. "Ultimately, man should not ask what the meaning of his life is, but rather must recognize that it is *he* who is asked. In a word, each man is questioned by life; and he can only answer to life by *answering for* his own life; to life he can only respond by being responsible."[6] The meaning of his life is not to be found in actualizing the self, but in transcending it. Frankl insists that self-actualization as such is an impossible goal; it can only be expected *in* and *through* self-transcendence.

According to his theory of logotherapy, we can discover meaning in our lives in three different ways: 1) by doing a deed, 2) by experiencing a value, and 3) by suffering. The first, the way of achievement, is obvious enough. The second and third require further elaboration. We experience a value by experiencing some*thing,* as in nature or in art, or by experiencing some*one,* as through love. "Love is the only way to grasp another human being in the innermost core of his personality."[7] It is by the spiritual act of love, Frankl maintains, that one is enabled to see the essential delineations of the other. One sees not only the actual but the potential as well and by one's love enables the other to actualize these potentialities. The energy of this second way is great enough to flood a life with meaning.

The third way, the way of suffering, is the most difficult, and yet the meaning derived from it is, says Frankl, the deepest meaning. This is meaning that can be discovered only when confronted with an inescapable fate, an unavoidable situation, an irreversible loss. What matters above all is one's attitude toward suffering. Man's main concern is neither pleasure nor the avoidance of pain; it is to find meaning in his life. He is even ready to suffer so long as his suffering has meaning. "Suffering ceases to be suffering in some way at the moment it finds a meaning, such as the meaning of a sacrifice."[8]

Akira Kurosawa's *Ikiru* shows us—and by showing, challenges us to embrace a similar process—a man who discovers meaning in all three of Frankl's ways, notably the first, by doing a deed, but doing it in such a way that he experiences love

STILL 17: *Ikiru*
Directed by Akira Kurosawa.
Mr. Watanabe (Takashi Shimura), a terminal cancer patient for whom life has been sheer bureaucratic drudgery, finds meaning in his last days working for the completion of a children's park. His inner serenity is transparent in this peaceful shot of the dying man, swinging in the snow, celebrating his victory over death.

and transforms the nature of his suffering. Stricken with incurable cancer, Mr. Wantanabe (Takashi Shimura) spends his remaining days personally overseeing the construction of a playground that City Hall, in its indifference, had previously blocked. As a bureau chief, he had contributed to the tangle of official red tape; now he cuts through it all, doing a deed that can only be seen as a work of love for young children. Man's existence, Kurosawa reminds us, is limited: The only way for him to redeem the time is to make the most urgent use of the day that is given to him. The film's choice of physical reality—specifically of a park for children as the goal of Watanabe's action—suggests that we must work, and thus live, *for* others.

In Elia Kazan's *East of Eden* the second way, the way of love, is powerfully enacted. The film is a retelling of the biblical story of Adam and Eve and their two sons, the story of the Trask family set in Southern California on the eve of the First World War. Cal (James Dean) feels himself rejected by his father (Raymond Massey) at every turn. This feeling of rejection is repeatedly emphasized by a pattern of visual composition of frames that shows him at diagonal odds with the physical world around him. Cal is like his mother, Kate, who has left the family for a life of sin; therefore Cal is "through and through bad," whereas his brother Aron, who resembles their self-righteous father, is good. Life without love is not only devoid of meaning for Cal; it also makes him irrational. When he precipitates the film's final tragedy—his brother's going off to war in a deranged state, his father's paralysis by a stroke—he confesses humbly, "It's awful not to be loved, it makes you mean." But he knows he is still free to choose. He turns to his father in his father's need; and when the stricken Adam accepts him, Cal's existence is suddenly ablaze with meaning. He is no longer at odds with reality; erect and self-assured, he blends perfectly with the upward thrust of his father's bedstead. The mythical journey of Cal-Cain is superficially between the brooding coast of his mother's sin and the sunlit valley of his father's righteousness, but only to adjust our vision to the coexistence of good and evil in each of us. Everyone is a sad, but hope-filled mixture of both; one accepts another despite the evil in him only if one acknowledges and transcends the evil in oneself.

Frankl's third way, the way of suffering, is the most mysterious. Like Frankl, Sol Nazerman in Sidney Lumet's *The Pawnbroker* is the only one of his immediate family to survive the Nazi concentration camp. Unlike Frankl, Nazerman (Rod Steiger) is driven into the shell of his own tormented self. We find him twenty years later running a pawn shop on the fringe of New York's Spanish Harlem. His manner is a cold and impersonal shield standing between him and the reach of pain. It also stands between him and meaning. Meaning deserted him by way of suffering; it returns by the same route. When his young Puerto Rican assistant gets shot in a holdup that the boy himself, out of spite, helped stage, Sol discovers that he is not past pain, not past caring. As his hand comes crashing down upon the counter and impales itself upon the spike meant for his customers' IOUs, meaning is glimpsed in an agony beyond his own. We see with Sol "a vision of what was, what is, and what ought to be."[9]

Any attempt to discover meaning in life is deeply related to hope. Hope is the wellspring of all vitality. Without hope one imagines that there is no inner strength, no outside help, to call upon. Without hope one decides that, even if there were such strength or help, "*there is no use,* no good, no sense in action or in life. Here we are up against the lack even of a wish to do or to live."[10] The hope that concerns us here is what has been called a fundamental hope as something quite distinct from the plurality of all our ordinary hopes. It is the difference between "I hope" and "I hope that. . . ." The latter has reference to all the possibilities that this world can offer, to a specific value corresponding to a specific desire, whereas the former apparently has no such object. It has to do, not with what a person *has,* but with what he *is.* It has to do, in fact, with the salvation of the human person.[11]

Strange as it may seem, fundamental *hope* asserts itself most tellingly only when all our *hopes* collapse and lose their meaning. The experience is observed by a number of writers. Joseph Pieper finds it in controlled studies of people "for whom hope had become a problem in a unique way—the psychological situation of persons incurably ill, and of those who have attempted to take their own lives."[12] Viktor Frankl finds it in a Nazi death-camp: "In a last violent protest against the hopelessness of imminent death, I sensed my spirit piercing through the enveloping gloom. I felt it transcend that hopeless, meaningless world, and from somewhere I heard a victorious 'Yes' in answer to my question of the existence of an ultimate purpose."[13] Erich Fromm finds it in what he calls the dynamic psalms, as in Psalm 22 ("My God, my God, why have you forsaken me?") where the movement "starts in some despair, changes to some hope, then returns to deeper despair and reacts with more hope; eventually it arrives at the very deepest despair and only at this point is the despair really overcome." He concludes with the paradox that "despair can be overcome only if it has been fully experienced."[14] That paradox makes itself keenly felt in a film like Luis Buñuel's *Nazarin.*

There is no doubt that Nazario (Francisco Rabal) is perfectly sincere. His hopes are modest. He wants to live the life of a priest in Mexico of the nineteenth century exactly as he imagined Christ would have lived it, giving out of his poverty, relying on the goodness of God, preaching, praying, reproving. Unlike Christ, he is detached from everything human. He presumes to enter the mystery of love without loving. Wanted only by the police (for having given refuge to a whore who had murdered another in a brawl), he sets out on a pilgrimage with the intention of serving the poor. When he is finally taken prisoner, the meaning of his life is challenged in a way that nothing had led him to expect. Two prisoners play good and bad thief to his suffering Jesus. The latter, a parricide, abuses him verbally and physically, so severely that the priest cannot find it in his heart to forgive him without at the same time despising him. When the "good thief" comes to his aid, Nazario, desperately clinging to his priesthood, asks him if he would like to change his life. The man surprises him with a question: "Would you like to change yours? What use is your life really? You're on the side of good and I'm on evil. And neither of us is any use for anything." Nazario is clearly shaken to his depths. The ground has been taken out from under him. He collapses, with all his hopes, into the black hole of meaninglessness.

In the final sequence, Nazario is taken under guard to trial. As we see him walking along the road, his face reflects nothing but the emptiness within him. A woman is selling fruit on the side of the road, a Veronica who comes forward to offer him a pineapple with her blessing. He looks at her, confused, unable to understand, as if the offer were some obscene intrusion from a world that had already died in his heart. A second time he refuses, but when she turns away, he takes her by the arm. We see him in close-up looking at her intently. Then he takes the pineapple and holds it in the crook of his arm like a precious gift. As he is led away to the sounds of drums, his face is wet with tears: hope has begun to build again, a fundamental hope that creates anew the wish to live, the will to meaning. A single act of kindness may be enough to open the door of the future again.

Hope keeps man on the road to meaning; it keeps him in relationship to his beginning and end, where he comes from, where he goes. By the same token, despair and presumption are his alienation from these poles of his existence. Despair and presumption can be said to constitute man's original sin, and as such they distort all his relationships—to himself, to his neighbor and world, to his God.

In this perspective, the search for meaning becomes a journey toward reconciliation. The personal dimension of that search addresses the issue of man's alienation from self: it impels him to a sense of his own worth. This is the impulse so evident in Cal's behavior in *East of Eden.* The social dimension responds to man's alienation from neighbor and world: it urges him to form community. Sol Nazerman's glimpse of "what ought to be" at the end of *The Pawnbroker* is inextricably bound to such an urge. The religious dimension responds to man's alienation from his beginning and end; it pulls him into the future, into the depths of God. The embryonic Star Child that rises above the earth in *2001: A Space Odyssey* is enveloped in mystery: a reality greater than his own urges him to pass beyond himself and unfolds in the center of his being.

The search for meaning surely begins with the attempt to sense one's own worth. We are not born with that sense, and in this world of ours we never perfectly achieve it: We are always on the way, on a pilgrimage toward self-realization. That pilgrimage is marked by three essential experiences: (1) by trusting and mastering the world around us, (2) by being loved, and (3) by loving. The child very soon finds himself immersed in the world of things. "This is mine" are among the first words he learns to say, and before he knows it, "This is mine" means "This is me." If he forgets his list of what is his, he will not know who he is. By extending himself over his little empire, he begins to define himself in terms of it. Some people never outgrow this experience, or else they revert to it in their adult years if the experiences of being loved and loving are suppressed.

Ordinarily, these two experiences follow quickly upon the initial experience of trusting and mastering the world. A child begins to sense his own worth when the adult world, especially in the person of his mother, bends over him in affection. He knows he is lovable because he is loved. When love is withheld, the road to self-acceptance is painful indeed. From the very beginning the child needs the other in order to become himself. He becomes himself in the other's presence. And as he matures, and learns to reciprocate love, he will tell others that they are lovable by loving them; they will become themselves in *his* presence.

In Anthony Pelissier's *The Rocking-Horse Winner,* Hester Grahame (Valerie Hobson) no doubt has for her son a certain instinctual love, but there is no time or place in her heart for the kind of love he needs and deserves as a person. The father is psychologically absent from the family. Unable to provide for it in the manner his wife demands, and not strong enough to impose a more reasonable level of living, he disappears as both husband and father. The son, in a sense, is compelled to assume both roles: the young Paul (John Howard Davies) must provide for his mother, and the way he goes about it, plunging to a climax on his wooden horse, is not without its sexual overtones. At the climax of his imaginary race, he becomes inspired; he is able to pick the winner of the next horse race. But there is no end to his mother's extravagance; the more money he wins, the more she wants, and Paul dies in his final effort to pick a winner. Hester had come to define herself in terms of that first human experience whereby "this is mine" becomes "this is me." The film's compositional motif is one of frames within frames, and the import is clear: Paul and his mother are trapped by her greed for possessions.

The social dimension of our search for meaning is already implied in the personal. Our relationship to ourselves, as we have seen, presupposes our relationship to others. These relationships spiral outward into a world of ever increasing complexity, a world that both invites and threatens, a world of communion in which we can be at home with ourselves and yet not be alone. "Only communion," Robert Johann remarks, "at once preserves the miracle of originality that is the person, while at the same time healing the isolation that became his lot when self-consciousness first wrenched him from the mothering embrace of nature."[15] The family, the neighborhood, the city, the nation, the world—these are the structures for community, and yet each one can become a prison. Do they free us or hinder us in our search for meaning? Do they help us create our future, or do they render us, in effect, futureless?

A man asking these questions a century ago would not have had to reckon with one important element that we must reckon with today. And that element is technology. There is no disputing that technology puts into the hands of man a power to create new forms of freedom, new images of the future—so long as it remains technology. What happens when technology becomes technologism, that is, when it ceases to be a tool and becomes instead a "savior"? When that happens, instead of liberating man, it envelops, conditions, and determines him. Man no longer simply uses technology; he becomes a part of the total technological system. Consequently, he becomes one-dimensional, as Herbert Marcuse describes him, "incapable of critical thinking and action, futureless and ahistorical, at home in a system that is now his home and his permanent tomorrow."[16]

And what if the system is threatened? Since it is the embodiment of all that is good, a god unto itself, it must preserve itself at all costs. It engages in that abuse of technology called modern warfare. It perpetuates and suffers the irrationalities of a *Slaughterhouse-Five.*

STILL 18: *Slaughterhouse-Five*
Directed by George Roy Hill.
Even though Billy Pilgrim (Michael Sacks) stoically announces that he has come "unstuck in time," Hill nonetheless shows us, ironically, that there are two aspects of human existence that everyone is inevitably stuck by—the consequences of technology (a clock pins Billy down) and death (the pointing machine gun suggests there is "a time" for "everyman").

As a result of the trauma of being captured behind German lines toward the end of the Second World War, Billy Pilgrim (Michael Saks) has become "unstuck in time." This device is somewhat clumsily rendered in Kurt Vonnegut's novel ("Billy blinked in 1945, traveled in time to 1958"), but George Roy Hill brilliantly exploits the possibilities of film in his direction of the screen adaptation: by skillful editing he jumps back and forth in time through visual association and sound overlap and the look of outer regard (Billy looks up from his typewriter through the window of his room at the snow-covered lawn: cut to the snowy scene itself, which we quickly perceive is behind German lines years earlier). A prisoner of German soldiers, all of them mere boys, he is taken to Dresden where he experiences the war's greatest single atrocity. The firebombing of Dresden is as fine a symbol of apocalypse as recent history has provided simply because of the enormity of its carnage. Dresden was an "open city"; it was undefended because it possessed no significant war industries or troop concentrations. Its art treasures and the splendor of its architecture had gained it the deserved title of "the Florence of the Elbe." The bombing of Dresden by what were then considered conventional weapons remains the greatest single destructive act not only in European history but also apparently in the recorded history of man-made catastrophes. The atomic bomb dropped on Hiroshima killed some 71,000 people and an incendiary attack on Tokyo (similar to Dresden) caused the death of some 84,000, whereas 135,000 people died as a result of the attack on Dresden. Is it inevitable that man's great technological achievements become the inferno of technologism? Are we incapable of controlling our world because we lack the foresight to project the consequences of our scientific dreams? Vonnegut does not imagine total catastrophe; he records history. What his humor contributes, though, toward the condemnation of man's pretensions and an expression of hope are more than amply conveyed visually in the affection with which Hill's camera records even the most bizarre of human tragedies.

The religious dimension pushes the personal and the social as far as they can go and then comes into its own. If the experience of being loved assures us that we are of value, the experience of God not only assures us, but actually creates that value. God's concern makes us be and be of value. If we are impelled into communion with others, our relationship to God not only provides the ground of our dignity as human beings but also becomes the very basis of fellowship. God stands in the same mutual relationship to every member of the community.

Inevitably, the religious dimension of man's quest for meaning raises the question of ultimacy. As Frankl puts it, are we sure "that the human world is a terminal point in the evolution of the cosmos? Is it not conceivable that there is still another dimension possible, a world beyond man's world; a world in which the question of an ultimate meaning of human suffering would find an answer?"[17] The question, then, becomes not so much, Is there a God? but rather, Is there a God to hope in? Is there a deathless source of power and meaning? For Sam Keen, the question of God can be posed in no other way:

> To deny that there is a God is functionally equivalent to denying that there is any ground for hope. It is therefore wholly consistent for Sartre to say that human beings "must act without hope," or for Camus to warn that hope was the last of the curses which Pandora took from her box. If God is dead, then death is indeed God, and perhaps the best motto for human life is what Dante once wrote over the entrance to hell: "Abandon hope, all ye who enter."[18]

If there is any ultimacy to the meaning that man so passionately desires, only God can provide it.

The knight in Ingmar Bergman's *The Seventh Seal* wants desperately to believe in such a God, but everything tempts him to say no, and he hangs miserably between yes and no, as if over an abyss. "Religious faith," says Lynch, "has always taught man not only to know, but to be able to live in waiting, in a kind of darkness, making war on the desire of man to reduce the whole of reality, supernatural and natural, to his own limited way of knowing."[19] Antonius Block (Max von Sydow) returns from the devastation of the Crusades only to find that Death comes up to face him everywhere. He hopes to do "one

STILL 19: *The Seventh Seal*
Directed by Ingmar Bergman.
Antonius Block (Max von Sydow), a knight returning from the Crusades, questions Death (Bengt Ekerot), disguised as a priest in the confessional, about the silence of God. "Why, in spite of everything," the knight asks, "is [God] a baffling reality that I can't shake off?" Man seeks knowledge, but must settle for faith.

meaningful deed" before he dies, and that he does: he leads a simple family of travelling actors—Jof, Mia, and their baby Mikael—to safety. Unlike the knight, Jof (Nils Poppe) never feels the need to stop living in order to ask the meaning of life. Life, rather, questions him. As for that other "dimension" that Frankl alludes to, Jof is in constant communion with it: for him, God *is*. If God is calling, why can he not be heard? If he lives in light, why can he not be seen? Paradoxically, Bergman suggests, it is the man of simple faith who sees and hears.

In Ken Russell's *Altered States,* scripted by Paddy Chayefsky,[20] the passion for ultimate meaning becomes a reckless obsession. Eddie Jessup (William Hurt) is a maverick professor at the Harvard Medical School who is feverishly intent upon reaching back through consciousness to the very origin of things. He is convinced that all our states of consciousness are as real as our waking states. Why couldn't they then be externalized? Using a variety of unorthodox means, including hallucinogenic drugs and immersion in an isolation tank filled with warm salt water, he makes several terrifying journeys back into time—back to primitive man, to the ape man, to chaos. He makes these journeys not only internally, in the world of the imagination, but externally, in the world of verifiable fact. Has he gone too far? Will he ever be able to return? He does, thanks to the far-reaching love of his wife. What about the ultimate meaning of things? There is none. There is nothing at the beginning and there is nothing at the end. There is only human love. Twenty years ago Paddy Chayefsky gave us the same message in his play *The Tenth Man.* When an agnostic lawyer becomes the tenth man in the exorcism of a dybbuk (evil spirit) that possesses a girl he has grown to love, he too falls on the floor as if possessed. Emerging from the experience, he says: "I feel as if I have been reduced to the moment of birth, as if the universe has become one hunger."[21] At the end, when he leaves with the girl, one of the exorcists says: "An hour ago, he didn't believe in God; now he's exorcising dybbuks." Another man remarks: "He still doesn't believe in God. He simply wants to love. And when you stop and think about it, gentlemen, is there any difference?"[22]

When you stop and think about it, any answer to the question of ultimate meaning that is not open to mystery is bound to be suspect.

To be open to mystery: the image of journey resonates with that attitude of mind; the experience of film at its deepest level prompts that response. Quest is the archetypal image for the furthest reach of the human spirit, perhaps never more powerfully expressed than in Dante's *Divine Comedy,* which opens at the end on "the love that moves the sun and other stars." Such images never quite disappear from the human psyche. According to Mircea Eliade, they may wear a different mask, but their function remains the same. The most abject nostalgia, he says, discloses the nostalgia for paradise. In the same way, the most timorous journey can disclose the journey of the mind to God, who is inexhaustible mystery; and the most ordinary experience of motion, as in film's inevitable portrayal of quest, can open our hearts to mystery. Archetypal images may become "disguised, mutilated or degraded, but are never extirpated." Even in their depleted state, they "present to us the only possible point of departure for the spiritual renewal of modern man. It is of the greatest importance, we believe, to rediscover a whole mythology, if not a theology, still concealed in the most ordinary, everyday life of contemporary man; it will depend upon himself whether he can work his way back to the source and rediscover the profound meanings of these faded images and damaged myths."[23]

To be open to mystery: without that attitude of mind the quest for meaning never truly begins and never rightly ends.

PART III

Directors and the Varieties of Religious Sensibility

WILLIAM PARRILL

Robert Altman

ROBERT ALTMAN is not, at least in any traditional sense, a religious film maker: he does not deal obviously with theological problems, he has no apparent interest in transcendent experience, and he seldom uses traditional religious imagery.[1] True, Altman is fond of saying that one of his first directing jobs was a commercial for the Catholic Bishops Fund, but his relish in the story is more an indication of his love of incongruity than of any feeling for institutionalized religion. Altman may justly be regarded—and has been—as a secular artist whose chief interest in the church is in its role as a social institution.

Altman's clerics are either ineffectual or self-serving or both. In *M*A*S*H,* the priest, Dago Red, is lovable but eccentric. He mistakes the sounds of the love-making of Hot Lips and Major Burns for "The Battling Bickersons" and is last seen blessing a Jeep. In *McCabe and Mrs. Miller,* the Presbyterian preacher drives McCabe at gunpoint out of the church, where he has taken refuge from the men who are trying to kill him, toward what they both know is nearly certain death. In *A Wedding,* the doddering bishop who performs the high-church ceremony at the beginning of the film is presented as a figure of fun throughout. He is a senile old man who stumbles through the ritual, is unable to locate the bathroom, carries on a conversation with a corpse, and grumbles when asked to give a blessing. In the same film, a second clergyman, presumably a fundamentalist, tells a bizarre story of his religious conversion. While in a Holiday Inn in Arcadia, West Virginia, he heard the voice of God speaking on late-night television and saying, "Enough is enough." Altman's portraits of the clergy, hardly numerous considering the number of films he has made, are primarily satirical and illustrate only the social function of the church. The church is simply another institution held up for scrutiny and shown to be inadequate.

Yet the situation is hardly as simple as it seems at first glance. Altman's films preserve, like forms embedded in prehistoric ore, traces of his Catholic upbringing. His pervasive interest centers on the public groupings that hold men together, and his films show the forces that attack those institutions from without and within. Indeed, his "American" films may legitimately be interpreted as large-scale questionings of our public celebrations. That Altman regards these celebrations as necessary and that they are ritualistic is clear in *Nashville.* By contrast, his "European" films show the breakdown of character and the descent into schizophrenia that occur when the institutions and rituals of society are absent or inoperative; for example, *Three Women* and *Quintet* present the attempts of a broken society and battered individuals to manufacture rituals to replace those which have been lost. Thus, if Altman's films are not religious in the stricter sense, I would certainly maintain that they are in the larger sense of their concern with ritual and celebration.

There are at least two Robert Altmans: the first is a great American original who makes wide-ranging and provocative films, often satiric in nature, about American life: *Countdown* (1967), *M*A*S*H* (1969), *Brewster McCloud* (1970), *McCabe and Mrs. Miller* (1970), *The Long Goodbye* (1973), *Thieves Like Us* (1974), *California Split* (1974), *Nashville* (1975), *Buffalo Bill and the Indians* (1976), *A Wedding* (1978), *A Perfect Couple* (1979), and *Health* (1981, but filmed in 1977); the second, and lesser, is an imitator of the great Europeans, particularly Bergman, who keeps remaking *Persona: That Cold Day in the Park* (1969), *Images* (1972), *Three Women* (1977), and *Quintet* (1979). *Popeye* (1980) is a musical romp that seems to fall somewhere between the two. All the "American" films are ensemble pieces that deal with the interactions of people within society. The "European" films are more private, deal with small groups, and lack local color. Only *Three Women* is set in America, and its hospital locale and desert landscapes are metaphors of the spirit and not slices of Americana. The films of the two Altmans are so different that they hardly seem the work of the same man, but certain crucial films, *Three Women, Quintet,* and *Brewster McCloud,* clarify the interrelationship.

Altman's "American" films celebrate corporate identity through group action, including ritual and its chief component, celebration: *Countdown,* the united effort to make a successful moon landing; *M*A*S*H,* a united assertion of life in the face of the "loads of meat" (Altman's phrase) being brought into the hospital camp daily by helicopter; *McCabe and Mrs. Miller,* the building of the town of Presbyterian Church around its chief institutions, the whorehouse, the church, the saloon, and the volunteer fire station; *Nashville,* the political rally as a paradigm of society; *Buffalo Bill and the Indians,* the Wild West show as a celebration of American ideals; and *A Wedding,* a social occasion centered around a rite that no longer seems to have much meaning for its celebrants.

The idea of celebration is particularly evident in *Nashville.* This film is worth considering in this context, not only because it is one of Altman's most satisfying films, but also because it expresses ideas of communal celebration implicit in several other films. According to Richard H. Rupp, "celebration is ultimately a religious act, although it has many secular manifestations. It is an act of praise—an action founded on love and leading to individual renewal."[2] *Nashville* fits nicely within the terms of this definition.

Nashville is an ensemble film that covers the lives of twenty-four people during the four days leading up to a political rally in Nashville, Tennessee, for a populist presidential candidate, whom we never see, and ending with the arbitrary shooting, not of the presidential candidate, but of a famous and fragile country and western singer. The sacrificial nature of the singer's being shot is shown by the fact that the killer decides to shoot her on the spur of the moment because she sings a song about her family. As the most sympathetic character in the entire film, the singer is the surrogate of the people at the political rally (and of the viewers of the film), and her sacrifice, however unwitting, renews the society and prepares it for the days to come. The concluding song, "It Don't Worry Me," asserts that the traditional ideals of American society will survive despite—I would argue "because of"—the trauma the society has just undergone.

When *Nashville* appeared, it was advertised as a "celebration," and many people who went to it expecting a paean to American virtues appropriate to the coming bicentennial year were disappointed. *Nashville* is not that, but neither is it the "put-down" of American society many took it to be. It is a depiction of the great celebrations by which American society renews itself. The film came at a dark period of American history, and its darkness represents not so much an attack on American society as an assertion of its fundamental integrity, a foundation on which to build. Assassination may even be a periodic necessity for the renewal of American society. When Haven Hamilton, toupee gone, fancy outfit soaked in his own blood, says, "This isn't Dallas, this is Nashville," he is not being ironic; he is asserting, admittedly with great presumption, the wholeness of the society he represents. And the complex feelings of peace, relief, and acceptance that flood through the rally's audience—and through the film's audience—as they sing the song of renewal and then return quietly to their homes and families are ritualistic and celebratory in nature.

Altman's "European" films show the fragmentation of personality and the descent into madness that occur when ritual is absent and when the institutions of society become inoperative. The people in these films are dislocated; unlike the Indians in *Buffalo Bill,* they do not belong to the settings. Frances (*That Cold Day in the Park*) and Cathryn (*Images*) have fragmented their personalities and become schizophrenic. But against odds and without any help from society, Milly (*Three Women*), Essex (*Quintet*), and Brewster McCloud attempt an artificial integration of personality. These attempts are a reflection of the drive toward wholeness that is the goal of the religious process. Based as they are merely on the demands of the individual will, they are doomed from the start, but the desire of the Altman protagonists for psychological wholeness is so great that they sometimes achieve limited success.

Marsha Kinder has written perceptively of *Three Women*: "The main creative task for the entire personality is to recreate a vital self in spite of the sterile environment and the impoverished cultural imprinting it has absorbed."[3] Milly's integration of personality is accomplished without the help of society. Her rebirth from the swimming pool is symbolic and ritualistic, but it is not specifically Christian, and it is religious only in the most general sense. At the end of the film, the three women have become one, but their success is a retreat from society, in effect, a return to the womb. It may indeed be schizophrenic. It does not show the renewed hope for an enriched society represented by the communal ritual of *Nashville,* or even the more limited affirmation of the shared ritual of the fire fighters in *McCabe and Mrs. Miller.*

In *Quintet,* the traditional shared values that hold society together have disappeared, and society has invented a brutal game to take the place of religion and to give coherence to life in a future ice age. Essex achieves a bloody revenge after his paramour, the last pregnant woman on earth, is killed by a player of Quintet—a complicated game of hide-and-seek which one wins by killing off the other players. Lacking any foundation in religion or genuine communal feeling, the game is only a bloody pastime, the last attempt of a spiritually dead society to justify its existence.

After gaining his revenge, Essex decides to set out by himself. When told by the Quintet referee that he will be killed, he says, "You know that, I don't." In the last scene, he disappears in the field of ice, a figure growing smaller and smaller and gradually becoming lost among the frozen forms. The image is rich in literary associations: it suggests the alternate but ancient vision of hell as a frozen waste and the conclusion of Edgar Allan Poe's *The Narrative of Arthur Gordon Pym.* These associations are relevant, but Altman characteristically does not insist on them. He does not have to. As an image of man's indomitability in the face of terrible odds, the conclusion of *Quintet* can stand alone.

Alone among Altman's films, *Brewster McCloud* combines Altman's satiric vision of modern America and his search for the wholeness of personality which only metaphysical certainty can give. With the help of his supernatural mother, Brewster, the half-human bird man of the Astrodome, is train-

STILL 20: *Brewster McCloud*
Directed by Robert Altman.
Robert Altman's satiric eye takes on the folly of American technology. In a film with multiple layers of mythic meaning, Brewster (Bud Cort) foolishly attempts to fly—man's earliest, but enduring mode of transcending his limits through technology. His futile efforts are circumscribed by the static, impersonal beauty of the Astrodome.

ing himself to fly. But he falls in love with a human girl, has sexual intercourse with her — the closest thing humans "have to . . . flying"[4] — loses his powers, and crashes to death within the enclosed wonder of the modern world, where he could not have flown far anyway. *Brewster McCloud,* although often cited by Altman as his favorite among his films, is not an artistic success. The satiric and the supernatural elements of the film never come together. But the image of Brewster, with his health foods, his complicated harness, and his elaborate exercises, attempting through sheer determination to fly, is Altman's most moving image of the human will released from the demands and restraints of society.

Robert Altman is in many ways the most protean and difficult of modern American commercial directors. He is also the most gregarious. The virtues he celebrates are always communal, and isolation is invariably shown through the separation of the self from society and from its healing rituals. This image of separation, however negative, has evident biblical roots; and, although Altman has not yet made a film of unequivocal religious affirmation, he has given us striking visions of spiritual isolation as well as secular analogues of ritualistic renewal.

BIBLIOGRAPHY

Billman, Carol W. "Illusions of Grandeur: Altman, Kopit and the Legend of the West." *Literature/Film Quarterly* 6 (1978), 253–61.

Gabbard, Krin. "Altman's *Three Women:* Sanctuary in the Dream World." *Literature/Film Quarterly* 8 (1980), 258–64.

Jacobs, Diane. "Robert Altman." In *Hollywood Renaissance.* Cranbury, N.J.: Barnes, 1977, pp. 63–96.

Kass, Judith W. *Robert Altman: American Innovator.* New York: Popular Library, 1978.

McClelland, C. Kirk. *On Making a Movie: Brewster McCloud.* New York: New American Library, 1971.

Parrill, William. "Mrs. Kennedy's Gloves." *New Boston Review* 4 (Sept. 1978), 7–8.

Rudolph, Alan, and Robert Altman. *Buffalo Bill and the Indians.* New York: Bantam Books, 1976.

Tewkesbury, Joan. *Nashville.* New York: Bantam Books, 1976.

MICHAEL BIRD

Ingmar Bergman

To speak of a religious perspective in the cinematic work of Ingmar Bergman leads to the fundamental question: can one detect a continuous point of view in films as diverse as *The Seventh Seal, Persona,* and *Scenes from a Marriage*? Is it at all reasonable to speak of a consistent vision that embraces not only the explicitly religious films but also those which, in some critics' eyes, indicate an abandonment of interest in the religious subject altogether?

Contrary to many interpretations that tend to divide Bergman's work into a religious and a "secular" phase, and taking exception even with certain remarks of the director himself (to the effect that after the completion of films such as *The Seventh Seal* and *Winter Light* he no longer was preoccupied with the question of God), my contention is that Bergman's total cinematic work—not merely a few selected examples—is amenable to a theological interpretation and that, while each film must be allowed to stand on its own as a completed aesthetic achievement, at the same time there is a pervasive spiritual search which gives unique movement and texture to all of these distinct cinematic works.

Bergman's spiritual outlook cannot be divorced from his intellectual and artistic milieu. Heir to the theatrical-literary world of Ibsen and Strindberg, with their unrelenting explorations of the theme of spiritually corrupted society and its microscopic equivalent in the family, Bergman has behind him a rich cultural resource for his own cinematic probings. A particular preoccupation of Bergman—the role of women as bearers of suffering and truth—has its background in the works of Ibsen and other writers at the close of the nineteenth century. The distance from *A Doll's House* to *Scenes from a Marriage,* revealed in a facial close-up or the sound of a closing door, is a short one indeed.

The visual dimension of Bergman's art—its textures, lines, tonalities, compositions—suggests a graphic indebtedness to the artistic tradition of Ensor, Munch, Kokoschka. The painterly representation of human anguish at the spiritual as well as at the physiological level—the chill, the shudder, the primal scream—has its powerful antecedents in the late-nineteenth-century artistic traditions of northern Europe. Is not *The Passion of Anna* in a certain sense a cinematic amplification of Edvard Munch's "The Scream," one of the most acoustically expressive statements achieved in painting? Of course the artistic tradition that in part infuses Bergman's outlook harkens back to a yet earlier period, recalling the foreboding and portentous world of those artists of the Northern Renaissance—Dürer, Holbein, and Grünewald. One cannot help but feel the presence of certain numinous elements of Dürer's "Knight, Death and the Devil" in *The Seventh Seal* or of Grünewald's forceful "Isenheim Crucifixion" in *Winter Light*. These celluloid masterpieces leave us with the haunting suspicion that a Bergman film is to contemporary cinema what the woodcut was to nineteenth-century art—an awesomely compressed expression of graphic power.

While the artistic, literary, and dramatic tradition provided Bergman with a vivid and agonizing perspective on the broken humanity of a fallen world, this view received further intensification from the theological tradition, focusing upon the reality of sin and depicting the vast, unbridgeable chasm separating men and women from God as well as from each other. This corrosion of human deed and reason had been articulated nowhere with such force and eloquence as by Søren Kierkegaard, that Danish theological firebrand and unloved prophet of the nineteenth century who, as the "father of modern existentialism" (though he himself was an intensely committed Christian), was to have inestimable influence upon twentieth-century art and ideas. The Kierkegaardian picture of abysmal despair, suffering, and the pervasive experience that he called the "sickness unto death" is not without its dramatic and cinematic corollary in the aesthetic works of Ibsen, Strindberg, and Bergman.

Yet the most profound influence upon Bergman (to be sure,

the one that he has continually tried so desperately to renounce) is the Lutheran theological tradition into which he was born. Reared by an autocratic father who was an ordained clergyman, Bergman came to know well the Lutheran emphasis upon the utter fallenness of humankind, in which the image of God was not merely stained but thoroughly shattered. This introspective milieu, although theoretically disposed toward the theme of the love of God, was imbued in practice all too often by the fear of man.

If one wishes to address the question of a spiritual focus in the overall work of this brilliantly diverse cinematic artist, one must take into account two of his own statements, both of which might be superficially taken as impediments to any such investigation. One of these is his publicly announced repudiation of the Lutheran milieu within which he was nurtured. The other is Bergman's brief reference to certain of his more explicitly religious films as a passing phase in his artistic exploration, to which he has no intention of returning.

There is, to be certain, a narrow definition of religious experience—particularly the theistic description (religion as assent to the notion of the existence of God)—within which one could include perhaps few films other than *The Seventh Seal* and *Winter Light* as truly religious investigations, because the question of God's existence arises at one point or another. There is, however, also a broad definition of the religious dimension, even a Christian religious experience, within which the continuous struggle and search in every major Bergman film emerge as the expression of a profound spiritual quest. This is the religious experience which, as the theologian Paul Tillich claims, exists both inside and outside the historic church and cultus, occurring in the hearts of men and women as a restless striving for ultimate unity with the unconditional ground of being itself. The distinction between narrow and broad appears in the thought of this creative theologian of culture as the difference between the God *of* theism and the God *above* theism. For Tillich, those elements often considered to be the denial of religious affirmation—doubt, despair, anxiety—are in fact necessary experiences within faith itself. The commonplace definition of faith as belief in God is insufficient, in the view of Tillich, because the word *God* is at best a symbolic reference to that which is beyond conceptualization altogether. Tillich offers an alternative formulation of faith as "the state of being grasped by ultimate concern."[1] This articulation of religious experience has the merit of making the object of faith truly absolute and unconditional (not merely a particular notion of "God"—what Bergman in several films calls an "echo-God"). The continual concern about the insufficiency of any particular definition of man's ultimate concern—God, love, truth, expressed religiously as doubt—is itself a consequence of the desire for a deeper encounter with the ultimate depth underlying the surface of experience. In this event, doubt is not the loss of faith, but rather the consequence of being engaged by ultimate concern, as it strips away all preliminary and finite pretensions at knowledge of the divine. For Tillich, *God* is a symbol for God. The word points to but does not exhaust the reality. Between the finite concept (the God of theism, the product of a process of logical argument) and the infinite reality of the Absolute there is encountered an abyss of doubt, testifying to the sufficiency of the latter and the insufficiency of the former. If doubt is essential to the experience of faith, the universal experience of anxiety and alienation is itself grounded in the awareness of the limits of human finitude and the intuition of an infinite depth behind the world of appearances.

The problem of existential doubt in the films of Ingmar Bergman has theological implications in its traditional connection with the notion of God as Totally Other, hence beyond comprehension and controlling knowledge. The paradoxical association of doubt with mysterious presence appears in *The Seventh Seal* (1956) in a manner strangely reminiscent of the Old Testament story of the suffering of Job. Indeed, Job's situation was painful not so much because of the remoteness but rather because of the very nearness of God. Job could not rail with such fury against a God who did not exist for him. Similarly, when Antonius Block utters his famous cry in the "confessional scene" in *The Seventh Seal*—"I want knowledge, not faith, not suppositions, but knowledge; I want God to stretch out his hand toward me, reveal Himself and speak to me"—it comes as something of a surprise that he also asks the seemingly contradictory question, "Why can't I kill God within me?"[2]

We have in this and similar cinematic moments a profound portrayal of the anguish of the questioning individual in the face of the mystery of the "hidden God," the *deus absconditus.* It is not surprising that this theme, so precious to Luther, should dominate the artistic work of the cinematic heir to that theological tradition (despite his own claims to have left it all behind).

No film makes more explicit the theme of Christian doubt than *Winter Light* (1962), which has generally been considered Bergman's most direct treatment of the ecclesiastical expression of religious life. It would almost appear that this film is a veritable Continental Divide, down whose one side flow the religious streams of the early films, and from whose other side spring the waters of his later films of a purportedly secular nature. This all-too-frequent dichotomization of religious and non-religious phases in the director's work is surely called into question by a fascinating irony in this particular film: it is the supposed agnostic Märta who, in the final moments of this Bergman journey, kneels in what is one of the most moving and evocative instances of a cinematic "prayer." Through a series of parallel images showing Märta's bowed head in juxtaposition with that of Thomas, and her "prayer," which, by overlapping both of the visual images, serves thereby to unite them, Bergman has managed to create a modern saint who in her existential doubt gives paradoxical expression to Tillich's "God who appears when God has disappeared in the anxiety of doubt."[3] At the same time, Märta becomes the prototype for those profoundly agonized women in the later films. To be certain, there are external shifts in his cinematic work—from cosmos to domicile, from rural to urban context, from men to women, from religious cultus to post-Christian culture. But the underlying search for that Ground of Being, that Depth which lies at the root of all experiencing—the spiritual preoccupation with Ultimate Concern—this theme pervades the entire cinematic work. Later films such as *Cries and Whispers* (1973) and *Face to Face* (1976) are among the most refined ex-

STILL 21: *Winter Light*
Directed by Ingmar Bergman.
Tomas Eriksson (Gunnar Bjornstrand) and his agnostic parishioner Marta Lundberg (Ingrid Thulin) converse on a cold, desolate field next to Tomas's church, their positions accentuating the distance between them. Her refusal to accept his icy rejection—that persistence in human communion—may finally kindle within him love's winter light.

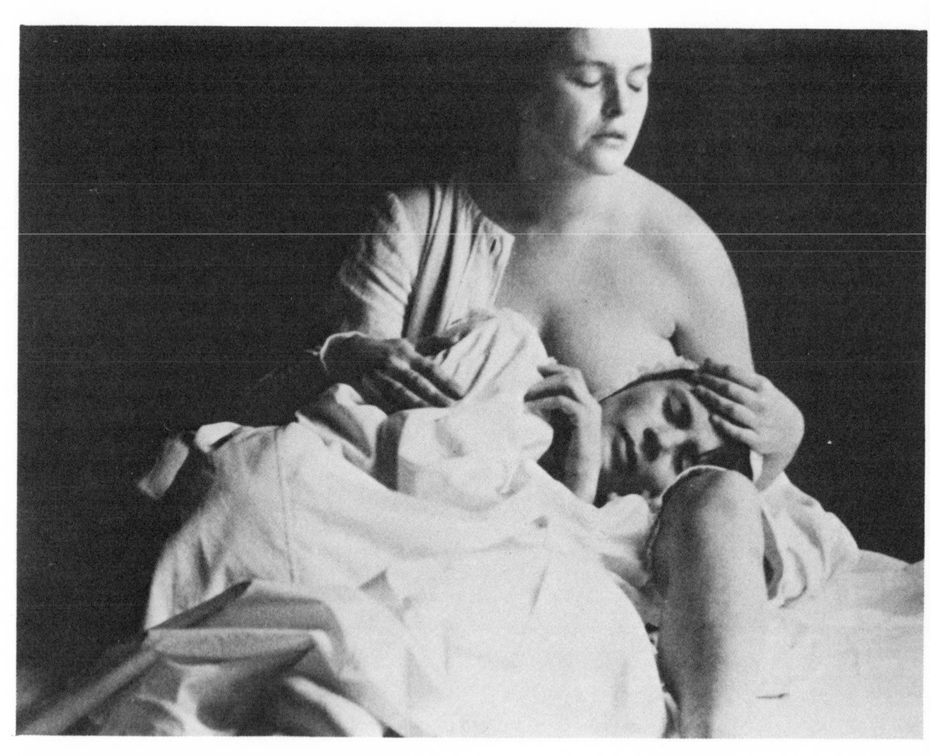

STILL 22: *Cries and Whispers*
Directed by Ingmar Bergman.
When Agnes (Harriet Andersson), dying from cancer, awakens moaning in the middle of the night, it is the simple maidservant Anna (Kari Sylwan) who comforts her—not one of Agnes's obsessed, guilt-ridden sisters. The ironic allusion to the Pietà is unmistakable: comfort in suffering may come from the least expected source.

pressions of the "chamber film," a genre developed by Bergman with exquisite sensitivity. *Autumn Sonata* (1979) accomplishes by way of domestic intimacy and musical evocation a striking return to the latent hopefulness and redemptive power of *Wild Strawberries* (1957), that unsurpassable masterpiece already hallowed by the vintage of a quarter of a century.

Bergman's cinematic work from beginning to end is endowed with that painfully prophetic quality of "un-earthing": it digs beneath the surface of culture, habit, belief, and convention in order to allow a profound truth to reveal itself. This unearthing is likely to be experienced as agonizing ordeal, threatening to remove necessary structures of survival. At the same time it is a calculated risk dedicated to the goal of stepping beyond the raw needs of survival to the promise of meaningful existence. Un-earthing is, then, a stage in the spiritual pilgrimage toward heaven. This destruction of finite barriers in the search for the infinite has been expressed by the philosopher Paul Ricouer in his perception that "an idol must die in order that a symbol of Being may speak."[4] Such is the function of doubt in Bergman's cinematic explorations; it is a dynamic factor clearing the way for the human encounter with "the God above God."

BIBLIOGRAPHY

Adams, R. H. "How Warm Is the Cold, How Light the Darkness?" *The Christian Century,* 16 Sept. 1964, pp. 1144–45.

Bergman, Ingmar. *Face to Face.* Trans. Alan Blair. New York: Pantheon, 1967.

______. *Four Screenplays: Smiles of a Summer Night, The Seventh Seal, Wild Strawberries, The Magician.* Trans. Lars Malmstrom and David Kushner. New York: Simon & Schuster, 1960.

______. *Four Stories: The Touch, Cries and Whispers, The Hour of the Wolf,* and *The Passion of Anna.* Trans. Alan Blair. New York: Anchor Books, 1977.

______. *Scenes from a Marriage.* Trans. Alan Blair. New York: Pantheon, 1974.

______. *The Serpent's Egg.* Trans. Alan Blair. New York: Pantheon, 1977.

______. *The Seventh Seal.* New York: Simon and Schuster, 1968.

______. *Three Films: Through a Glass Darkly, Winter Light, The Silence.* Trans. Paul Britten Austen. New York: Grove Press, 1969.

______. *Wild Strawberries.* New York: Simon and Schuster, 1969.

Brightman, Carol. "The Word, the Image, and *The Silence.*" *Film Quarterly* 17, No. 4 (1964), 3–11.

Dahlberg, Bruce. "The Bergman Trilogy." *Christianity and Crisis,* 6 July 1964, pp. 135–39.

Donner, Jorn. *The Personal Vision of Ingmar Bergman.* Trans. Holger Lundbergh. Bloomington: Indiana Univ. Press, 1966.

Gibson, Arthur. *The Silence of God: Creative Response to the Films of Ingmar Bergman.* New York: Harper and Row, 1970.

Gill, Jerry H. *Ingmar Bergman and the Search for Meaning.* Grand Rapids: William B. Eerdmans, 1969.

Steene, Birgitta. "Archetypal Patterns in Four Screenplays of Ingmar Bergman." *Scandinavian Studies,* Feb. 1965, pp. 58–76.

Suttor, Timothy. "Religious Dialectic in Bergman." *The University of Windsor Review* 9 (Fall 1973), 67–81.

Ulrichsen, Erik. "Ingmar Bergman and the Devil." *Sight and Sound* 27 (1958), 224–30.

ERNEST FERLITA

Luis Buñuel

"I'M not a Christian, but I'm not an atheist either," Luis Buñuel says. "I'm weary of hearing that accidental old aphorism of mine 'I'm (still) an atheist, thank God.' It's outworn. Dead leaves." He recalls a film he made in 1951 called *Mexican Bus Ride*; it was about a village too poor to support a church and a priest. "The place was serene, because no one suffered from guilt. It's guilt we must escape from, not God."[1]

Buñuel expressed this conviction at the age of seventy-seven in 1977, working on his film *That Obscure Object of Desire*. It is a conviction already felt in the very first film he made, *Un Chien Andalou* (1928). Done in collaboration with Salvador Dali, the film is an experiment in surrealism that unfolds with the logic of a dream, its images proliferating in provocative association, generally sexual in character. What it seems to say is that "normal" relations between the sexes are out of the question, and the reason for this is the guilt generated and fostered by church and society. In one very remarkable scene, the young man "goes into a frenzy, kicks aside the furniture, and, seizing two ropes, pulls an incredible pile of debris, driftwood, two startled clerics, and a pair of grand pianos decorated with suppurating dead donkeys toward the girl. It is an unforgettable image of the dead weight of the past, the burden of the repressed contents of his psyche."[2] Buñuel aims to lift that burden and to free natural man. (Paradoxically, he expresses admiration for William Golding's *Lord of the Flies* where "natural man" is himself the problem.)[3]

Born at the turn of the century into a wealthy family in the small town of Calanda in northern Spain, Buñuel attended the Jesuit College in Saragossa and then the University of Madrid, where he read Freud. "I suppose Freud was our patron saint," he says of the associations he later formed in Paris.[4] After *Un Chien Andalou,* he made *L'Age d'Or,* a story of frustrated

STILL 23: *L'Age d'Or*
Directed by Luis Buñuel.
Buñuel is one of cinema's trenchant critics of aristocratic decadence. His imagination, formed by a Catholic education, has yielded some of the most devastating images of the church's excesses. Here, the skeletons of bishops become the "rock" upon which the golden age is built.

love in a New Rome that is just as repressive as the Old, and in 1932 *Las Hurdes,* a documentary about the erosion of hope in an ignorant people too poor to know what bread is. As Peter P. Schillaci observes, the major themes of Buñuel's lifetime concern had already emerged in basic outline: "The attack on organized religion, the affirmation of a natural humanity seldom given voice, the fascination with human deformity, perversion, and the capacity for evil—all were there."[5]

There followed a period of obscurity spent mainly in the United States, to which he came after the Spanish Civil War broke out. He did things related to film but made no films himself. His productivity began anew in Mexico where he made close to twenty films between the years 1947 and 1960. Outstanding among them are *Los Olvidados* (1950) and *Nazarin* (1958). He returned to Spain to make two of his best: *Viridiana* (1961) and *The Exterminating Angel* (1962). For the next ten years he worked in France, producing seven films including *Belle de Jour* (1966) and *The Discreet Charm of the Bourgeoisie* (1972). In 1977, he returned to Spain to do *That Obscure Object of Desire.*

The "forgotten ones" of *Los Olvidados* are the deprived young who are caught in the whirlpool of poverty and ignorance. Love, which might have given meaning to their lives, never takes root, never flowers. Unloved by his mother, Pedro (Alphonso Mejia) makes friends with the older Jaibo (Roberto Cobo), who teaches him to cheat and steal. But Jaibo's brutal murder of an honest worker is too much for Pedro; he goes to work with a silversmith. When Jaibo falsely accuses him of stealing a silver knife, Pedro is sent to reform school. Further provocation induces him to inform against Jaibo and to go himself in pursuit of him. Jaibo brutally kills him; later, the police kill Jaibo. Pedro's body, thrown into a sack by others who come upon the scene, is left to lie forgotten upon a refuse heap. *Los Olvidados,* which André Bazin describes as a film that "allows conscience no avenue of escape," won Buñuel an award for best direction at Cannes in 1951.[6]

In 1958, *Nazarin* won the Grand Prix at Cannes; three years later *Viridiana* won another Grand Prix. Both are what Schillaci calls "reverse morality plays." Both Nazario and Viridiana are frustrated practitioners of "pure" Christianity. The priest Nazario (Francisco Rabal) tries to serve the poor in Mexico as he thinks Christ would have done. All his efforts to do good either are dismissed or actually provoke evil. Viridiana (Silvia Pinal) is a novice in religion who leaves the convent to serve the poor at the residence of her Uncle Jaime (Fernando Rey); the effect of her charity is only to provoke an orgy of eating and drinking and lusting. Nazario, stripped of his official priesthood, discovers his humanity in a woman's good deed; Viridiana, stripped by beggars, puts aside her religious aspirations. She lets down her long hair and goes to Jorge, her worldly cousin (Francisco Rabal), and joins him and his mistress in a game of cards: a picture of humanity that hardly inspires confidence.

Belle de Jour is said by critics to represent Buñuel's complete mastery of the surrealist style. By that same token, it is probably the most difficult of all his films, mixing as it does reality and fantasy and providing the viewer with two contrasting endings. Of course, the heroine, played by Catherine Deneuve, is two contrasting persons. Morning and night she is Severine, the frigid wife of the charming Pierre (Jean Sorel); but in the afternoon she becomes Belle de Jour in a brothel patronized by the rich. When Marcel (Pierre Clementi), a young thug of a patron, falls in love with her, he begs her to come away with him. She refuses. Marcel shoots Pierre; the police shoot Marcel. Marcel dies, but Pierre is paralyzed for life. In one ending of the film, Pierre, immobile, sheds a tear; in the other, he rises from the wheelchair, apparently cured. Whatever the reality of it all—how much of it is Severine's sick imaginings?—Buñuel would seem to be leveling his aim at the moral schizophrenia of our age.

For *That Obscure Object of Desire,* Buñuel went back to a project he had attempted in the fifties but had abandoned after a disagreement with the producer—the filming of a late-nineteenth-century novel by Pierre Louÿs, *La Femme et le Pantin.* The novel had been adapted for the screen three times before, the third version being the best known, Josef von Sternberg's *The Devil Is a Woman* (1935), starring Marlene

Dietrich. When Buñuel pulled out in the fifties, the producer hired another director and came out with a *A Woman Like Satan* (1958), starring Brigitte Bardot.[7] Buñuel was to have used Maria Schneider for Conchita, the femme fatale of his 1977 version, but she withdrew after the third week of shooting and the project was almost scrapped again, but then he decided to cast *two* actresses in the role, one French (Carole Bouquet), the other Spanish (Angela Molina), with a third actress speaking the French dialogue for both of them, as if daring us to draw some conclusion from the way of this one woman about all women. Fernando Rey plays her puppet, and the film proceeds by a series of deft jerks on the strings, each of them priming him for sexual surrender, but again and again the arousal of expectation is comically frustrated. At the end it appears that Conchita may at last have given in, but a terrorist bomb throws everything in doubt. The terrorist activity of the RAIJ (Revolutionary Army of the Infant Jesus), in which Conchita seems to be implicated, erupts at several points during the action of the film. Both expressions of passion, the political and the sexual, are replete with absurdity.

Buñuel is a moralist, but he does not preach: he turns the cold, audacious eye of his camera upon the reality of our world and into the world of our dreams.

BIBLIOGRAPHY

Durgnat, Raymond. *Luis Buñuel.* Berkeley: Univ. of California Press, 1968.

Fieschi, Jean-André. "Luis Buñuel." In *Cinema: A Critical Dictionary, The Major Film-Makers,* Vol. I. Ed. Richard Roud. New York: Viking Press, 1980, pp. 167–80.

Gilliatt, Penelope. "Profiles (Luis Buñuel)." *New Yorker,* 5 Dec. 1977, pp. 53–72.

Harcourt, Peter. "Luis Buñuel: Spaniard and Surrealist." In *Six European Directors.* Baltimore: Penguin Books, 1974, pp. 102–34.

Kael, Pauline. "That Obscure Object of Desire." *New Yorker,* 19 Dec. 1977, pp. 128–30.

Sarris, Andrew. "*Viridiana*" and "*Belle de Jour.*" In *Confes-*

sions of a Cultist: On the Cinema, 1955–1969. New York: Simon & Schuster, 1971, pp. 53–60, 353–59.

Schillaci, Peter P. "Luis Buñuel and the Death of God." In *Three European Directors*. Ed. James M. Wall. Grand Rapids: William B. Eerdmans, 1973, pp. 111–224.

NEIL P. HURLEY

Charles Chaplin

To see in the Chaplin persona an image of the Hebrew prophet may seem extreme, but that is mainly due to the fact that film criticism within America has not addressed itself to the discernible religious motifs in the films of Chaplin. French film critics such as Maurice Pontet and Jean d'Yvoire see in the work of Chaplin the theme of the wandering Jew.[1] Chaplin himself referred to his Jewish ancestry through his mother, thus establishing some foundation for the scriptural flavor in the best of his films. First of all there is the concern for the underdog—the orphan in *The Kid,* the blind flower girl in *City Lights,* the distressed woman in *Modern Times,* the suicide-prone ballerina in *Limelight.* There is too the theology of reversal implicit in the Hebrew canon—defeat is turned into victory as in the Suffering Servant songs of Isaiah. Hope always persists, despite apparent failure. The little tramp is eternal victim and, ironically, eternal victor.

The unquestionable David-Goliath motif in the Chaplin films of the silent era celebrates the underdog. Despite his frail physique, he triumphs over the obese employer, the buxom matron, the brawny gangster. He is a symbol of spirit opposing matter, the ethereal versus the corporeal. In *Easy Street* (1917), out of love for a minister's daughter, Chaplin's persona becomes a policeman; he not only succeeds in subduing the powerful law-breaker by asphyxiating him with a gas-burner, but also converts him to honesty. The victory is even more complete than that of David over Goliath, for instead of killing the enemy he recruits his allegiance. In *The Pilgrim* (1923), Chaplin, significantly enough, delivers a moving sermon by enacting in pantomime the battle of David and Goliath. A fugitive from prison, he finds himself in the pulpit by force of circumstance and manages to surpass in eloquence the efforts of the superiorly trained but hypocritical minister.

Little David conquers again. In this same film we see too an instance of how Chaplin impressed his audience with the lesson that the arm of Providence is never foreshortened. Escaping from the law, the Chaplin character crosses the Mexican border only to meet an oncoming band of hostile bandits. He races back to the border; the audience senses the dilemma and feels enclosed within the ever-narrowing trap. Once at the border, however, Chaplin straddles it, with one foot in Mexico and one foot in the U.S.A.; thus he continues his flight laterally along the boundary line. One thinks of Solomon's wisdom in determining the true mother in the dispute over the child. Chaplin's solutions are invariably unusual and creative.

The little tramp always seems to find a door in the walled-up cubicle of society. Over, under, around, or through the set walls of convention that it had erected—the way did not matter, as long as Chaplin made his escape from social restrictions. And having once escaped he beckons the audience to follow him down the rosy dawn of tomorrow. The scene that most typifies the hope he held out to people is the last one in *Modern Times* (1936) where, hand-in-hand with Paulette Goddard, he turns his back on mass-production society to disappear down the unending road which leads into the hopeful horizon of the future.

It is in *Modern Times, The Great Dictator,* and *Monsieur Verdoux,* though, that we see Chaplin's prophetic quality and his rebellious nature at their boldest. Whereas in *Modern Times* the aesthetic and functional aspects of his art remain in delicate balance, in the latter two pictures the message dominates the art. In his anti-totalitarian *The Great Dictator* (1940), Chaplin directs his message upstage and his art down when, at the end of the film, he puts aside his characterization to fling blunt questions directly at the audience. To appreciate the mordant nature of *Monsieur Verdoux,* one must not lose sight of the stormy times Chaplin's personal reputation was passing through in the U.S.A. Chaplin had been critical of American mores and folkways and refused to become a naturalized citizen after thirty years' residence in America. His Soviet sympathies, moreover, had been aired in a congressional investigation in 1940. The final estrangement of Chaplin from

America came in 1952 when the State Department refused him a return visa upon the occasion of his visit to London for the premiere of *Limelight*. He then took up residence in Switzerland.

These facts help to explain the nihilism of *Monsieur Verdoux* (1947), the most negative film Chaplin ever produced. In it he plays the part of a man who, forced out of work by an acquisitive, insensitive social order, begins supporting his family by marrying and successively murdering a number of rich widows. Monsieur Verdoux is, basically, the little tramp come back in disguise to take revenge on those flighty women who would not have him, to take by violence what society in its callousness had denied him, to fight hypocrisy and cunning with its own arms. The tenor of the film is best grasped by Verdoux's own remarks: "I shall see you all very soon" (addressed to the court after receiving the death sentence); "one murder makes a villain, millions a hero"; "I am at peace with God, my conflict is with man" (to the priest). One critic has said of the film: "This time there is no long road to the horizon, no pretty girl for companion, no pathetic fatalism. It is a stark march to death."[2]

In *Limelight* (1952), we have a film of beauty and genius, and a message of a new dimension. Reflecting Chaplin's own life, the film portrays the renewal of purpose an aged trooper (Calvero) finds in trying to restore confidence to a disillusioned young dancer (Terry). In the dramatic death of Calvero and the prayer to the Unknown God at the moment when the dancer wavers in her performance, we perceive a new element in Chaplin's prophetic career—the conviction that losing one's life is really saving it.

Chaplin reverted to bleak prophecy in his second to last film, *A King in New York* (1957). The shades of bitterness and negative witness evident in *Monsieur Verdoux* reappear in this satire of American society, its fear of heterodox thinking, its worship of success, its entrapment in mass-thinking and chaotic forms of recreation. The theme of the wandering Jew is also discernible: the King of Estrovia finds refuge and popularity in America only to be stigmatized because of his friendship with a small boy who has been investigated by Congress for Communist sympathies. Chaplin comes across as a Hosea or Jeremiah calling society, in this case America, to repentance for its materialism and its paranoid reactions to divergent social arrangements.

Chaplin's exile in Switzerland reminds us of another twentieth-century artist, James Joyce, whose credo aptly fits the career of Chaplin: "I will try to express myself in some mode of life or art as freely as I can and as wholly as I can, using for my defence the only arms I allow myself to use—silence, exile and cunning."[3] A child of poverty with a Hebraic sense of mission, Chaplin not only pushed cinematic art to exalted heights, but also gave witness to the hope of a utopian social order in which the individual would not have to surrender his dignity in the face of wealth, social status, mechanization, totalitarianism, or consumeristic democracy.[4] For those condemned to a life of quiet desperation in the darkness of industrial society, the little tramp is a "pillar of fire."

Chaplin is the "arch-rebel" figure in the history of cinema.[5] Roger Manvell sees this religiously inspired rebellion as central to Chaplin's work, holding that his screen philosophy is "so deeply-felt that it has at times become almost messianic."[6] Chaplin's most intensely messianic work is *The Great Dictator,* where at the end Chaplin doffs the disguise of the humble Jewish character (who looks like Hitler and substitutes for him) in order to plead with the audience for active resistance to totalitarian governments such as the Third Reich.

From 1914 to 1940, Chaplin's films clearly exalt the "common man." The biblical messianism is undeniable and merits further research. Whenever the tramp touches the poor, the oppressed, the physically handicapped, they are cured. The parallel with Jesus' healing activity is obvious. In that remarkable film *City Lights* (1931), Chaplin helps a blind flower girl have her sight restored. The last scene contains the most touching "close-up" in film history—Chaplin's anguished face as he realizes that the girl now knows him for what he is, not the millionaire whose role he earlier feigned, but a social outcast. Her touch made her realize that this was the benefactor to whom she owed so much. The theology of reversal has never been so sublimely portrayed.

STILL 24: *City Lights*
Directed by Charles Chaplin.
The biblical paradox of strength in weakness and the irony of reversed fortune are often the substance of Chaplin's archetypal adventures of the tramp. The blind flower girl (Virginia Cherrill), whose sight he helps to have restored, in turn accepts him for what he is rather than the millionaire he claims to be.

We have, of course, Chaplin's own testimony regarding the influence of the Bible in his life.[7] In his *Autobiography,* he tells of reading the Gospel account of Jesus' love and pity for the poor and little children. It was these "luminous and appealing" impressions of Jesus—unmatched in his early life—that influenced him to incorporate the themes of love, pity, and humanity into virtually all his films.

BIBLIOGRAPHY

Chaplin, Charles. *My Autobiography.* New York: Simon & Schuster, 1964.

Huff, Theodore. *Charlie Chaplin.* New York: Henry Schuman, 1951.

Manvell, Roger. *Chaplin.* Boston: Little, Brown, 1974.

Tyler, Parker. *Chaplin, Last of the Clowns.* New York: Vanguard Press, 1948.

JOHN R. MAY

Francis Coppola

IN an April 1975 address to the Arts Club of Chicago, Pauline Kael made the point that "almost every interesting American movie in the past few years has been directed by a Catholic." She was speaking specifically of Francis Coppola, Martin Scorsese, and Robert Altman, and her thesis seems at least emotionally plausible when one realizes that Coppola's *The Godfather Part II* had just won an Academy Award for best film of 1974 and Altman's *Nashville* had just been released. The "sensual richness" of their backgrounds had enhanced their capacity, she said, to do what films do best—"enlarge our experience." Of *The Godfather* films and *Nashville,* she said pointedly: "You get the sense of American epics, of directors really dealing for the first time with the American experience, and dealing with it truthfully."[1]

What makes Kael's thesis interesting in this context is not that she implies Coppola's films are somehow Catholic—she does not—but rather that she senses a relationship between his religious background and a certain sensual richness that is linked, at least for Kael, to cinematic truth. There was indeed a sensual richness to Pre-Vatican II Roman Catholic ritual. Born of immigrant parents, Coppola is first-generation Italian-American, and the ethnic and cultural vitality that shaped his artistic sensibility was inextricably wedded to traditional Catholicism.

There is, however, another and more important aspect of Coppola's religious background that has found its way at least unconsciously into the design of his films—the sense of an orderly and therefore cogent world, one in which mythos and ethos are mutually complementary[2]—and in this regard Coppola's films are certainly catholic, if not Catholic. Coppola like many great directors is both scriptwriter and director; *Finian's Rainbow* (1968) is the only one of his films whose screenplay he did not at least coauthor, and it is perhaps no coincidence that it is the least memorable of his major films.[3] A 1940s musical with a simplistically liberal attitude toward racial inequality, it was tragically ill-suited for release as a film in the year Martin Luther King was assassinated.

The ordered world of Coppola's films should not be confused with the fatalism that one often hears associated—incorrectly I think—with Roman Catholicism. Fatalism suggests a world in which events are predestined, but Catholics among Christians of various sects certainly have no monopoly on predestination; the so-called Catholic fatalism seems more narrowly to imply a tragic destiny (typified perhaps by Catholic preference for, even obsession with, crucifixes as opposed to the naked cross), and even though Coppola's characters often suffer for their transgressions, they neither embrace suffering readily nor seem overly fated to it. What suffering there is is more obviously explained by the inevitable interplay of actions and consequences.

There is also in the world of Coppola's works a strong sense of irony, and in this instance too Coppola's imagination is at least broadly catholic. There is not only the irony of unexpected developments or thwarted purpose but also that of the coexistence of contraries. It is irony of his latter sort that William Lynch discovers at the heart of Christian faith. "Faith's imagination," Lynch writes, "composes reality with irony and with ironic images."[4] It is the wisdom of faith to realize that there is no other way to imagine reality than to hold together opposites in the same image.

Irony is in fact at the heart of Coppola's cinematic imagination; it is the way he orders the world of his films, and it was that way from the beginning. While he was still a graduate student at UCLA, he directed three "nudie" films[5] (all reputedly milder than most films rated PG today). One called *The Peeper* (circa 1960), about a voyeur who finds out that girls are posing for pin-ups near his house, shows a blend of humor and irony. Everything the man does to get a closer, if not clearer, look backfires. One sequence shows him hauling a gigantic telescope up to his room, but the best it produces is a navel in close-up.

Coppola's first feature film was an exploitation film, *Dementia 13* (1963), filmed in England and produced by Roger Corman, who was a Maecenas to many aspiring young directors in those days. Whereas *Dementia 13* has all of the standard horror movie clichés, it reveals Coppola's preoccupation with the family—this one decidedly more psychopathic than the Corleones—and offers a kind of zestful, though bloody parody of thwarted purpose. Even the revelation of the killer, as Myles and Pye point out, is more confusing than the mystery itself.[6]

You're a Big Boy Now (1967) is about an innocent young man's passage toward maturity in New York City. Released in the wake of *The Graduate,* it was completely engulfed by it, but it served at least two practical purposes in Coppola's career—it satisfied the thesis requirements for his M.F.A. from UCLA and it earned him an invitation from Warner Brothers to direct *Finian's Rainbow.* Yet the film has its merits, not the least of which is its diversification of the energies of a Mrs. Robinson into four women—a possessive mother, a passive girlfriend, an obsessive landlady, and an aggressive actress. The film's visual trope is appropriately enough the cage—library elevator, disco birdcage, and prison cell—that Bernard must be liberated from as from the limits of his univocal imagination.

In *The Rain People* (1969) and later in *The Conversation* (1974), which Coppola directed between installments of *The Godfather,* he deals with complex moral problems faced by individuals in contemporary society. Both films are tightly structured and as such reveal Coppola's awesome capacity to construct an ordered filmic world more clearly perhaps, though less subtly, than he did in *The Godfather* films and *Apocalypse Now. The Rain People* is about a young mother-to-be who in trying to flee one responsibility—her pregnancy—picks up another and even greater one—responsibility for a brain-damaged ex-football player who teaches her, ironically, more than she apparently wants to know about the sacrifice love entails. In *The Conversation,* an expert in electronic surveillance learns, of course too late, what it is like living with total paranoia when his expertise is turned against him.

The Godfather films and *Apocalypse Now* are epic presentations of Americana, the family and the nation, as metaphors for the horror of human duplicity. Just as *The Godfather* and its sequel are only superficially about the Mafia and Italian-Americans, so *Apocalypse Now* is about the Vietnam war only on the level of plot. Each of these works is a masterpiece of visual texture and cinematic structure. *The Godfather* (1972) is framed by a family's participation in religious celebrations intercut with scenes exposing the conspiracy of the human heart. The ecclesiastical rites provide maximum irony when contrasted with secrets revealed: marriage, in the beginning, creates the familial bond that needs the conspiracy of the brotherhood to protect it; and baptism, at the film's end, is the new birth that signs the total duplicity of brothers born to kill one another. With perfect subtlety and utter irony, Coppola reverses the chiaroscuro contrast of the framing sequences: secrets that are born in the shadows of an inner room are revealed finally in bright daylight as marriage alfresco yields to the darkness of the church.

While *The Godfather*'s excellence is due in large part to Coppola's ability to hold sin and sacrament together in an integral ironic image of perverted innocence, *The Godfather Part II* succeeds because Coppola trusts the central irony of the artistic process: less is more. Rejecting a script titled *Death of Michael Corleone,* he opted for a narrative that would reveal the total emptiness of Michael's success by showing him as a living corpse.[7] Moreover, Coppola achieves his cinematic contrast here not through the framed juxtaposition of rituals, but through a central flashback to Don Vito Corleone's youth. Thus *The Godfather* links the old Don Vito with Michael as a young man, and *Part II* shows the older Michael and younger Vito. In either case, the end is in the beginning.

Although *Apocalypse Now* (1979) lacks the structural finesse and visual symmetry of *The Godfather* films, there is a greatness to the film that perhaps only time will acknowledge, one proportionate to the intensity and depth of its vision. Like the novel by Joseph Conrad it is based on, it follows the meandering course of a river—into the heart of darkness.[8] Captain Willard (Martin Sheen) has been commissioned by his military superiors to "terminate" Colonel Kurtz (Marlon Brando) and

STILL 25: *Apocalypse Now*
Directed by Francis Coppola.
Colonel Kurtz (Marlon Brando) offers Captain Willard (Martin Sheen) an explanation, but no apology, for his "uncivilized" behavior in ruling his Cambodian jungle army of renegade American forces and Montagnard natives with the rage of a demented deity. "You have a right to kill me," Kurtz says, "but you have no right to judge me."

thus to put an end to the "unsound methods" of his Cambodian jungle kingdom. Kurtz, like his literary antecedent, had shown great promise as a leader of men: "He was a good man, a good humanitarian man, man of wit and humor," the consigning general acknowledges. Instead, sent on one of civilization's savage missions, Kurtz has become an embarrassment to his country—gone beyond, as he puts it, "their timid lying morality." He has in fact presumed to make himself a god, or allowed himself to be made one. Because he has gazed too long into fire ("*they* train young men to drop fire on people"), he is hypnotized by its destructive power.

Coppola's great gamble with *Apocalypse Now* is to have given his work a mythic dimension not shared by its literary source; from Sir James Frazer's *The Golden Bough*—a copy of which we glimpse among Kurtz's books—he has appropriated the mythic ritual of the killing of the divine king. John Tessitore has made a helpful correlation between the imagery of the long final sequence and Frazer's specific references to Cambodia's mystic Kings of Fire and Water (curiously enough the principal Judaeo-Christian agents of apocalypse).[9] Thus, Coppola transforms Marlow / Willard's temptation by casting him in the role of the new god. "The man-god must be killed as soon as he shows symptoms that his powers are beginning to fail," Frazer writes, "and his soul must be transferred to a vigorous successor before it has been seriously impaired by the threatened decay."[10] Willard emerges from the river as he begins to stalk his prey, and the gesture is purely symbolic. After he has slashed Kurtz to death with a type of machete—a scene intercut with slow-motion shots of the ritual slaying of a sacred cow—Kurtz's people, a motley mixture of Montagnard natives and renegade special forces, kneel in unison for their expected theophany. But Willard passes *through* them and returns to his boat.

If Colonel Kurtz has succumbed to ultimate horror, he has at least had the "clear mind" to revolt consciously against civilization (which in Conrad is pitted against savagery) by exposing *its* festered heart for all to see. "You have a right to kill me," he tells Willard, "but you have no right to judge me." And, though Willard rejects the divine kingship, he has experienced enough of the "moral terror" of existence to be affected by it himself: he signals his complicity by cutting off radio communications with his command base. The air strike, therefore, proceeds on precautionary schedule without regard for the success of his mission—the sinister irony of a world run by "sound" methods. (The code names for base and boat are appallingly appropriate—"Almighty" and "street gang" respectively.) Thus Kurtz's command—"Drop the bomb! Exterminate them all!"—is carried out. Though the film itself ends in darkness, an apocalypse of napalm explodes behind the credits like some celestial garden in time-lapse bloom.

Conrad's *Heart of Darkness* offers unreconciled extremes—a Kurtz who looks straight into the heart of existence (in its savage state) and succumbs, and a Marlow who is too civilized to look. With portraits of two ravaged hearts in varying degrees of presumption, Coppola holds the extremes together in ironic tension—in the pattern of his truly catholic imagination.

BIBLIOGRAPHY

Coppola, Eleanor. *Notes.* New York: Simon and Schuster, 1979.

Denby, David. "Stolen Privacy." *Sight and Sound* 43 (1974), 131–33.

Farber, Stephen. "Coppola and *The Godfather.*" *Sight and Sound* 41 (1972), 217–23.

Jacobs, Diane. "Francis Ford Coppola." In *Hollywood Renaissance.* Cranbury, N.J.: A.S. Barnes, 1977, pp. 97–122.

Johnson, Robert K. *Francis Ford Coppola.* Boston: Twayne, 1977.

Pye, Michael, and Lynda Myles. "Frances Coppola." In *The Movie Brats: How the Film Generation Took Over Hollywood.* New York: Holt, Rinehart, 1979, pp. 66–111.

Rule, Philip C. "Italian Connection in the American Film: Coppola, Cimino, Scorsese." *America,* 17 Nov. 1979, pp. 301–4.

Yates, John. "Godfather Saga: The Death of a Family." *Journal of Popular Culture* 4 (1975), 157–63.

JOHN R. MAY

Federico Fellini

No contemporary film director has been as blatant as Federico Fellini in his use of religious material. There is a wild exuberance to his imagination that is unmatched in the history of cinema, and some of his most memorable scenes employ religious images of varying sorts. Who could forget, once seen, the opening sequence of *La Dolce Vita* (1960) when the statue of Christ the Laborer, borne by helicopter across the Roman skyline, appears majestically above the dome of St. Peter's while the bells of the great Basilica toll triumphantly? Or the moment in *Fellini Satyricon* (1969) when Encolpio and Ascylto, wandering aimlessly through the pagan night, see the fractured head from a mammoth statue of a Roman god, filling the passageway it is being rolled through? Or, finally, conveying a sense of the wonder of a purposeful creation, the final scene of *La Strada* (1954), as Zampano kneels alone on the shore of the ocean, humbled by the majesty of the universe?

Anyone inclined to confuse the literal treatment of explicit religious elements with the genuine religious sensibility of a work of art may, however, come away from Fellini's films with the conviction that he is flippant about religion, if not positively antagonistic. Critics have been quick to note Fellini's apparent anti-clericalism. It is true that every one of his films has at least a shot, usually a scene or a sequence, that parodies a certain type of religious mentality, the one of course that Fellini knows best, Italian Catholicism. As early as *I Vitelloni* (1953), he demonstrated his capacity to satirize the juxtaposition of religious ideal and the reality of human observance: Fausto tries to seduce his benefactor's wife amid packed statues in the back of a religious goods store. The swindlers in *Il Bidone* (1955) dress as priests to secure the trust they need for their con game; Cabiria joins a pilgrimage to pray for a miraculous cure of the "disease" of prostitution. An apparition of the Virgin is faked by two mischievous children in *La Dolce Vita.* Hermaphrodite in *Fellini Satyricon,* powerless to restore a grotesquely maimed war hero, simply dies; in keeping with the pre-Christian setting of the film, Fellini transposes his generic concern with Christian hypocrisy to the shrine of a ludicrous albino demigod. In *Roma* (1972), he treats us to an outrageous ecclesiastical style show, featuring neon-trimmed copes and miters, while *Amarcord* (1974) exposes clerical curiosity over the details of adolescent sex.

Yet for all this, Fellini is scarcely harder on clerical hypocrisy than he is on any other form of it. Organized religion, at its best, is still *man's* response to God, and therefore never more than a historically conditioned, fallible understanding of the divine. It was Paul Tillich who reminded us that we should not confuse religion with God, and it stands to reason that it is even more foolish—and Fellini knows this—to equate clerical performance with even the best of organized religions. Fellini's often playful use of explicit religious material aside, there is a fundamentally religious, specifically Christian, sensibility in all his films.

Fellini has commented on what he considers the thematic unity of his films. In an interview with Pierre Kast, he put it this way: "At bottom, I am always making the same film, to the extent that what arouses my curiosity, what interests me definitively, what unlatches my inspiration, is that, each time, I am telling the story of characters in quest of themselves, in search of a more authentic source of life, of conduct, of behavior, that will more closely relate to the true roots of their individuality."[1] Although one cannot automatically assume that an artist does what he claims to do, Fellini is clearly the master of his art in this instance. What he expresses in psychological terms can, from the perspective of Christian theology, be seen as an affirmation of hope.

At least two specific cinematic techniques recur in Fellini's films as visual bases for this affirmation of hope: one springs from his restless camera, the other is evident in his mise-en-scène of encounter. The former includes persistent movement of the camera as well as movement within the frame; the latter points to Fellini's tendency to represent the offer of grace through his protagonist's encounter with innocence in some form. Moraldo in *I Vitelloni* meets the mysterious young railway worker; for Zampano in *La Strada,* it is the guilelessness of Gelsomina's face; Marcello in *La Dolce Vita* is drawn to Paola, the "Umbrian angel."

Circular movement is an archetypal image in Fellini. Its metaphysical root is not the enclosure of a deterministic world; it springs rather from primitive religious symbolism of wholeness or communion. This is undoubtedly why, in two specific and notable instances, Fellini takes his circle from the circus. In *The Clowns* (1970) it is an actual circus ring: the mock funeral for a lazy clown erupts suddenly into a wild celebration of triumph, one of Fellini's most potent evocations of resurrection. And as soon as Guido in *8½* (1963) decides to abandon an inane science fiction project, his creative powers appear to return as he unites all the personalities from his life (the film's whole cast) in a circular dance.

Nowhere in Fellini's oeuvre is the dual motif of movement and innocence so poignantly brought together as in the closing scene of *The Nights of Cabiria* (1956). The film, like Cabiria's character, develops through an intensifying rhythm of promise, disillusionment, and renewed hope. Cabiria (played by Fellini's immensely talented wife, Julietta Masina) barely escapes with her life in the opening sequence when her faithless lover snatches her handbag and shoves her into a stream. Determining to ply her trade more successfully, she shifts her evening promenade to a more fashionable sector of Rome. She is taken in by a famous actor, who has just had a violent public argument with his mistress; the anticipation of entertaining such a wealthy customer is shattered when his mistress returns unexpectedly and Cabiria has to spend the night hidden in the actor's bathroom. With hope in a completely new life, Cabiria joins a procession to a shrine of the Virgin Mary: the miracle she seeks is less tangible—though apparently more realistic—than that of the crippled pimp who shares the scene. We are no doubt to assume—at least for the time being—that her prayer is as unanswered as his when the procurer throws away his crutches and collapses.

Still pursuing other possibilities, Cabiria visits a burlesque

STILL 26: *La Dolce Vita*
Directed by Federico Fellini.
A statue of Christ the Laborer, borne by helicopter, is shown against the ruins of Roman aqueducts in the electrifying opening sequence of Fellini's contemporary vision of apocalypse. The presence of explicit Christian elements raises the question of religious meaning even though a film may not be specifically religious in the final analysis.

STILL 27: *La Dolce Vita*
Directed by Federico Fellini.
Two persistent strands of religious symbolism in Fellini's masterpiece are typified in this frame by the ambivalent union of water and woman – both give life, both consume and destroy. Sylvia (Anita Ekberg), devouring earth mother, and Marcello (Marcello Mastroianni) are re-united in the pre-dawn freshness of the waters of the Trevi Fountain.

house, accepts the hypnotist's invitation to be put into a trance, imagines herself dancing with a man called Oscar, and worriedly seeks a protestation of love. Before an answer comes, the trance is broken, and she awakens to the derisive laughter of the audience. Outside the theater, a young man whose name—he claims—is Oscar carefully begins the process of winning her confidence. On the day they are to be married (she has unfortunately brought all of her money), in woods high above the sea, Cabiria realizes Oscar's true intentions. Unable to push her off the cliff as he had evidently planned, he simply takes her bag and abandons her, grief-stricken, on the floor of the forest. The way is set for the climactic wedding of movement and encounter.

Moving slowly back onto the road, Cabiria is approached, passed, and then led by a group of dancing, singing youths. In their passing, they circle Cabiria and serenade her. The gay innocence of their movement coaxes Cabiria to smile through her tears. The camera moves toward Cabiria, whose stride quickens; a close-up of her face, tilted slightly by the wisdom of experience, discloses the troubled joy that will be the ground of her future.

The naysayers who mark the decline, if not the demise, of Fellini's creative powers from the period following *8½* are doubtlessly asking more of him than they have of other *auteur* directors. No artist can produce a *La Dolce Vita* every time he sets to work. They are certainly not being fair to the thematic and cinematic symmetry of his oeuvre. Where particular scenes fail or individual films fall below the artistic excellence he has achieved, it is not from an absence, but rather an excess, of imagination. Fellini persists in his fondness for freaks (*Fellini Satyricon*) and clowns (*The Clowns*), variations of the same affirmation of spirit over flesh; in his obsession with women (*Juliet of the Spirits,* 1965; *City of Women,* 1981) and man's reification of them (*Casanova,* 1977); in satirical comment on society (*Orchestra Rehearsal,* 1979); in his remembrance of things past (*Roma* and *Amarcord*); and most consistently, and successfully, in his celebration of the sights and sounds of his native Italy.

BIBLIOGRAPHY

Bergtal, Eric. "The Lonely Crowd in *La Dolce Vita.*" *America,* 7 Oct. 1961, pp. 13–15.

Bondanella, Peter E., ed. *Federico Fellini: Essays in Criticism.* New York: Oxford Univ. Press, 1978.

Boyer, Deena. *The Two Hundred Days of 8½*. Trans. C.L. Markmann. New York: Macmillan, 1964.

Fellini, Federico. *La Dolce Vita.* New York: Ballantine, 1961.

______. *8½*. New York: Ballantine, 1964.

______. *Juliet of the Spirits.* New York: Orion, 1965.

______. *La Strada.* New York: Ballantine, 1970.

______. *Three Screenplays: I Vitelloni, Il Bidone, The Temptations of Doctor Antonio.* New York: Orion, 1970.

______. *Fellini on Fellini.* Trans. Isabel Quigley. New York: Delacorte/Seymour Lawrence, 1976.

Gorbman, Claudia. "Music as Salvation." *Film Quarterly* 28 (Winter 1974), 17–25.

Harcourt, Peter. "The Secret Life of Federico Fellini." In *Six European Directors.* Baltimore: Penguin Books, 1974, pp. 183–211.

Ketcham, Charles B. *Federico Fellini: The Search for a New Mythology.* New York: Paulist Press, 1976.

Navone, J. "Fellini's La Dolce Italia." *Commonweal,* 15 March 1963, pp. 639–41.

Salachas, Gilbert. *Federico Fellini.* Trans. Rosalie Siegel. New York: Crown, 1969.

Steel, Ronald. "Fellini: Moviemaker as Moralist." *Christian Century,* 19 April 1961, pp. 488–90.

Taylor, John Russell. "Federico Fellini." In *Cinema Eye, Cinema Ear.* New York: Hill and Wang, 1964, pp. 15–51.

Zucher, Wolfgang M. "The Clown as the Lord of Disorder." *Theology Today* 24 (Oct. 1967), 306–17.

NEIL P. HURLEY

Alfred Hitchcock

ALFRED HITCHCOCK's signature can be summed up by the phrase, "Things are not what they seem to be." There are mercurial shifts in mood and atmosphere in a Hitchcock film, but most of all there is a consistent, recognizable dualism at work according to which characters rise and decline in moral performance. Unlike the heroes and heroines of a D.W. Griffith movie, Hitchcock's protagonists undergo interior development. Thus, in the quintessential Hitchcock film, the leading players grow as crisis teases out of them strengths that were not evident earlier.

This melioristic principle of character betterment is particularly clear in *Suspicion* (1941) and *North by Northwest* (1959), in which Cary Grant portrays irresponsible men whom circumstances raise to heights of sober courage and mature response. In *Notorious* (1946), Devlin (Cary Grant), a federal agent, helps save Alicia Huberman (Ingrid Bergman), an American spy, from her loose ways. In *The Birds* (1963), Melanie Daniels (Tippi Hedren) is a fashionable member of the idle jet set. Mitch Brenner (Rod Taylor), a lawyer, helps her to find her deeper self as they experience the inexplicable attack of the gulls and crows in Bodega Bay above San Francisco.

While Hitchcock has been noted for suspense, he is really more concerned with mystery—not of the "whodunit" kind, but of primordial forces that break into the most commonplace lives and alter their direction. The religious notion of fate and redemption recurs enough in Hitchcock's filmography to merit comment. In *I Confess* (1952), a Canadian priest (Montgomery Clift) is bound by the seal of confession not to disclose the identity of the real killer who is willing to let the incriminated curate be accused of his crime. The role of the scapegoat is fraught with sacred implications just as it affords, in this instance, an unusual basis for a spine-tingling plot. In *The Wrong Man* (1957), Hitchcock chose an actual incident to underscore the paradoxical intertwining of destiny and providence. Manny Balestrero (Henry Fonda), a bassist at the Stork Club, is falsely accused of hold-ups. After his arrest and detention, his wife (Vera Miles) has a breakdown. The movie broods with expressionistic techniques—shadows, source lighting, nighttime scenes, and confined spaces. Then, suddenly, while Manny is praying to the Sacred Heart of Jesus, there is a dissolve—a man is seen walking toward Manny. He looks like Manny but is not. He is the true criminal. When Manny is released, he must care for his mentally disturbed wife. Hitchcock is obsessed with the vagueness of the law and the possibility of miscarriages of justice.

Hitchcock blends compassion with psychological realism. He shows understanding for the most case-hardened people—except, curiously, for Central European spies, saboteurs, and intelligence agents. All are Nordic, menacing, and humorless. Apart from this, however, Hitchcock demonstrates repeatedly that human beings not under contract to some bureaucracy have interior lives and that passion and precarious moods can move them from evil into goodness, from mediocrity into heroism.

Cary Grant's fickle Madison Avenue adman in *North by Northwest* is prototypical. Roger Thornhill has alcoholic tendencies (three-martini luncheons), is divorced, and apparently unscrupulous (he cons a woman out of a taxicab). Suddenly, he finds himself in the center of an espionage plot involving foreign agents and the CIA. His purpose becomes firmer, an illustration of that recurrent law of Hitchcock films—the greater the danger, the stronger (ideally) the moral fiber exhibited.

Another is his belief that we trust appearances too much. *Psycho* (1960) is a watershed film not only in cinema history, but also for confirming the peculiarly Catholic subtext of many of Hitchcock's films. The crux of *Psycho* is the mutability of human nature—how scene, circumstances, and historical genesis transmute motives and consequently behavior. Both Norman Bates (Anthony Perkins) and Marion Crane (Janet Leigh) have peculiar psycho-histories. There is a traveling shot in the opening scene that makes us voyeurs (as does *Rear Window*), mobilizing our eyes to enter a motel room to witness a noonday tryst. Thus Hitchcock sets up the rationale for Marion's theft—she loves a married man who needs more money for his divorce. Marion is normal and Hitchcock makes us identify with her dual temptation—adultery and embezzlement. His compassion is achieved from understanding the mutability of human motivation.

In Catholic theology intentions are tantamount to deeds, so that attempted suicide is as grievous a sin as suicide itself. Hitchcock possesses a psycho-spiritual skill that depends largely on this distinction. Things are not as they appear since we can never judge the inner world of others, nor do the Gospels advise us to judge others. Midway in the film we begin to transfer our allegiance from Marion Crane to the youthful motel proprietor, Norman Bates, with his "golly-gee" innocence and dedication to caring for his invalid mother. Integrity versus moral blemish. This is the contrast Hitchcock gives us—and the audience overtrusts its feelings, overconfides in appearances. For Marion has repented of her defalcation in the lonely motel.

The film's perspective shifts. Marion puts aside the stolen money and undresses for her shower. Norman Bates, from his room crowded with stuffed birds, watches her through a peephole. Things are not what they seem. Interior worlds have changed—the nice boy is seen as lustful, a potential aggressor, while the thieving, adulterous woman appears as regenerated and as such as a pitiable victim. The famed shower scene is a passion scene—not only of blood lust, but also of innocence unjustly punished. Hitchcock's suspicion that the wrong persons are arrested, persecuted, and killed is reaffirmed. The wrong woman dies. And the culprit? It turns out to be not Norman's jealous and demented mother, but the psychotic son himself with his split personality. There are really no serious moral offenses, Hitchcock insinuates in *Psycho,* only people whose lives are blown about like ships in a gale.

Hitchcock is known for psychological suspense, but even a cursory review of films such as *The Lodger, Saboteur, I Confess, The Wrong Man, Vertigo,* and *Marnie* reveals deep moral

STILL 28: *Vertigo*
Directed by Alfred Hitchcock.
Scottie Ferguson (James Stewart), victim of "vertigo," descends the steps of the bell-tower after the woman of his dreams has fallen, apparently to her death. Hitchcock's meticulous composition supports his ironic point that appearances inevitably deceive; there is no delving *into* the psyche of another.

and theological concerns. If Christ is "the wrong man" in terms of Christian theology, then the movies of Hitchcock (trained in an English Jesuit school) bear a curiously inexplicable affinity to Christ the victim. They are certainly more than entertainment. Guilt, victimhood, and moral mutability through conversion and character development are part of Hitchcock's signature. The art of an *auteur* director, Hitchcock's films contain horizons of meaning that are deeper than critics have been able to detect thus far. As such they provide a firm basis for the proposition that theology is not alien to the cinema, that religious insight is a hermeneutical tool for fuller, richer understanding of many of cinema's most enduring artists. Hitchcock stands in the front line of such film makers.

BIBLIOGRAPHY

Anobile, Richard J., ed. *Alfred Hitchcock's "Psycho."* New York: Avon/Flare Books, 1974.

Durgnat, Raymond. *The Strange Case of Alfred Hitchcock.* Cambridge: MIT Press, 1974.

LaValley, Albert J., ed. *Focus on Hitchcock.* Englewood Cliffs, N.J.: Prentice-Hall, 1972.

Naremore, James. *Filmguide to "Psycho."* Bloomington: Indiana Univ. Press, 1973.

Spoto, Donald. *The Art of Alfred Hitchcock.* New York: Hopkinson & Blake, 1976.

Truffaut, François. *Hitchcock.* New York: Simon and Schuster, 1967.

Wood, Robin. *Hitchcock's Films.* New York: Barnes, 1965.

PAUL TIESSEN

Claude Jutra

IT is in his two great feature films, both set in a Quebec of the past, that Claude Jutra (b. 1930) has brilliantly demonstrated his sensitivity to a distinct religious ethos and to characters motivated and shaped by that ethos: in *Mon Oncle Antoine* (1970), set in the late 1940s, and in *Kamouraska* (1972), set in the mid-1800s. These films, by Quebec's but also doubtlessly Canada's greatest film maker, were his third and fourth feature films. Jutra's career began about a quarter-century before these films were made, when he was experimenting with short films to please himself, as he finished a formal education in medicine. It is, however, the way Jutra has creatively explored his characters', his own, and his audience's sensitivity to religious archetypes in his major film, *Mon Oncle Antoine,* that is of greatest interest here.

Jutra grew up in a society where even film reflected the demands of the church, and his own work was always in distinct contrast to such, or any other, external demands. The Quebec feature-film industry was unusually busy, and very much in league with the Roman Catholic church, in the very years during which Jutra began to make short films. The nineteen features made between 1944 and 1953 in Quebec for the most part shared explicit religious themes and motifs. Many featured a priest who had something of the appeal of a "cowboy in a cassock,"[1] in Pierre Vérroneau's phrase. Aesthetically and emotionally, these films were not inspiring, and "the genre that aroused the most reaction was the weepy melodrama, highly moralistic with curious sado-masochistic overtones"; they reflected a dark period in the life of Quebecers, "suffocated by Catholic values of penitence, atonement, forbearance and self-sacrifice."[2]

When a new, youthful generation of directors turned once again to feature films in Quebec, about a decade after the earlier boom had ended, many of them emphatically swept away, and went far beyond, not only the thematic icons but also the stylistic conventions of their predecessors and revealed new influences and attachments such as the French "new wave." Claude Jutra, who had been out of Canada in the late 1950s, led the way.

From the beginning of his career Jutra was interested always in new, often abstract, film forms, and he won a Canadian Film Award for his experimental piece *Mouvement Perpétuel* in 1949. In the mid-fifties, while making films for the National Film Board of Canada, Jutra acted in the comical pixilation short *A Chairy Tale* (1957); he co-directed it with the famous animator Norman McLaren, whose formal, abstract work Jutra admired greatly. Then, moving away from the relatively thin film world of Canada, Jutra made *Anna la Bonne* in France, a short film produced in 1959 by François Truffaut; in 1961 he made the hour-long *Le Niger: Jeune République* in Africa with the "cinema-direct" film maker Jean Rouch.

Returning home and finding a vigorously new political and cultural climate, Jutra decided, as Martin Knelman puts it, "to pull off something startling—a privately financed film made in cinema-direct style with real-life characters acting out their own story."[3] The film was *À Tout Prendre* (1963); in it Jutra included a portrayal of himself, "unflinchingly and unflatteringly in a tense love affair with a black model named Johane."[4] With this first feature effort, he led the move toward a contemporary urban film, in which the priest had lost his important and flattering role.[5] To it can be traced the structurally adventuresome work, examining a contemporary secular marriage, *Pour le Meilleur et pour le Pire/For Better and for Worse* (1975), Jutra's fifth feature, and, to date, the last in the context of his Quebec culture.

Wow (1969), Jutra's second feature, again used techniques of improvisation, this time in a portrayal and celebration of the world of the teenager. Like his short *Rouli-Roulant* (1966), *Wow* is a comic, satiric treatment of the oppression of joyous urban youth by local officialdom. In fact, *Wow* and *À Tout Prendre*—like Jutra's next two features, *Mon Oncle Antoine* and *Kamouraska*—might have been "dedicated to all victims of intolerance." In the epic period film *Kamouraska,* for example, Jutra deals with a woman who is the "new Quebec wresting herself free from the ancient priest-ridden one," expressed largely by the household of the woman's mother and three maiden aunts, "dressed in corsets of pieties."[6]

It is *Mon Oncle Antoine,* based on an original script by Clément Perron, that is still Jutra's, probably Canada's, masterpiece. Here, Jutra himself, in turning away from the modern city to life in a small asbestos-mining town in post-war Quebec, had to deal with a world in which the institutional church was still intact and prominent. And he dealt with it sensitively, subtly, warmly, in the manner of a Jean Renoir. However, it is quickly apparent that Jutra (in the manner of Renoir's treatment of the classes in, say, *The Rules of the Game*) is satirizing the institution and its many forms of control, however endearingly he presents them, throughout the film. What is still more interesting, and my main point here, is Jutra's use of the iconography and patterns of the very thing he is satirizing—the church, Christianity—to present an alternate means of the people's salvation; for him, any spiritual salvation they might achieve must be gained in social, political, and economic terms, in terms of dealing with the oppression of *l'Anglais,* the owner of the asbestos mines.

Most critical responses to *Mon Oncle Antoine,* especially in English-speaking Canada, have stressed the film's rich documentary sense of time and place, or the archetypal quality of its rites-of-passage theme. Although critics have here and there acknowledged the political statement of the film, they have tended to play down its importance.[7] The film is, in fact, a bold, urgent expression of Jutra's political agenda and, in its "warmth," essentially ironic. Jutra's images of life, death, and rebirth in the Christian context are central in expressing the film's political implications not only for the period it represents, but also for the period in which it was made.

Mon Oncle Antoine is a story of the initiation of a young boy, Benoit, who works for his Aunt Cecile and his Uncle Antoine, the undertaker and general-store owner in the isolated town controlled by the "English" mining company and the Roman Catholic church. His succession of perceptions, or discoveries, many involving the cradle and/or the coffin, lead him beyond a state of mischievous and careless innocence, although it is not entirely clear, finally, to what. Near the opening of the film he watches with some amusement his uncle's crude treatment of a corpse in a coffin, just after he has observed the polite rituals of a religious funeral. A little later he observes the triteness of religious observances when his aunt reconstructs the nativity scene—with a damaged Jesus in its cradle—amongst the Christmas decorations in a store window.

In the context of the film's political concerns, it is apparent that Jutra is depicting a religious life that is a death-in-life, regardless of how endearing or comical he is with his material. Even the warmth of the general store (a place complex in meanings and where, more than in the church, is found the community's spiritual center) is lost for us when we come to see it as a place filled with secretive silences, expressed, for example, by Antoine's (like the priest's) private retreats into drinking, by the voyeuristic and leering sexual gestures of one employee, by the preying parasitism of the father of another employee, a young girl to whom Benoit is attracted. This lethargic and paralyzed little world, where miners frolic with children in the asbestos-touched snow outside the store, is, as long as he remains entirely within it, the inheritance awaiting Benoit, who watches its parade of foibles.

The one adult male who actually can list the forces that oppressively exploit and reinforce the paralysis of the community is Jos Poulin, a biblical "Joseph" figure and father of the family around which the film's alternate plot is built. According to him, it is church and *l'Anglais,* priest and "boss," who assure the victimization of the people. His comment on the beer he drinks—"Here's another one the English won't get"—is punctuated by a zoom shot through the window of the bar to the grayish church outside. Jutra further extends his satiric statements from church to *l'Anglais* by showing the English-speaking mine owner haughtily engaged as a giver of trinkets the day before Christmas.

But Poulin, though his instincts are the right ones, does not find any mechanism to deal with the destructive forces he can identify. He, too, simply retreats and becomes a hewer of wood in some distant wilderness. It seems as though his withdrawal only hastens his family's pathetic loss in the death of their eldest son, a boy about as old as Benoit. Jutra seems to be saying that if new life is to come to the community, it will come through the boy Benoit, who at first observes events from some distance, but finally, though just for a moment when he lifts the dead boy, touches—literally and figuratively—his world.

It is in association with the Poulin family that the images of birth and death remind us most authentically of parallel Christian images, and certainly arouse a great deal of sympathy in the viewer. When the dead boy is dropped into a tiny coffin, with Benoit suddenly clutching his naked ankles, the boy's cold limbs, starkly exposed by the harsh lighting in the sequence, and his neck, bent by the tightness of the coffin, suggest Caravaggio's and Rubens' paintings titled "Entombment of Christ." That his mother's name is Elise suggests, too, the boy's link with John the Baptist. The question is clear: will Benoit become the savior?

Returning with the coffin at night to the general store, Benoit accidentally lets it drop from his sleigh into the snow. Later that night he dreams that he is in a coffin, from which his own body, dressed as an altar boy, rises in longing for a fulfillment, here expressed sexually. Suddenly he is awakened: he must help in the search for the lost coffin. His earlier, lighthearted journey to the Poulin house becomes now a darker journey, a more perilous quest for death in the night.

When the searchers cannot find the lost coffin, they come finally, on Christmas morning, to the Poulin house; with Benoit, the viewer advances, through a subjective, hand-held camera, accompanied by a nervous, tense drumming music, to a window of the house. Benoit peers through the window and sees the boy in his coffin, which is also now a crèche, with his neck still bent. The camera pans along the members of the stunned family, to the father kneeling in silence and the mother standing. The camera moves up to her staring eyes, reminiscent of the Madonna's as she holds her newborn child

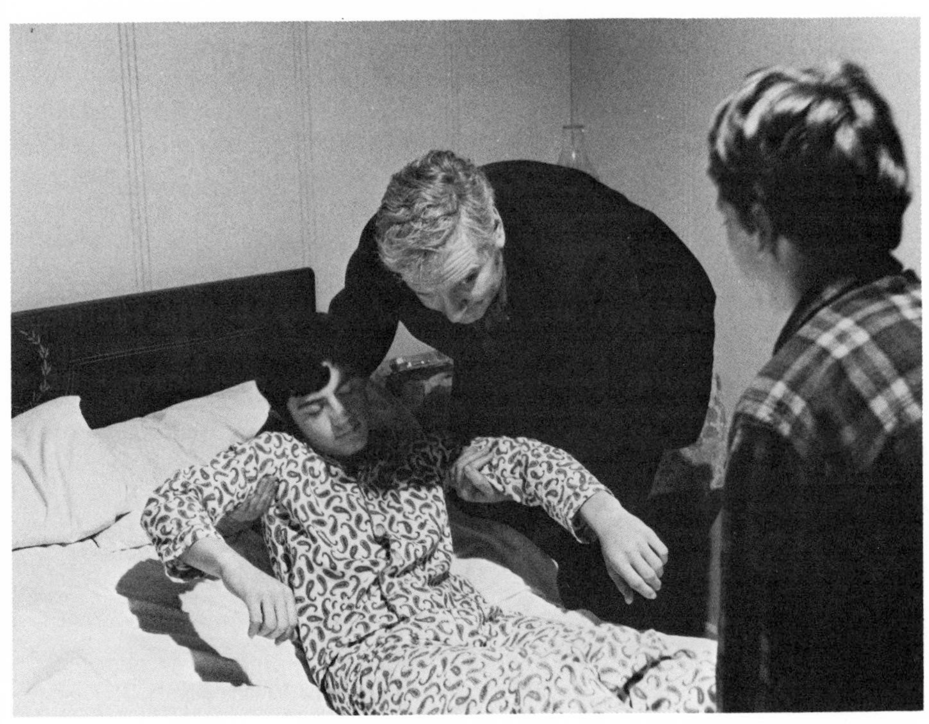

STILL 29: *Mon Oncle Antoine*
Directed by Claude Jutra.
Benoit (Jacques Gagnon) and his Uncle Antoine (Jean Duceppe), the undertaker, lift the body of the Poulin boy from his death-bed to place it in a coffin. This encounter with death becomes Benoit's most significant contact with life's threshold to maturity. Jutra's classic variation in the mythic pattern of death and resurrection deserves a much wider audience.

while looking away from him, challenging the viewer with her gaze. She stares out at Benoit, it seems, and at the viewer.

But in the last shot we are left watching the watcher, Benoit, as he gazes—with typical inscrutability—through the dirty glass at the people who helplessly surround the dead body. The associations are overwhelming. Yet amid a Christmas morning scene of despair and futility, the viewer has the sense that some new life is surely imminent; some awareness must follow this otherwise senseless death. Will the boy, watching the bewildered family, reach levels not only of feeling but also of vision beyond that of the father, Jos Poulin? It is not at all clear; Benoit does not say, Jutra does not help. But when Jutra forces the viewer to confront this question, he is also forcing him to move beyond sympathy for the bereaved "holy family" and seek a vision—necessarily a political vision—that will fulfill Joseph Poulin's and the community's needs in their inarticulate cry for help.

BIBLIOGRAPHY

Elder, Bruce. "Claude Jutra's *Mon Oncle Antoine.*" In *Canadian Film Reader.* Ed. Seth Feldman and Joyce Nelson. Toronto: Peter Martin, 1977, pp. 194–99.

Hofsess, John. *Inner Views: Ten Canadian Film-Makers.* Toronto: McGraw-Hill Ryerson, 1975.

Knelman, Martin. *This Is Where We Came In: The Career and Character of Canadian Film.* Toronto: McClelland and Stewart, 1977.

Véronneau, Pierre, and Piers Handling, eds. *Self Portrait: Essays on the Canadian and Quebec Cinemas.* Ottawa: Canadian Film Institute, 1980.

WILLIAM PARRILL

Stanley Kubrick

THE mature films of Stanley Kubrick, perhaps the most technically accomplished and certainly the most enigmatic of current American film directors, show the desire of the self to achieve rebirth in other than its present form. The rebirth itself is not necessarily what the participant desires, is never precisely what he imagined it would be, and is sometimes bitterly ironic or unsatisfactory. The films before *2001: A Space Odyssey* (1968) circle gingerly and ironically around the idea of rebirth, but *2001*, one of the boldest films of the commercial cinema, shows the evolution of mankind from "the dawn of man" at the beginning of the film to the birth of the star child at the end. In succeeding films, *A Clockwork Orange* and *The Shining,* Kubrick examines the attempt of the individual self, as opposed to the collective self of *2001,* to be reborn from the ashes of the old.

In Kubrick's films, the existing order is shown as pervasively corrupt, but the self, lacking in opportunity, sees the new order only imperfectly. The possibilities of rebirth, submerged as genre or disguised as irony, are perceived, often unclearly, by the protagonist, who yearns for rebirth with a passion that allows him in at least two instances to transcend space and time.

Rebirth is, of course, a concept central to all religions,[1] and while Kubrick's films are far from doctrinaire—indeed, they examine the idea of rebirth from several points of view—their main thrust is toward transcendence, that is, toward the desire to move away from the three dimensions in which we are trapped across space and time toward a higher form of existence. Rebirth may be either subjective, that is, take place within the individual, or objective, outside the individual. In Kubrick's films the two types tend to merge into each other, and only *2001* shows rebirth occurring outside the imperious demands of the individual ego. In *2001,* rebirth is not connected to the individual, but to the race.

In *Killer's Kiss* (1955) and *The Killing* (1956), rebirth centers around the idea of the "big strike," which is a staple of *film noir.* The "big strike" will turn around a wasted life and give it meaning. Davy Gordon in the former film unrealistically thinks that he will become a boxing champion, and Johnny Clay in the latter plans a daring robbery which will set him up for life. Of course, neither succeeds, and the desire for a new life need not here be interpreted as evidence of rebirth. *The Killing* owes more to John Huston's *The Asphalt Jungle* (1950) than it does to any philosophical or religious concepts.

In *Paths of Glory* (1957), the execution of the three French soldiers chosen by lot and convicted of dereliction of duty in a hopeless attempt to take the Ant Hill, a highly fortified German position, brings no change in the corrupt status quo. The stalemate in the darkest days of World War I continues. Dax's impassioned attempt to save the soldiers fails, and, at the end of the film, he walks back in total despair to his command. He stands in a tavern doorway and hears a timid girl sing a German song. Gradually, the French soldiers quiet down. The girl's innocence and the song, sung in a language they do not understand, remind them of their homes and loved ones. Such an ending, though it hardly represents rebirth, reminds the audience that even in the darkest times hope is not dead and goodness will survive.

Although *Spartacus* (1960) is the only film by Kubrick that makes extensive use of explicit Christian symbolism, it is also the only film over which he lacked complete artistic control. Kubrick has in effect disowned the film, but we may note in passing the clearly religious conclusion in which Variana shows the crucified Spartacus their young son and tells him, "This is your son. He is free." She repeats the word *free* as the head of the dying Spartacus falls back against his chest. Symbolically, the ending asserts Spartacus' immortality both through his own resurrection and through the freedom of his son. The revolt of the slaves is a failure, and the freedom of the son is at best only a limited victory over a corrupt system. Kubrick's reservation about the film and its unsatisfactory and anticlimactic conclusion[2] — one that can hardly have pleased the director — make *Spartacus* an uneasy vehicle to support generalizations about Kubrick's films.

Rebirth is given an ironic twist both in Vladimir Nabokov's novel *Lolita* and in the screenplay for Kubrick's film (1962).[3] Humbert Humbert, the middle-aged European seducer turned American emigré, is condemned to a cycle of fascination for and frustration by "nymphets," young girls caught in the fitful transition between childhood and pubescence. Thus, his love for them, even in the unlikely event it achieves fulfillment, can never be permanent. The concept of rebirth is ironically transferred from the protagonist to the object of his affections. The change that she undergoes is real and desirable, but it removes her from his consideration. Thus, his suffering is constant, but not, like that of Jack Torrance in *The Shining,* eternal; however, neither does he find the peace with which Torrance is periodically rewarded.

Lolita represents in Jungian terms a female personification of the unconscious,[4] and Claire Quilty is a distorted mirror image of Humbert Humbert himself. As erotic fantasy, *Lolita* represents Kubrick's most persuasive portrayal of the anima, the female element in a male psyche; it is unfortunate that the censorship of the time prevented a more robust portrayal which would have made the fragmentation of personality convincing.

At the end of *Dr. Strangelove, or How I Learned to Stop Worrying and Love the Bomb* (1964), the world is destroyed by a nuclear holocaust after a number of bumbling and ineffectual attempts by both the Russians and the Americans to prevent the activation of "the Doomsday Device." The black comedy, played strictly for laughs, concludes with Dr. Strangelove, the German scientist turned American adviser, pleading that, if anyone is left, "ten women for every man" be put in mine shafts, and with General Turgidson, the fanatical patriot, arguing that "we cannot allow a mine shaft gap." Over the concluding image of a nuclear blast, a song tells us that "we'll meet again, don't know where, don't know when." In Kubrick's universe, nothing is final — not even total nuclear catastrophe.

To this point in his career, Kubrick had circled around the

idea of rebirth, approaching it gingerly from a number of directions, but in *2001: A Space Odyssey* he made it the center of the film. The film is divided into four parts: (1) "The Dawn of Man," dealing with the evolution of mankind's ancestors; (2) the near future, recounting the digging up of a strange device at the Tycho crater on the Moon: (3) the Jupiter mission eighteen months later and the struggle with Hal the computer; and (4) "Jupiter and Beyond the Infinite," dealing with man's future evolution and his metamorphosis into the Star Child, presumably a new and more advanced form of life. Presiding over each of the four parts is a mysterious black monolith.

The monolith is an extraterrestrial force that appears at important moments and alters man in crucial ways, instigating or at least speeding up the evolutionary process. Although the monolith cannot be reduced to a single meaning,[5] the film clearly deals with the evolving cycles of death and rebirth; and Kubrick himself has said that "the God concept is at the heart of *2001*."[6] The film is pessimistic about individual men, but optimistic about the future of the race. Through the help of some mysterious outside force, mankind's future lies beyond the stars in a cycle of creative rebirth whose end no man can see.

After these grandiose speculations about the future of the race, Kubrick made a trio of films dealing with the ravening self's yearnings for rebirth. In different ways, the science fiction film *A Clockwork Orange,* the costume drama *Barry Lyndon,* and the horror film *The Shining* show rebirths so hedged with qualifications that the possibilities of the individual self are largely denied. Only in *The Shining* is the protagonist successful in any positive way, and here he has abrogated his self, never strong anyway, in favor of a community of maniacs.

A Clockwork Orange (1971), closely based on the novel by the Catholic writer Anthony Burgess,[7] parodies true rebirth. Alex, a demonic figure moving vigorously through a corrupt society, is consumed by his twin loves, violence and Beethoven. Imprisoned by a benevolent superstate, he is given the "Ludovico Treatment" and conditioned against violence. Released, he is helpless before his enemies. In the end, Alex has

STILL 30: *2001: A Space Odyssey*
Directed by Stanley Kubrick.
In the film's second episode, a routine excursion to an outpost on the moon to discover the origin of an unusual signal is interrupted by the appearance of the black monolith, a recurring symbol of mystery that reminds technological man of the folly of his efforts to control his destiny.

been emotionally deconditioned and is "himself again," but he is a pawn of the socialist state. Without free will, man is a "clockwork orange" and any true rebirth is impossible; there is only the appearance of renewal within a closed circle of deterministic variations.

Barry Lyndon (1975), based on a picaresque novel by William Thackeray, is Kubrick's most beautiful and enigmatic film. Barry Lyndon, née Redmond Barry, hardens himself to the world around him, becomes a soldier, a gambler, and an adventurer who lives by his wits, marries wealth, and is destroyed either by an awakening conscience or by a desire for rebirth and regeneration after the death of his young son. In a duel with his stepson, Lord Bullingdon, Barry, after the terrified Bullingdon misfires, discharges his pistol harmlessly. But Bullingdon, who has the next shot, refuses to accept mercy and shoots his stepfather. Although Barry survives, he loses a leg as a result of the wound and lives out his days drinking and gambling on a pension from his wife. The film is narrated from such a distance that the viewer is hard pressed to read Barry's true motivation, but the view that Barry wishes to begin a new life by showing compassion to Bullingdon is contradicted neither by the film itself nor by Kubrick's other films.

The Shining (1980), loosely based on a pulp horror novel by Stephen King, is Kubrick's darkest parable of rebirth. Jack Torrance, would-be writer, reformed alcoholic, and abuser of wife and young son, takes a job as winter caretaker of the Overlook Hotel, an elaborate resort hotel high in the Colorado Rockies. The Overlook has sinister powers over people with evil desires and weak wills and draws them inexorably into its past – or presides perhaps over periodic reincarnations of evil. Torrance's freezing to death at the center of the garden maze, a frequent symbol of the unconscious,[8] suggests his assimilation by the Overlook ghosts and perhaps by the hotel itself. The film's final shot, which shows Torrance as one of the revelers in a wall photograph from the 1920s, confirms the hypothesis of periodic rebirth. Despite the fact that Wendy, his wife, and Danny, his young son, have escaped, the cycle of evil has not been broken, but will continue, presumably as long as the Overlook lasts – and perhaps beyond.

In Kubrick's films, the individual will is subsumed into that of the group. The films represent not a triumph of the individual will but a triumph of the mass will represented by a corrupt society or by science. Paradoxically, however, Kubrick is obsessed with the idea of renewal. If his presentation of rebirth is still so hedged with qualification that a sense of affirmation is muted, he is too great an artist to have ruled out permanently all possibility for creative rebirth.

BIBLIOGRAPHY

Agel, Jerome, ed. *The Making of Kubrick's "2001."* New York: New American Library, 1968.

Clark, Arthur C. *The Lost Worlds of "2001."* New York: New American Library, 1972.

______. *2001: A Space Odyssey.* New York: New American Library, 1968.

Geduld, Carolyn. *Filmguide to "2001: A Space Odyssey."* Bloomington: Indiana Univ. Press, 1973.

Kagan, Norman. *The Cinema of Stanley Kubrick.* New York: Grove Press, 1972.

Kubrick, Stanley. *Stanley Kubrick's "A Clockwork Orange."* New York: Ballantine Books, 1972.

Phillips, Gene D. *Stanley Kubrick: A Film Odyssey.* New York: Popular Library, 1975.

Taylor, John Russell. "Stanley Kubrick." In *Directors and Directions: Cinema for the Seventies.* New York: Hill and Wang, 1975, pp. 100–35.

Walker, Alexander. *Stanley Kubrick Directs.* Rev. ed. New York: Harcourt, Brace, 1972.

WILLIAM PARRILL

Sam Peckinpah

SAM PECKINPAH is a powerful but largely instinctive artist whose films, through the use of romance, furnish patterns of conduct appropriate for a heroic age. The virtues that he celebrates—loyalty to the self and to a small band of followers, friendship, physical bravery, personal integrity, absolute commitment to keeping one's word—have been celebrated in literature for three thousand years and, indeed, still form the backbone of many works of popular literature. But Peckinpah states them in such extreme fashion that he antagonizes many people. His morality is a radical one because most people no longer believe that the heroic virtues have much relevance to the complexity of twentieth-century life. Thus, Rudolph Wurlitzer, who wrote the script for one of Peckinpah's films, can speak of Peckinpah's "reactionary theatricality," and Dustin Hoffman can speak of Peckinpah as a gunfighter born out of his time.

Peckinpah combines a radical morality with ancient tradition. By insisting on the relevance of ancient patterns of storytelling to modern life, Peckinpah keeps alive a nearly moribund narrative tradition and gives his stories an integrity generally lacking in low mimetic forms. Peckinpah insists on the reality of myth for modern man. René Wellek and Austin Warren, in their authoritative *Theory of Literature,* write: "In a larger sense, myth comes to mean any anonymously composed story a society offers its young of why the world is and why we do as we do, its pedagogic images of the nature and destiny of man."[1] Although it could be argued that the movies are the modern counterpart of the anonymous stories of the past, Peckinpah is clearly no anonymous artist. His film style is immediately distinguishable, but his films otherwise fit easily within the range of this definition. It may be bitterly ironic that the "story a society offers its young" these days is likely to be visual and that few think of Peckinpah as a moral guide, but that is what he is nonetheless.

For Peckinpah, the test of a narrative is its validity as an embodiment of myth. Myths assert manhood, they show patterns of integrity, heroism, and bravery, and they reenact in narrative form patterns for our young. It follows from the latter proposition that corruption of the young is always in Peckinpah's films the highest form of corruption, and Peckinpah returns to the theme compulsively until *Cross of Iron* (1977), a film in which the analysis of the corruption of the young becomes a central theme. Earlier films treat the subject in less, but still striking, detail. For example, the corruption of the two Hedden children is a minor, but significant, pattern in *Straw Dogs* (1971). The boy models himself after his father in the wrong ways: he is a peeping tom and has already learned to drink. And the girl, lacking proper guidance, seduces the village idiot and pays dearly for her deficiencies.

The process of corruption begins at an early age. We remember the nursing mother with the cartridge belt strapped to her shoulder in *The Wild Bunch* (1969). The newspaper today carries a photograph of a child, perhaps five, with a pistol tucked into his pocket. A boy plays admiringly with the big pistol of Mapache, a sodden bandit chief (*The Wild Bunch*). CBS News shows African teenagers training for guerrilla warfare. Peckinpah does not invent such happenings: he merely records them. But, and this is the greatest irony of all, the recording has caused the public to believe that he approves.

Models of conduct are likely to be extreme; after all, they embody extreme situations. Peckinpah stated the simple truth when he said that he does not approve of the Wild Bunch, but I think that it would be more accurate to say that, while he does not approve of them, he does admire them because they live "according to certain codes."[2] They are like the barbaric heroes of the epic. According to M.I. Finley in *The World of Odysseus*: "The age of heroes, . . . as Homer understood it, was a time in which man exceeded subsequent standards with respect to a specified and severely limited group of qualities."[3]

STILL 31: *Cross of Iron*
Directed by Sam Peckinpah.
As a captured Russian youth (Slavco Stimac) surrenders his harmonica to the German Corporal Steiner (James Coburn), the glance they exchange acknowledges war's saddest necessity—the abuse and corruption of youth. The boy's innocence accentuates the senseless horror of war even if Peckinpah's Puritan code elsewhere extols the opportunities for courage that war inevitably provides.

Homer, however, was in a more fortunate position than Peckinpah because many men of his time, as Finley goes on to state, shared his assumptions and values.

Here, the famous distinction made by Philip Young about the writings of Ernest Hemingway seems helpful. Young distinguishes between the Hemingway hero and the code hero.[4] The Hemingway hero is based more or less on Hemingway himself, while the code hero embodies in extreme form certain standards of conduct and confronts the world of violence and death with bravery and dignity. Strictly speaking, there may not be any Peckinpah heroes, but Peckinpah has used certain parts of his background and experience in his films, most notably perhaps in *Ride the High Country* (1962).[5] And Benny in *Bring Me the Head of Alfredo Garcia* (1974) has been taken by Pauline Kael and others to be a portrait of Peckinpah himself.[6] Benny is a man on a quest, he wears reflective sunglasses (like Peckinpah), he fights aginst corrupt and vague corporate structures, he loves Mexico, and he dies in a shootout. While this is obviously not pure autobiography, it does not follow that it is pure fiction either.

Peckinpah's code heroes live by certain standards: they keep their word, they will not hang anyone, they keep their countenance in the face of death, they are intensely loyal to each other, and they regard betrayal as the highest crime; when betrayed, they seek personal revenge based on an Old Testament idea of retaliation. Adherence to the code is not by itself enough to elicit Peckinpah's approval, but a man who is ignorant of the code or who doubts its relevance to modern life is, like David Sumner in *Straw Dogs,* a man who can be imposed on, abused, and perhaps even eventually killed.

Like William Faulkner, Peckinpah grew up hearing the old stories told, the rambling anecdotes of a former time; and like Faulkner, he embodied many of them in his best works. And one cannot read the interviews in which Peckinpah speaks about his childhood without hearing in them the Old Testament strains of Protestant preachers, of camp meetings and stern admonitions, and of loyalty to one's country and to one's self.

The reasons Peckinpah became a radical moralist may never be precisely determined, but in retrospect it can be seen that *The Wild Bunch,* which appeared in 1969 at the height of the Vietnam involvement, is the film in which the process reaches its full development; that the two films that followed at yearly intervals, *The Ballad of Cable Hogue* and *Straw Dogs,* are lesser works that deal in somewhat doctrinaire fashion with concepts inherent in the earlier film; and that, having exhausted the concept of territory, Peckinpah turned to an examination of the possibilities for heroic action in the modern world. *The Wild Bunch* may be seen as an outgrowth of Peckinpah's earlier films, but I doubt that anyone could have predicted it from them before it appeared.

Many elements contributed to *The Wild Bunch*: Peckinpah's war experiences, the disappointments of *Major Dundee* (1965), his being fired from *The Cincinnati Kid,* his enforced vacation from directing and the resultant personal bitterness, the darkening of the country's mood during the Vietnam conflict, the influence of the novels of Ernest Hemingway and the films of John Huston, and the growing suspicion that man, by failing to understand his own deepest nature, is leaving himself open to the worst sort of trouble.

While we need not regard the films Peckinpah made after the territory trilogy (*The Wild Bunch, The Ballad of Cable Hogue,* and *Straw Dogs*) as failures, they seem, with two notable exceptions, to lack the sheer nervous energy and the love that the director lavished on his earlier works. *Junior Bonner* (1972) is a beautifully sustained but minor work. *Alfredo Garcia* is a cankered and bitter, though eminently defensible, film. *The Killer Elite* (1975) is a routine project which never quite becomes a Peckinpah film; and *Convoy* (1978), which shows Peckinpah examining the mythical basis for the comparison between the trucker and the cowboy, ends by rejecting the analogy almost completely.

The next two films show Peckinpah in full command of his awesome battery of cinematic skills. *Pat Garrett and Billy the Kid* (1973), while it adds little thematically to the earlier westerns, is in some respects the definitive Peckinpah western, and much of the film is without equal in the whole range of his work. Unfortunately butchered by the studio, it was not a commercial success, and our knowledge of it must be pieced together from the theatrical release, from the television version, and from what has been written about it.

Cross of Iron (1977), which I believe to be the greatest of Peckinpah's films and the one that most completely expresses his philosophy, has never achieved anything like the recognition it deserves. The enormously ambitious film represents no less than an analysis of the causes of Germany's corruption and an extension of that analysis to include the continuing corruption of the world today. It is also an amazingly detailed reconstruction of the look and feel of war, a series of graphic illustrations of the terrors of modern warfare which concludes with a dance of death, a vision of hope for the future, and finally a vision of the heroic possibilities of war.

The situations in *Cross of Iron* are extreme, the range of morality narrow but stern, instructing us through myth and preparing us for the fierce times to come. Peckinpah's films will not solve problems of energy and inflation, but if the old times should ever return, if man's survival ever depends upon his physical courage and the loyalty of his friends, then Peckinpah's films and the lessons they embody will seem warnings beyond price.

Peckinpah is descended from a pioneer family with close ties both to the law and to traditional Protestant morality. Time in military school seems to have yielded paradoxically a love of ritual and a distrust of authority. In my opinion, the increasing darkness of the later films reflects a soured Protestantism attempting to come to grips with the moral ambivalence of the modern world. Peckinpah is a radical moralist, and his moral position is an outgrowth of his intense belief in the priority of the individual, a belief that he demonstrates with relentless vigor, and of his need to establish a minimum standard of personal conduct, a kind of bedrock morality in a world in which moral standards have been eroded.

BIBLIOGRAPHY

Kitses, Jim. *Horizons West: Anthony Mann, Budd Boetticher, Sam Peckinpah: Studies of Authorship Within the Western.* Bloomington: Indiana Univ. Press, 1970.

McKinney, Doug. *Sam Peckinpah.* Boston: Twayne Publishers, 1979.

Miller, Mark Crispin. "In Defense of Sam Peckinpah." *Film Quarterly* 28, No. 3 (1975), 2–17.

Parrill, William. *Heroes' Twilight: The Films of Sam Peckinpah.* Hammond. La.: Bay-Wulf Books, 1980.

Pettit, Arthur G. "Nightmare and Nostalgia: The Cinema West of Sam Peckinpah." *Western Humanities Review* 29, No. 2 (1975), 105–22.

Ross, T.J. "Death and Deliverance in the Western." *Quarterly Review of Film Studies* 2 (Feb. 1977), 75–87. See reply by William Parrill, *QRFS* 4 (Summer 1979), 379–82 and (Fall 1979), 507–8, and Ross' reply (Summer 1979), 382–88.

Seydor, Paul. *Peckinpah: The Western Films.* Urbana: Univ. of Illinois Press, 1980.

Simmons, Louis Garner. "The Cinema of Sam Peckinpah and the American Western." Diss. Northwestern Univ., 1975.

Wurlitzer, Rudolph. *Pat Garrett and Billy the Kid.* New York: New American Library, 1973.

TIMOTHY L. SUTTOR

Ken Russell

In contemporary patriarchal societies, technological control of sex has replaced mental or spiritual control, virtue as it was formerly called. Justice and chastity should ensure sexual order, but instead clothing does. Although we have abandoned sex censorship of literature, for practical purposes we retained until recently enough film censorship, not of thought or act, *but of flesh,* to preserve the patriarchal dogmas—mythologize woman, especially nude, and equate indecency with sex. Hollywood's self-administered censorship under the Hays Code, 1934–1964, together with the vice-punished-virtue-rewarded formula made American films, with something close to a global monopoly during that period, simply an extension of Victorian melodrama. Since all this was done in the name of religion, the net result was to make religion appear to involve an impaired sense of reality.

The filming of *Women in Love* (1969) by a group of major English talents was a dramatic and certainly decisive event in the history of film mores. Ken Russell's realistic focus on the male nude quite simply challenged the existing patriarchalism and male chauvinism. Russell is the director who has been most free of that vision and who, in consequence, has troubled the film-finance establishment most and has indeed been harassed by them.[1] His challenge to the prevailing Victorianism led him naturally and inevitably into a long series of studies of artists and of their relations to the establishment, tradition, and the erotic. For it is to great art that the modern world has entrusted the task of religious inquiry—and "serious film" is a case in point.

Russell began his career in television from 1962 to 1968, with programs on Elgar, Rossetti, Isadora Duncan, Delius, Bartok, and Prokofiev. His carefully documented TV piece "The Dance of the Seven Veils," on Richard Strauss, appears to have been suppressed by the BBC after one airing in 1970. "You can't do Tchaikovsky," U.S. producer Harry Salzmann later snapped at Russell; "Dimitri Tiomkin's gonna do that and he's already writing the music."[2] And United Artists is said to have remained cool until he put the story to them as that of a homosexual who marries a nymphomaniac. But by then he had directed *Women in Love.* Even that, however, failed to win United Artists' money to back *The Devils* (1971), which left its immense risks and profits to Warner Brothers. But Russell belonged neither to the market nor to the financiers, as *The Music Lovers* (1970), *Mahler* (1974), and *Valentino* (1977) showed; they all keep an unrelenting eye on the sins of big finance as well as of artists and ordinary people, and especially on film's own "sin," the Hays (or any other) code masquerading as conscience. The alternative to decency as defined by codes is not indecency; it is thought. It may also be worship.

Russell describes his Catholicism, to which he was converted, as more lapsed than Catholic in "their" sense of the word; but, of course, he has chosen to be the outsider in relation to the church establishment as much as he is one in relation to established opinion and money. His interviews with John Baxter show him sharply critical of the church's attitude to the presentation of religious material in film. "Unless it's a laudatory, anaemic, mealy-mouthed, simpering piece of work with no blood in it at all, they're terrified" (108). He further comments: "People in this country are afraid of laughing at religion for fear of offending . . . who? Certainly not God, who must have the biggest sense of humor of us all" (203).

When his images fail to penetrate his milieu, Russell does not normally try to win a way for them with words; however, his observation on *The Devils* shows it to be closely related conceptually to *Altered States* (1981), a decade later:

> Saint Francis took vows of poverty and chastity and founded an order to which the Church gave a lot of publicity, but if Grandier had become a saint instead of being declared a heretic and an order had been founded on *his* concepts—because he did have a brilliant mind, quick, free, forward-looking, sexy, uninhibited and unbigoted—the Church might have at least succumbed to his sort of

> thinking and Catholicism might have been a religion worth living by. . . . The only thing I really regret . . . is that the real core of the film, the Rape of Christ, was cut out. . . . Naked nuns tear down a wooden figure of Christ and throw themselves on it, having it in every possible way. Then Mignon goes up into the roof and masturbates looking down on the orgy below. Both Warner Brothers and the censor thought it was too strong so I took it out. . . . But it was really central to the whole thing, intercut as it was with Grandier finding both himself and God in the solitary simplicity of Nature. Overripe, perverted religion going as bad and wrong as it can possibly become, with the eternal truth of the bread and wine and the brotherhood of man and god. . . . (204–10)

Grandier may not have been exactly a Joan of Arc or a Thomas More, but he was a hero and a martyr who tapped the springs of honesty in his culture and put an end to its phoney religiosity and phonier indignation. The fictional Jessup of *Altered States* is given the wisdom—religious, erotic, cosmic—that the historical Grandier was killed for seeking.

In *The Devils,* obscenity is not naked nuns; it is techniques of torture and punishment that have changed much less with the passage of time than we wish to believe. John Trevelyan, the censor who enabled Russell to get what he did through the censorship committee, led him to understand that his most antagonistic censors were actually agnostics. In the modern world the road to holiness is perfectly clear, as Russell recalls: "Of all the dozens of hours I spent arguing the pros and cons of this and that with John only one moment still sticks in my mind. 'I'm afraid we can't have Vanessa saying "cunt,"' he said. 'It's taken me ten years of fighting just to get "fuck" accepted. I'm afraid the British public isn't ready yet for "cunt"'" (210).

If Russell thinks that the church is confused, he is sorrier still for a world that, having set aside saints and sacraments, has put artists and arts in their place. There is by now no artistic medium he has not savaged: dance in *Isadora Duncan,* literature in *Dante's Inferno* and *Women in Love,* sculpture in *Savage Messiah,* music in half-a-dozen major productions, and at last film itself in *Valentino.* "Every composer I used fell

STILL 32: *The Devils*
Directed by Ken Russell.
Father Grandier (Oliver Reed), whose sensuality is virtue rather than vice in Russell's vision, is a saint made by adversity. However rebellious his resistance to Cardinal Richelieu's attempts at centralization or unorthodox his ministry to the nuns of Loudon, his excesses pale by comparison with the ruthlessness of the Inquisition.

into the same pattern. He had great aspirations, lost them and/or was double-crossed, and sold out at the end" (228).

The Music Lovers is the biography of an idea, the idea central in most modern religious perversion, that genius—or rather perhaps the work it finally effects as our one door open to the absolute—can dispense with humor, truth, and honor. His recoil from the hell of Tchaikovsky's life made Russell perhaps too gentle with the stage in *The Boy Friend* (1972); he made up for it, however, in *Tommy* (1975) and *Lisztomania* (1975) and has yet to be forgiven by the critics who live by the credo that art is absolute. A stern moral perception, humor in abundance without cynicism, and the absence of any respect whatever for traditional packaging of drama into separate bundles labeled tragedy, comedy, and farce make the philosophy undergirding Russell's films at once human and robust. "All my films," he says, "are choreography."[3] The remark is more than autobiography; it is a key to film criticism itself, and particularly to the way in which aesthetic values lead, as nature intended, to religious values. Only through form and pattern can words, music, and images yield silence. It is time to reread the *Poetics,* so long misread by men (the gender is intentional) who failed to notice Aristotle's dancers.

All this has guaranteed Russell, like Bergman and Fellini through the 1950s and Antonioni into the 1960s, a tough fight with the American film conscience and the critics who like to think they voice it. Paradoxically, *Valentino,* a study of the patriarchal state of mind called Hollywood, was financed by Hollywood money, five million dollars to be exact, thus proving two points: first, if you "spill the beans," no one will believe you, for the truth about the U.S. film industry *is* unbelievable; second, if a company does not like its own creation, the people inside the industry (a term that ironically includes film reviewers too) feel obliged to prove it right and make the film a box-office failure. United Artists, who had owned the dying Valentino and now owns Russell's indictment, would rather sustain a loss than disturb the universe.

Unlike the artist, the star is not the creator of his own stardom. He provides a point round which the fantasies of millions crystallize; he is manipulated by mass emotion he cannot handle; but if he is smart, there is money in it. Valentino was, by common consent, the great star of the silent era. He was not smart. He was, so to speak, made to order to illustrate Russell's vision of a victim who, because he disbelieves his cult surrounding, becomes a savior figure. He is the Grandier of film-as-a-sickness-of-conscience, a symbol for the human condition in terms of film culture.

Altered States, an apparently harmless combination of sci-fi special effects and old-fashioned horror techniques, is actually a cosmic dance, myth in the deepest sense, a Man-Woman dance where He and She are cosmic forces and the real plot is the theological structure of the visions. The dance consists of a relentless interrogation by the modern scientific world view of childish bible-with-crucifix piety. If the mind travels back through the cosmos of Darwin and Einstein, what ultimate reality will it discover? None at all, of course, because modern science is not the road to God. But neither apparently is modern religion, because it is too afraid of philosophy, beauty, *and* science. Still Eddie Jessup has something metaphysical going for him—Emily, the timeless enigma-sphinx of his vision, Eve to his Adam. The couple, true to each other by first being true to truth, is a greater theophany than a million visions. Though erotic, their bond transcends the erotic, transcends them, transcends the universe. "Even sex is a mystical experience for you," Emily half chides Eddie before they marry; the word *even* shows how decently brought up she is. But the final image of the film tells us, no less than the two who embrace, of a mystic truth no human will can cancel.

Fortunately, in film as in Greek tragedy, there is always a chorus, the movie audience itself, however small. Watching Russell's films, we can purge our vision. Theology is, after all, purged vision. In Russell's theology, the base of our troubles is not so much original sin as an almost insurmountable distaste for reality.

BIBLIOGRAPHY

Atkins, Thomas R., ed. *Ken Russell.* New York: Monarch Press, 1976.

______. ed. *Sexuality in the Movies.* Bloomington: Indiana Univ. Press, 1975.
Baxter, John. *An Appalling Talent: Ken Russell.* London: Michael Joseph, 1973.
Fisher, Jack. "Three Paintings of Sex: The Films of Ken Russell." *The Film Journal* 2 (Sept. 1972), 33–43.
Gomez, Joseph A. *Ken Russell: The Adaptor as Creator.* New York: Pergamon Press, 1977.
Phillips, Gene D. "Fact, Fantasy, and the Films of Ken Russell." *Journal of Popular Film* 5 (1976), 200–10.
______. *The Movie Makers: Artists in an Industry.* Chicago: Nelson-Hall, 1973.
Wilson, Colin. *Ken Russell: A Director in Search of a Hero.* London: Intergroup Publishing, 1974.

BART TESTA

François Truffaut

AMONG film makers whose work has received treatment by critics considering the religious dimension of cinema, a particularly complex figure is François Truffaut. The leading student of André Bazin, Truffaut reflects in his films his own belief that human consciousness and experience must be bound to language and culture. For Bazin, human consciousness is directly grounded in Being, and for him the special role of film is to express this grounding in a manner free of "those piled-up conceptions, that spiritual dust and grime," which our culture has imposed upon our grasp of reality.[1] In contrast to his mentor, Truffaut believes rather that experience is always mediated by culture and that human consciousness is constituted by language. This conviction is increasingly evident during the progress of Truffaut's career, attaining mature expression in *Fahrenheit 451* and *The Wild Child.*

Bazin's film theory was evolutionary. He argued that the tradition of "faith in reality" exerted pressure on the history of film such that there was a gradual withering away of cultural accretions on the essential photographic realism of the film medium. Bazin expressed this theory by writing a history of film style that showed the realist tradition progressively displacing the tradition based on "faith in montage and the image." Certain of Bazin's views come to forceful expression in Truffaut's critical writings, as, for example, in his discussion of two adaptations of Georges Bernanos' novel *The Diary of a Country Priest,* one by the leading French scenarist Jean Aurenche (it was never filmed) and the famous version later made by Robert Bresson.[2]

In his comparison,Truffaut reveals how close he is to Bazin and even establishes his argument by drawing upon Catholic phenomenological film criticism that had extended Bazin's realism into an explicitly theological approach to film.[3] He draws on this critical school's position that film can go beyond psychology to express religious consciousness. Truffaut adapts this view to support his own contention that the *auteur* can share and express Bernanos' religious sensibility in film. Conventional French film makers, represented for example by Jean Aurenche, had thought such a sensibility in a novel to be "unfilmable."

The "certain tendency" Truffaut uncovers is that the French cinema of the fifties is dominated by a tradition of quality in which the work of a few scenarists determines the aesthetics of French film as a whole. The position developed by Aurenche and others is that many classical novels are at least in part impossible to convey to the screen unless mediated by psychological realism, a system of equivalents devised by the scenarist. Nevertheless, as Truffaut points out (citing Bazin's "The Stylistics of Robert Bresson"), the finished Bressonian adaptation of Bernanos is totally faithful, thus proving that the "unfilmable" is but a determination made within the narrow confines of certain formulas. Truffaut then sarcastically suggests that the whole tradition of quality is but an impoverished set of formulas that allows script writers to dominate the directors who shoot their scripts. Consequently, when adaptations are made, says Truffaut, all novels seem to be the same novel since they have to conform to the same formula and their vision of human nature is limited to psychological realism. In contrast, the *auteur* like Bresson, when he sets out to do an adaptation, struggles to find true filmic equivalents and achieves greater fidelity because, paradoxically, he exercises greater freedom.

Truffaut's first three feature films indicate the kind of cinema he was to make over a twenty-year span. *The 400 Blows* (1959) opens the autobiographical Antoine Doinel cycle starring Jean-Pierre Léaud, to which Truffaut returned periodically through the 1960s, concluding with *Love on the Run* (1979). *Shoot the Piano Player* (1960) initiates the series of genre films that run through the 1960s and seem to have ended with the nearly self-parodic disaster *Such a Gorgeous Kid Like Me* (1972). *Jules and Jim* (1961) is the first of two Henri-Pierre Roché adaptations; the second is *Two English Girls* (1971). Both works deal with the agonized passage from the romanticism of the nineteenth century into the modern period. Close to the Roché films are the curious *The Story of Adele H.* (1975), based on the journal of Adele Hugo but thematically treated as a gloss on both the Roché films and the Doinel cycle, and *The Green Room* (1978), based on Henry James' "The Altar of the Dead." *The Wild Child* (1969) stands somewhat apart from the kinds of films Truffaut has made, almost as a thematic essay, though it too is a film based on a journal, from the eighteenth-century Doctor Itard, whom Truffaut himself plays in the film. *Day for Night* (1973) and *The Last Metro* (1980), appearing after several lesser works, are Truffaut's *hommages* to film and theater respectively.

Seeds are planted in *The 400 Blows* that spring up in the subsequent Doinel films and separate Antoine from the tradition of the Bazinian realist hero. The love of the child Antoine for Balzac anticipates the growth of the character into a "symbolizer" who does not confront his reality but dreams and insists on his romantic projections. Truffaut both sympathizes with and chides this later Antoine. The sympathy is everywhere —in Antoine's quirky loves, in his comic eagerness and aching seriousness, and in his immersion in the working world around him, most often figured by Truffaut as a social collective (a figure borrowed from Renoir), such as the detective office in *Stolen Kisses* and the courtyard in *Bed and Board.* The recurring critique of Antoine is placed by Truffaut in those privileged moments where Antoine's direct encounters with women divest him of the enchanted image he has projected on them.

In *Bed and Board,* Antoine becomes a novelist of autobiographical persuasion. This not only cues the viewer to his cultural self-interpretation and to the privileges of language as his special medium, but Antoine's novel-writing also doubles the process of the Doinel cycle as a whole, reflecting the ethical problems of Truffaut's autobiographical cinema. James Monaco in *The New Wave* (1976) sees this doubling as a self-reflexive meditation on the role of the film maker[4]; one might also add that it expresses Truffaut's deliberate "fall" from the aspiration of a direct realism into the complexities of the languages of writing and film. The reflexivity of Antoine, however self-involved, points out that the films, too, are the products of reflection, that they are constructed bits of language: in short, that they are writing.

Monaco observes, "Our main sense of [Antoine] in *Bed and Board* as in *The 400 Blows* is deeply colored by his isolation."[5] But this isolation is of a new sort, for it is grounded in Antoine's novel-writing rather than on his bold dash for freedom as in the earlier film. Still, the novel itself is being written in service to that dash, for Antoine is now reinventing himself through memory, through writing. In this way, *Bed and Board* recalls the solitude of *The 400 Blows* not only to remind us of Antoine's irreducible humanity, but also to acknowledge his growth from an unguarded child into a self-mythologizing artist. And that artist is now re-creating the child just as Truffaut himself re-created himself as Antoine.

That Truffaut has refused to allow the cycle's resolution in *Bed and Board* to stand, but takes it back with *Love on the Run,* marks just how far he has moved from Bazin, for whom a character's growth should lead to a reconciliation with Being, to facing reality itself. Truffaut never allows this final reconciliation; his characters remain forever self-complicating. Why? Because for Truffaut there is no humanity outside culture, no "really real," no "ground of being" to which human consciousness has access. There is for Truffaut only the ethically frail, much-flawed means of language that we have all inherited from our culture.

Outside the Doinel cycle, Truffaut also mounts a somewhat more systematic consideration of his concerns with the exploration of characters as inheritors of culture and users of language, and he sometimes does so with greater urgency than is found in the gently unfolding story of Antoine. It is in *Fahrenheit 451* and *The Wild Child* that Truffaut's theological anthropology is most fully thematized. At stake here is the question of what constitutes the human and what connects the individual to reality. For Truffaut, reality is always mediated by culture, the "producer" of meaningful language, even though its results are ambiguous: for language loses the reality that it opens to love at the same moment it discloses it. This is why Truffaut at once celebrates and criticizes Antoine's romanticism, for Antoine's love would be impossible without a specific cultured language to evoke it and give it form even as it distorts love and has to be corrected—by, humanly enough, the beloved.

The expository sequences of *Fahrenheit 451* are surprisingly undramatic. The absence of books and of all but the most functional language has reduced the people of the future into unfeeling, sedated monads, typified by the hero Montag (Oscar Werner) and his wife, Linda (Julie Christie). In films within the dystopian subgenre of science fiction movies (like *THX 1138* or *Nineteen Eighty-four*) to which this Truffaut film belongs, interpersonal love, the bearer of authentic humanity, is conventionally placed in rebellious opposition to the inhuman coldness of the futurist society. But Truffaut sets up a conflict on a very different plane, between culture and society. The characters in this film remain as impersonal as the society around them. The acting is muted and even Montag's relationship with Clarisse (also played by Julie Christie) is cold.

The film narrates Montag's discovery of literature through which he discovers his human identity. Eventually, he and Clarisse move to the fringes of society where they join the book-people, those who individually memorize a single book and become that book, even changing their names. And it is there, among the book people, that human discourse, and with it humane existence, is resumed as recitation. Not human nature or its usual manifestations, love, rebellion, or freedom, but human *work,* the work of culture and language, is the basis of humanity discovered and cultivated in *Fahrenheit 451.*

Truffaut treats the same theme, though with far greater depth and grace, in *The Wild Child.* Some have seen the life of Victor before his capture as a nature idyll. But Truffaut clearly does not. Although, as Monaco reports, Truffaut has toned down the violence originally planned for the opening sequences, the finished film still shows Victor either desperately struggling to survive or rocking back and forth in his tree-top perch in an autistic trance. The middle of the film, while hardly a paean to civilized society, shows that the boy is reviled as subhuman precisely because he fails to live up to the

STILL 33: *Fahrenheit 451*
Directed by François Truffaut.
Nowhere has Truffaut better expressed his thematic preoccupation with language as the basis of human consciousness than in this futuristic parable. In an anti-intellectual totalitarian state, Montag (Oscar Werner) contributes to the survival of culture by memorizing the books he will become.

myth of the noble savage—the very myth that predisposes viewers to misread the film's opening as an idyll.

Dr. Itard (Truffaut himself) proves to be the serious representative of human culture. Itard conceives humanity to be the product of work, the labor of education. Once Victor arrives at Itard's home-laboratory, and his senses are loosened from the rictus his constant struggle for survival has induced, *The Wild Child* becomes the story of the acculturation of the boy, a process that consists of his learning language (broadly understood to include table manners, dress codes, and so on) and each step in this process is accompanied by Victor's emergence as a human personality.

Itard's journal, read off-screen to cover ellipses and to double for narrative with commentary, at times expresses the doctor's doubts about the benefits of civilization, but the film moves inexorably toward the disclosure of Victor's soul, the final experiment Itard performs. This is the painful sequence in which Itard unjustly punishes Victor during one of his lessons. The boy rebels, thus showing he has the power to tell right from wrong. It is no accident that this episode should become the final experiment, for the emergence of personhood in Truffaut's cinema does not occur through any exfoliation of human essence but through the power of language to expose the soul.

The Story of Adele H., also from a "found text," the solipsistic journals of Adele Hugo, reverses the process of *The Wild Child*. We are told through titles that Adele invented her own language. She is shown writing obsessively throughout the film, inventing a whole universe of romance for herself and the military officer who has already jilted her—and will do so again and again. Eventually, Adele leaves the real world, which she physically wanders through like a specter, and enters wholly into a fantasy universe. In a sense, she is an extreme version of what Antoine could have become had he lived in a period of high romanticism as Adele did. Next to *Two English Girls* and *The Green Room, Adele H.* is easily the darkest, most pessimistic of Truffaut's films, for it relentlessly traces, with immense tenderness and detail, a descent into what for this director could only be a damnation—the delusion of language itself. Its inevitable successor, *The Green Room,* is a long meditation on a dying sensibility that seems in space to exist in the anteroom of hell, in time to teeter on the edge of muted apocalypse. Julien Davenne (Truffaut) sinks into an obsessive contemplation of his dead wife; another woman, Cecilia, speaks to him of life and the future, but unlike so many Truffaut heroines, she fails to draw Julien out of his symbolized universe.

Over the span of two decades, and a diversity of film themes and subjects, Truffaut has constructed a cinematic opus that both derives from and departs from his mentor André Bazin. The spirituality of these varied works, beginning in psychological realism, tends toward an evocation of a religious transcendence (or depth) through images of fugitive flights, the act of writing (a re-invention through memory), the struggle between a romantic past and a modern present, between rapture and realism. There is no articulated spirituality in that there is no readily recognizable relationship of events and images to an ultimate reality or ground of being. Rather what emerges is the gently latent possibility that one comes face to face with the problem of individual and collective destiny only when confronted with the catastrophic threat of the deterioration and ultimate loss of language and culture. Truffaut's ambiguous evocations invite, in fact require, bringing to these films an independent theological judgment which for Bazin and the films of the Neorealists and Bresson would have been inherent in the artistic work itself.

BIBLIOGRAPHY

Allen, Don. *Truffaut.* New York: Viking Books, 1974,

Graham, Peter, ed. *The New Wave.* New York: Doubleday, 1968.

Insdorf, Annette. *François Truffaut.* Boston: Twayne, 1978.

Jebb, Julian. "Truffaut: The Educated Heart." *Sight and Sound* 41 (Summer 1972), 144–45.

Millar, Gavin. "Hitchcock vs. Truffaut." *Sight and Sound* 38 (Spring 1969), 82–88.

Monaco, James. *The New Wave: Truffaut, Godard, Chabrol, Rohmer, Rivette.* New York: Oxford Univ. Press, 1976.

Truffaut, François. *The Adventures of Antoine Doinel: Four Autobiographical Screenplays.* Trans. Helen G. Scott. New York: Simon and Schuster, 1971.

______. *Day for Night.* Trans. Sam Flores. New York: Grove Press, 1975.

______. *Jules and Jim.* Trans. Nicholas Fry. New York: Simon and Schuster, 1968.

______. *The Story of Adele H.* Trans. Helen G. Scott. New York: Grove Press, 1976.

______. *The Wild Child.* Trans. Linda Lewin and Christine Lemery. New York: Washington Square Press, 1973.

NEIL P. HURLEY

Lina Wertmüller

LINA WERTMÜLLER, the first widely acknowledged woman film maker of world class, belongs to the Christian left—as do many of her compatriots in Italy. An inveterate movie-goer, she intersperses her films with both tributes to and touches borrowed from the most memorable directors and films. Like Alfred Hitchcock, Luis Buñuel, and Stanley Kubrick, she is an ironist, subverting the literal meaning of surface reality. Like Rosselini, De Sica, and Fellini, she celebrates (and satirizes) distinctively Italian scenes. Like Eisenstein, Visconti, and Pasolini, she has a socialist world view. And like Lubitsch, Renoir, and Bergman, she sees romantic love as crucial to social harmony.

Yet Lina Wertmüller's film signature is indelibly unique, neither a derivative product nor a residual pastiche of film nostalgia. In a Wertmüller film, "Whirl is King!" but only for a while, since order—of a sort—always surfaces, imposed by the fascist state, the Mafia, the Catholic Church, or the patriarchal family. She sees western civilization, most especially Italy, caught in the vortex of a giant whirlpool made up of the eddies of Christianity, capitalism, and Marxism. Whereas popular journals treat the spread of Eurocommunism and the crisis in western culture analytically, Wertmüller symbolizes these themes through private psycho-dramas, generally involving the "ups-and-downs" of a man and a woman in a romantic or erotic relationship. Wertmüller penetrates the motives, moods, and mechanisms of choice of recognizably ordinary people, and in so doing she ironically illuminates the contradictions of the social macrocosm.

One may wonder what her relevance is to a study of religion and cinema since by her admission she has turned her back on what she considers the rationalization of the Catholic faith she was educated into and has looked more toward mystery and disorder. In a significant interview, published by Ernest Ferlita and John R. May in *The Parables of Lina Wertmüller,* she nevertheless explains that whereas "all religions, in a certain sense, are the same with respect to the concept of man, i.e., of the man who achieves harmony," she is more concerned with "man in disorder . . . who even though he now and then makes mistakes is nonetheless growing in harmony with himself and the world . . . that seems to be rushing headlong toward destruction, lacking all good sense and reason."[1] The person searching for integrity, for wholeness in a time of political power and social disorder—that is the Wertmüller leitmotif, *la politique d'auteur,* her analogue to the religious question.

Despite the ribald caricatures played by Giancarlo Giannini and Mariangela Melato (her stock players), Wertmüller's films carry a liberating message, one of alternatives. Paulo Freire, the noted Brazilian educator, insists in *Pedagogy of the Oppressed*: "The oppressed suffer from the duality which has established itself in their inmost being. . . . The conflict lies in the choice between being wholly themselves or being divided between ejecting the oppressor within or not ejecting him. . . ."[2] Wertmüller's films provoke us and make us feel that we are accomplices. We are her characters: we experience guilt for the way things are; we are divided between alienation and authenticity.

In *The Seduction of Mimi* and *Love and Anarchy,* Lina Wertmüller seems to be saying that the acids of modernity are eating away the foundations of Catholic rural Italy, that somehow the acquisitive spirit and individual incentives must find a *modus vivendi.* Her radical disposition (both emotional and intellectual) inclines her toward a socialism "with a human face."

The operative word in the lexicon of Wertmüller's film dialogue is *order.* In *The Seduction of Mimi,* Mimi (Giancarlo Giannini) is a quarry worker in Sicily. When he loses his job for voting against a Mafia-backed candidate, he leaves his wife and becomes a metal worker in Turin. Drawn into the Communist party, he falls in love with the Leninist Fiore (Mariangela Melato). They live together and have a child. But fate pursues Mimi relentlessly, always in the guise of a

STILL 34: *The Seduction of Mimi*
Directed by Lina Wertmüller.
On the steps of the church, Mimi (Giancarlo Giannini) taunts the police sergeant whose wife Mimi has impregnated in revenge for the sergeant's having done the same to Mimi's wife. His facile plan to restore order through the honorable exchange of babies misfires, and chaos reigns once again.

Mafioso-like figure with a triangle of moles on his face (now a local don, later a Turin mobster, finally a Cardinal). Mimi is seen not only as a prisoner of powerful ruling elites, he is also a captive of traditional attitudes. A professed Marxist, he betrays his bourgeois background and tells his radical mistress: "My son must lack for nothing. . . . My son must be a king."

Mimi is ripe for the fascist principle of law and order at any price. As a foreman in a refinery in his own hometown, Mimi resists the idea of a strike by his men: "The gang's not striking. What we need is order." Later we see him after his imprisonment for a murder committed by a Mafia henchman: he has contracted with the Mafia boss to distribute leaflets to the quarry laborers with whom he had worked at the film's beginning. His rationale? To support his children. Fiore leaves him in disgust, driving off in her red van with the Communist hammer and sickle painted on its side. Order is what Mimi wanted, and he aligns himself with the traditional ruling powers to obtain it.

In *Love and Anarchy,* order is contrasted with political chaos. Wertmüller separates the public world of order ruled by Il Duce's security police chief Spatoletti (Eros Pagni), and the feminine world of the brothel with its colored rugs, loosely drawn curtains, and dimly lit bedrooms. Tunin (Giancarlo Giannini) feels drawn to overcome the security of the world (his mother's protective love and that of the dark-haired prostitute) in order to win his self-respect. Order keeps him from this—the order of the extended family, of class structures, of the state hierarchy. At one point Tunin complains poignantly: "Even the chickens laughed at me—the time comes when a man has to say 'enough.'" When arrested for anarchic aggression, he is tortured but refuses to talk. In Spatoletti's eyes he is a threat to order, but order without human dignity is not worth living for—at least in Tunin's eyes.

All Screwed Up (the original Italian title *Tutto a posto e niente in ordine* means "Everything's OK But Nothing Works") is a devastating critique of consumer society. Wertmüller's attack on mass production is all-out as we see steers in a slaughterhouse being ritualistically killed while the carcasses dance about suspended from overhead pulleys. Scene after scene unmasks urban technological society: older apartment houses surrounded by impersonal high rises, over-crowded tenements, the chaos of a restaurant kitchen, the economic burdens of large families and unwanted children, the erotic games played by men and women whose work is devoid of meaning, and the passion for consumer goods.

One scene stands out. A man, tired of his Sicilian girl friend's coolness, moves to ravish her; trying to protect herself, she grabs for the dislodged color TV lest it crash to the floor. Lying on the floor and supporting the off-balance set, she is an easy mark. Choices are difficult, and virtue an unaffordable luxury.

The central image in *All Screwed Up* is the restaurant kitchen, a miniature replica of society at large. Bodies hurl past one another with trays, and white-frocked chefs give orders to subalterns with self-conscious authority. Suddenly there is a bomb scare, perpetrated by a right-wing terrorist group. Then all cooks, waitresses, and employees look to the left of the screen, gazing expectantly. Is a new order emerging? What will happen? The boisterous sound track falls silent: it is a moment pregnant with revolutionary possibilities. Will some leader give the signal to attack? The tension mounts, then someone unexpectedly shouts an order for a customer. The old habits take over; everyone returns to his habitual role. Everything is back in place, but nothing is in order.

Swept Away presents an idyllic sequence in the lives of an upper-class woman and a Marxist worker who are stranded on a paradise island. The parenthesis in the lives of both is unreal, alternately violent and beatific, and shortlived; for in the prologue and epilogue, man is under the domination of women. In the state of primitive nature, the man expresses his natural physical superiority and elicits the love of the once-proud female. Gennarino (Giannini) wants to hail a passing boat to prove that Raffaela (Melato) will continue to love him back in civilization where social convention and historical tradition have made her his superior. She begs him not to signal the ship, but he ignores her plea. On the magic isle there is a state of anarchy where natural impulses can be allowed free rein. Back on the mainland the magnetic pull of habit blights their dream: he is nagged at and struck by his domineering blue-collar wife; she returns to her elegant but passive spouse. Once again, everything is in place, but nothing is in order.

Seven Beauties stars Giancarlo Giannini as Pasqualino, the proud, handsome Neapolitan who protects family honor and the virtue of his seven comely sisters. As it turns out, the sisters—and presumably the mother—all become prostitutes to raise money for his defense when he kills the lover of his eldest sister. The levity of the film changes into tragedy in the German concentration camp where Pasqualino is degraded in order to survive. Complete submission to the sexual requests of the oversized female Commandant is preferable to extinction. Then a German officer slaps a pistol into Pasqualino's hand with the order to shoot his best friend. How many of us, the film asks, would pull the trigger as Pasqualino does?

Wertmüller insists that honor and integrity are luxuries when survival is at stake unless one is totally committed, like Fiore the militant Communist in *The Seduction of Mimi,* Tunin in *Love and Anarchy,* and the anarchist Pedro in *Seven Beauties.* All serve as transcendental ideals of hope in a better future, whereas the antiheroes of *The Seduction of Mimi, All Screwed Up,* and *Swept Away* are Walter Mitty types who envision behavior they are unequal to when put under pressure.

The popularity of Communism in Italy is evidence that something is dying and something is being born. The cracks in the political, economic, social, and religious structures are real; and Wertmüller's genius is to register this change not in documentary fashion but in visual imagery of stunning artistry. Wertmüller's films represent screen power as did Frank Capra's populist parables of the New Deal period (*Mr. Deeds Goes to Town, Mr. Smith Goes to Washington, Meet John Doe*). Italian Catholic sensibilities prevail in the films of both —personal integrity and concern for social justice.

Wertmüller's films brim with political relevance and religious hope. Their significance is that they serve as symbolic backdrop for the transition to a new era in which Christianity, capitalism, and communism will combine to form a new social blueprint more apt for meeting real needs rather than those synthetic needs Wertmüller portrayed in *All Screwed Up.* The seeds of a new society are present and, as Wertmüller shows us, will emerge from the womb of history. Her religious philosophy is as important as her art and cannot be divorced from it. The artist has always served as a "distant early warning signal"; Lina Wertmüller is a contemporary example of this type of prophecy.

BIBLIOGRAPHY

Allen, Tom. "Announcing—Lina Wertmüller, Daredevil Aerialist." *America,* 7 Feb. 1976, pp. 99–100.

Bettelheim, Bruno. "Surviving." *The New Yorker,* 2 Aug. 1976, pp. 31–52.

Biskind, Peter. "Lina Wertmüller: The Politics of Private Life." *Film Quarterly* 28, No. 2 (1974–75), 10–16.

Des Pres, Terrence. "Bleak Comedies: Lina Wertmüller's Artful Method." *Harper's,* June 1976, pp. 26–28.

Ferlita, Ernest, and John R. May. *The Parables of Lina Wertmüller.* New York: Paulist Press, 1977.

Gerard, Lillian. "The Ascendance of Lina Wertmüller." *American Film* 1, No. 7 (1976), 20–27.

Jacobs, Diane. "Lina Wertmüller: The Italian Aristophanes?" *Film Comment* 12, No. 2 (1976), 48–50.

Simon, John. "Wertmüller's 'Seven Beauties'—Call It a Masterpiece." *New York,* 2 Feb. 1976, pp. 24–31.

Wertmüller, Lina. *The Screenplays of Lina Wertmüller.* Trans. Steven Wagner. New York: Quadrangle/New York Times Book Co., 1977. (Includes *The Seduction of Mimi, Love and Anarchy, Swept Away, Seven Beauties.*)

Notes

PART I

FILM AS HIEROPHANY

1. Mircea Eliade, *The Sacred and the Profane* (New York: Harper, 1961), 11.
2. Ibid.
3. Ibid., 12.
4. Paul Tillich, *Systematic Theology,* I (Chicago: Univ. of Chicago Press, 1951), 85.
5. Paul Tillich, *The Religious Situation* (New York: Meridian, 1956), 39.
6. Paul Tillich, *The Protestant Era* (Chicago: Univ. of Chicago Press, 1957), 60.
7. Ibid., 68.
8. Ibid., 78.
9. Ibid., 79.
10. Mikel Dufrenne, *The Phenomenology of Aesthetic Experience* (Evanston: Northwestern Univ. Press, 1973), p. 55.
11. Dufrenne's work is characterized by Edward Casey as the fulfillment of a trend: "In this respect, it is by no means accidental that his *Phenomenology* brings the decade to a close. For it represents a return to that fundamental and most concrete level of human experience which the Greeks had called aisthesis: 'sense experience.' After Baumgarten and Kant, aesthetic experience had become increasingly divorced from sensory experience. . . . In opposition to such aestheticism, Dufrenne attempted to restore a measure of the meaning of aisthesis by providing a base for aesthetic experience in the open availability of feeling and perception" (Edward Casey, Introd., *The Phenomenology of Aesthetic Experience,* by Dufrenne, p. xvi).
12. Ibid., 336.
13. Ibid., 534.
14. Ibid., 376–77.

15. Ibid., 377.
16. Ibid., 549.
17. Ibid.
18. Rudolf Arnheim, *Film as Art* (Berkeley: Univ. of California Press, 1971), p. 157.
19. Ibid., 8.
20. Ibid., 157–58.
21. Arnheim, *Film as Art,* 35.
22. Ernest Lindgren, *The Art of the Film* (London: George Allen and Unwin, 1967), 79.
23. V.I. Pudovkin, *Film Technique and Acting* (London: Vision, 1958), 86.
24. Georges Sadoul, *L'Invention du Cinéma,* as quoted in Siegfried Kracauer, *Theory of Film* (New York: Oxford Univ. Press, 1960), 31.
25. André Bazin, *What Is Cinema?,* I, trans. Hugh Gray (Berkeley: Univ. of California Press, 1967), 13.
26. Ibid.
27. Kracauer, *Theory of Film,* 39.
28. Ibid., 301.
29. Bazin, *What Is Cinema?,* 15.
30. Kracauer, *Theory of Film,* 23.
31. Bazin, *What Is Cinema?,* 165–66.
32. Amédée Ayfre, "Conversion aux Images?," in Henri Agel, *Le Cinéma et le Sacré* (Paris: Editions du Cerf, 1961), 12.
33. Alain Bandelier, "Cinéma et Mystère," as quoted in Amédée Ayfre, *Cinéma et Mystère* (Paris: Editions du Cerf, 1969), 86.
34. Ibid., 108.
35. Ibid., 16.
36. As quoted in Amédée Ayfre, "The Universe of Robert Bresson," in *The Films of Robert Bresson,* ed. Ian Cameron (New York: Praeger, 1969), 8.
37. Henri Agel, *Poétique du Cinéma* (Paris: Editions du Signe, 1960), 59.
38. Ibid., 14.
39. Ibid., 50.
40. Bandelier, "Cinéma et Mystère," in Ayfre, *Cinéma et Mystère,* 80–81.
41. Kracauer, *Theory of Film,* 233.
42. Ibid., 309.

43. Ibid., 298.

44. Ayfre, "The Universe of Robert Bresson," in Cameron, *The Films of Robert Bresson,* 11.

45. Ibid., 12.

46. Ibid.

47. Raymond Durgnat, "Le Journal d'un Curé de Campagne," in Cameron, *The Films of Robert Bresson,* 47.

48. Ibid., 48.

49. Ibid. Bazin describes this scene as the culmination of a spiritual pilgrimage: "The spectator has been led, step by step, toward that night of the senses the only expression of which is a light on a blank screen" (*What Is Cinema?*, 140).

50. Durgnat, "Le Journal d'un Curé de Campagne," in Cameron, *The Films of Robert Bresson,* 48. The use of montage here is certainly one of the cinema's more restrained examples of the principle.

51. Bazin, *What Is Cinema?,* 133.

52. Bandelier, "Cinéma et Mystère," in Ayfre, *Cinéma et Mystère,* 115–16.

53. Agel, *Poétique de Cinéma,* 8.

54. Ibid., 24.

55. Ayfre, *Cinéma et Mystère,* 17.

56. James Luther Adams, *Paul Tillich's Philosophy of Politics, Culture and Art* (New York: Harper and Row, 1965), 98.

57. Dufrenne, *The Phenomenology of Aesthetic Experience,* 339.

58. Agel, *Poétique du Cinéma,* 28.

59. Ibid., 8.

60. Ibid.

61. Eliade, *The Sacred and the Profane,* 11.

VISUAL STORY AND THE RELIGIOUS INTERPRETATION OF FILM

1. T.S. Eliot, *Essays Ancient and Modern* (New York: Harcourt, Brace, 1936); rpt. in *The New Orpheus,* ed. Nathan A. Scott, Jr. (New York: Sheed and Ward, 1964), 223–35. See also Cleanth Brooks, *The Hidden God: Studies in Hemingway, Faulkner, Yeats, Eliot, and Warren* (New Haven: Yale Univ. Press, 1963); John Gardner, *On Moral Fiction* (New York: Basic Books, 1978) — Gardner does not write, of course, from any acknowledged religious perspective, but rather from a viewpoint of "ethical" heteronomy; John Killinger, *The Fail-*

ure of Theology in Modern Literature (New York: Abingdon Press, 1963); Martin Jarrett-Kerr, *Studies in Literature and Belief* (London: Rockliff, 1954); Randall Stewart, *American Literature and Christian Doctrine* (Baton Rouge: Louisiana State Univ. Press, 1958); and Sallie McFague TeSelle, *Literature and the Christian Life* (New Haven: Yale Univ. Press, 1966).

2. Paul Tillich, *The Protestant Era* (Chicago: Univ. of Chicago Press, 1957), 55–65. See also Nathan A. Scott, Jr., *Modern Literature and the Religious Frontier* (New York: Harper, 1958); *Rehearsals of Discomposure: Alienation and Reconciliation in Modern Literature* (New York: Kings Crown Press, 1952); *Three American Moralists: Mailer, Bellow, Trilling* (Notre Dame: Univ. of Notre Dame Press, 1973); and Amos N. Wilder, *The New Voice: Religion, Literature, Hermeneutics* (New York: Herder and Herder, 1969); *Theology and Modern Literature* (Cambridge: Harvard Univ. Press, 1958)—in *The New Voice* Wilder modifies the theonomous assumptions of his earlier criticism and moves closer toward that variation on autonomy that perceives language, rather than faith, as the ground of the relationship between literature and religion.

3. R.W.B. Lewis, *Trials of the Word: Essays in American Literature and the Humanistic Tradition* (New Haven: Yale Univ. Press, 1956), 97–111. See also Robert Detweiler, *Story, Sign, and Self: Phenomenology and Structuralism as Literary-Critical Methods* (Philadelphia: Fortress Press, 1978); R.W.B. Lewis, *The American Adam: Innocence, Tragedy, and Tradition in the Nineteenth Century* (Chicago: Univ. of Chicago Press, 1955); *The Picaresque Saint: Representative Figures in Contemporary Fiction* (Philadelphia: Lippincott, 1959); and William F. Lynch, *Christ and Apollo* (New York: Sheed and Ward, 1960); *Christ and Prometheus: A New Image of the Secular* (Notre Dame: Univ. of Notre Dame Press, 1970).

4. Paul Schrader, *Transcendental Style in Film: Ozu, Bresson, Dreyer* (Berkeley: Univ. of California Press, 1972).

5. The biographical assumption, a fallacy of heteronomous interpretation, tends toward a facile equation of the artist's background—training, religious affiliation, theoretical persuasion—and artistic achievement. In this instance, one would assume that Schrader's celebration of transcendental cinema would shape his artistic creation. *Taxi Driver* and the more re-

cent films that Schrader has written and directed (*Blue Collar* and *Hardcore*) are anything but transcendental.

6. Charles Moeller, "Religion and Literature: An Essay on Ways of Reading," in *Mansions of the Spirit: Essays in Literature and Religion,* ed. George A. Panichas (New York: Hawthorn Books, 1967), 59–73.

7. Ernest Ferlita and John R. May, *The Parables of Lina Wertmüller* (New York: Paulist Press, 1977).

8. Huston Smith, *The Religions of Man* (New York: Harper and Row, 1958), 133.

9. John Dominic Crossan, *The Dark Interval: Towards a Theology of Story* (Niles, Ill.: Argus Communications, 1975), 53.

10. Ibid., 57.

11. Sheldon Sacks, *Fiction and the Shape of Belief* (Berkeley: Univ. of California Press, 1966), 7, 24–26.

12. For fuller treatment, see my *The Pruning Word: The Parables of Flannery O'Connor* (Notre Dame: Univ. of Notre Dame Press, 1976), Ch. 1, "The New Hermeneutic and the Parables of Jesus."

13. Herbert W. Richardson, "Three Myths of Transcendence" in *Transcendence,* ed. Herbert W. Richardson and Donald R. Cutler (Boston: Beacon Press, 1969), 98–113.

14. D.H. Lawrence, *Studies in Classical American Literature* (New York: Thomas Seltzer, 1923), 92.

THE ANALOGY OF ACTION IN FILM

1. The film that Wertmüller was working on at the time was *The End of the World in Our Usual Beds on a Night Full of Rain.* In one of the early sequences of that film, Giancarlo Giannini maneuvers Candice Bergen into the confessional booth of a baroque monastery, where he "confesses" his love for her. No doubt this is the scene Wertmüller had in mind when she asked me for the formula of "The Act of Contrition" (and in a later phone call, for that of "The Act of Love"). But she never used either as such.

2. Jan Kott, *Shakespeare Our Contemporary* (Garden City, N.Y.: Doubleday, 1966). Kott reduces *King Lear,* in effect, to Beckett's *Endgame.* Hamm in *Endgame* erases the mystery of the universe in a single breath when he says of God: "The bastard. He doesn't exist." But nowhere does Lear say that the

gods do not exist, that everything is absurd. For a fuller treatment of *King Lear,* see my *The Theatre of Pilgrimage* (New York: Sheed & Ward, 1971), 13–33.

3. Francis Fergusson, *Dante's Drama of the Mind* (Princeton: Princeton Univ. Press, 1953), 92.

4. William F. Lynch, *Christ and Apollo* (Notre Dame: Univ. of Notre Dame Press, 1975), 154.

5. Francis Fergusson, *The Idea of a Theater* (Princeton: Princeton Univ. Press, 1949), 113.

6. Ibid., 115.

7. William Shakespeare, *Hamlet,* with a psychoanalytic study by Ernest Jones (New York: Funk and Wagnalls, 1948).

8. See the chapter on *Wild Strawberries* in Ernest Ferlita and John R. May, *Film Odyssey: The Art of Film as Search for Meaning* (New York: Paulist Press, 1976), 48–54.

9. Ingmar Bergman, *Four Screenplays,* trans. Lars Malmstrom and David Kushner (New York: Simon and Schuster, 1960), 227. All subsequent page references, placed in parentheses after each quotation, are to this edition.

10. *The Screenplays of Lina Wertmüller,* trans. Steven Wagner (New York: Quadrangle/New York Times Book Co., 1977), 289. All subsequent references are to this edition.

11. Ernest Ferlita and John R. May, *The Parables of Lina Wertmüller* (New York: Paulist Press, 1977), 66–67.

12. Ibid., 80.

13. Ibid., 62–63.

14. Lynch, *Christ and Apollo,* 12. The dynamic relationship of descent and ascent forms the core of Lynch's brilliant study.

15. Lynch, *Christ and Apollo,* 181.

16. Quoted in *The Films of Robert Bresson,* ed. Ian Cameron (New York: Praeger, 1969), 96.

17. "Bergman in Exile," *New York Times,* 17 Oct. 1976, Sec. 2, 15.

18. Ferlita and May, *Parables,* 83–84.

19. Ibid., 85.

PART II

CINEMATIC TRANSFIGURATIONS OF JESUS

1. Theodore Ziolkowski, *Fictional Transfigurations of*

Jesus, Ch. 2, "The De-Christianizing of Jesus" (Princeton: Princeton Univ. Press, 1972), 30–54.

2. Robert Detweiler, "Christ and the Christ Figure in American Fiction," in *New Theology No. 2,* ed. Martin E. Marty and Dean G. Peerman (New York: Macmillan, 1965), 200.

3. Northrop Frye, *Anatomy of Criticism* (New York: Atheneum, 1968), 33–34.

THE DEMONIC IN AMERICAN CINEMA

1. Andrew M. Greeley, "Why Hollywood Never Asks the God Question," *New York Times,* 18 Jan. 1976, Sec. 2, p. 13.

2. John R. Frederick, *The Darkened Sky: Nineteenth Century American Novelists and Religion* (Notre Dame: Univ. of Notre Dame Press, 1969); Frederick J. Hoffman, *The Mortal No: Death and the Modern Imagination* (Princeton: Princeton Univ. Press, 1964); Harry Levin, *The Power of Blackness* (New York: Vintage Books, 1960); R.W.B. Lewis, "Days of Wrath and Laughter," in *Trials of the Word* (New Haven: Yale Univ. Press, 1965), 184–235; John McCormick, *Catastrophe and Imagination* (New York: Longmans, Green, 1959); John R. May, *Toward a New Earth: Apocalypse in the American Novel* (Notre Dame: Univ. of Notre Dame Press, 1972); Perry Miller, *Errand into the Wilderness* (New York: Harper and Row, 1964); Walker Percy, "Notes for a Novel about the End of the World," *Katallagete* 3 (Fall 1970), 5–12.

3. The term *figural,* from the Latin *figura,* is normally understood as referring to an established connection between a person or event within history that prefigures or mirrors another person or event, within or outside history, but in such a way that the first signifies both itself and the second while the second fulfills the first as in "Jonah is a *figura* of Christ" or "The Eucharist is a *figura* of the Kingdom as eternal banquet." Although figuralism in a Christian context developed out of a traditional eschatological model of earth and heaven, I feel that it may be broadened to accommodate less specific images of promise and fulfillment; thus figuralism is used here to include the prefiguration of ultimate revelation (however it may be made) of whatever endures as "mystery" in human existence.

4. See Nathan A. Scott, Jr., *The Wild Prayer of Longing: Poetry and the Sacred* (New Haven: Yale Univ. Press, 1971),

25. Scott calls ours "a world, indeed, which being independent of any *other* worldly plan or scheme of meaning, has ceased to be a *figura* of anything extrinsic to itself and is sealed off against any transcendental ingress from without."

5. John R. May, "American Literary Variations on the Demonic," in *Disguises of the Demonic: Contemporary Perspectives on the Power of Evil,* ed. Alan M. Olson (New York: Association Press, 1975), 31–47.

6. Anon., "Background Material on *The Exorcist*" (Burbank, Calif.: Warner Bros., 1973), 2.

7. Pauline Kael, "Back to the Oiuja Board," *New Yorker,* 7 Jan. 1974, p. 59.

8. Vincent Canby, "The Exorcist," *New York Times,* 27 Dec. 1973, Sec. 2, p. 1.

9. Harvey Cox, "Can We Live Together?" *National Catholic Reporter,* 29 Oct. 1969, p. 4.

10. According to Peter Fonda, "easy rider" is a Southern expression "for a whore's old man, not a pimp, but the dude who lives with a chick. Because he's got the easy ride. Well, that's what's happened to America, man. Liberty's become a whore, and we're all taking an easy ride." Elizabeth Campbell, "Rolling Stone Raps with Peter Fonda," in *Easy Rider,* ed. Nancy Hardin and Marilyn Schlossberg (New York: New American Library, 1969), 28.

11. Tom Wicker, "A Cascade of Greed, Cruelty, Hysteria," *New York Times,* 15 June 1975, Sec. 2, pp. 1, 15.

CINEMA, RELIGION, AND POPULAR CULTURE

1. My understanding of technological civilization has been deeply influenced by J. Ellul, *Technological Society* (New York: Vintage Books, 1964). See also the penetrating essay "The Work of Art in the Age of Mechanical Reproduction," in Walter Benjamin, *Illuminations* (New York: Harcourt, Brace, 1968).

2. Mircea Eliade, *The Forge and the Crucible: The Origins and Structures of Alchemy* (New York: Harper and Row, 1971), 172. See also "The Ontology of the Photographic Image," in André Bazin, *What is Cinema?* I, trans. Hugh Gray (Berkeley: Univ. of California Press, 1967) for its suggestive comments on the link between the arts and the quest for immortality.

3. Herbert Read, *Icon and Idea: The Function of Art in the Development of Human Consciousness* (New York: Schocken Books, 1965), 3.

4. Clyde Kluckhohn, "The Concept of Culture," in *Readings in Sociology,* ed. E.A. Schuler et al. (New York: Crowell, 1967), 77.

5. Quoted in Richard Schickel, "Good Ole Burt; Cool-eyed Clint," *Time,* 9 Jan. 1978, p. 48.

FILM AND THE QUEST FOR MEANING

1. Plato, *The Republic,* trans. Charles M. Bakewell (New York: Scribner's, 1928), 404–5.

2. *The Orestes Plays of Aeschylus,* trans. Paul Roche (New York: New American Library, 1962), App. IV, 218. Roche's translation of the definition is the best I know of: "Tragedy, then, is an imitation of an action that is serious, complete, and of a certain magnitude; in language embellished with every kind of artistic ornament, the several kinds being found in separate parts of the play; in the form of action, not of narrative; through pity and fear effecting the proper purgation of these and similar emotions." The definition appears in the sixth chapter of Aristotle's *Poetics.*

3. Adapted from the original script, as quoted in Gilbert Salachas, *Federico Fellini,* trans. Rosalie Siegel (New York: Crown, 1969), 127–29.

4. See Ernest Ferlita and John R. May, *Film Odyssey: The Art of Film as Search for Meaning* (New York: Paulist Press, 1976), for analyses of twenty-one films exploring the metaphor of the road as the visual component of spiritual quest.

5. Viktor E. Frankl, *Man's Search for Meaning: An Introduction to Logotherapy,* trans. Ilse Lasch (New York: Washington Square Press, 1963), xiii.

6. Ibid., 172.

7. Ibid., 176.

8. Ibid., 179.

9. Neil P. Hurley, *Theology Through Film* (New York: Harper, 1970), 128.

10. William F. Lynch, *Images of Hope* (New York: New American Library, 1966), 40.

11. Joseph Pieper, *Hope and History* (New York: Herder &

Herder, 1969), 25; Gabriel Marcel, *Homo Viator* (New York: Harper, 1962), 32.

12. Pieper, *Hope and History,* 26.

13. Frankl, *Man's Search for Meaning,* 63–64.

14. Erich Fromm, *You Shall Be as Gods* (Greenwich, Conn.: Fawcett, 1969), 163.

15. Robert Johann, *Building the Human* (New York: Herder & Herder, 1968), 83.

16. As paraphrased in Ruben A. Alves, *A Theology of Human Hope* (Washington: Corpus Books, 1969), 22.

17. Frankl, *Man's Search for Meaning,* 187.

18. Sam Keen, "Hope in a Posthuman Era," in *New Theology No. 5,* ed. Martin E. Marty and Dean G. Peerman (New York: Macmillan, 1968), 86–87.

19. Lynch, *Images of Hope,* 98.

20. Evidently dissatisfied with Russell's directing of his script, Chayefsky removed his name from the credits and used instead his actual given name, Sidney Aaron.

21. Paddy Chayefsky, *The Tenth Man,* in *Four Contemporary American Plays,* ed. Bennett Cerf (New York: Random House, 1961), 98.

22. Ibid., 100.

23. *Mircea Eliade, Images and Symbols: Studies in Religious Symbolism* (New York: Sheed & Ward, 1961), 11, 17.

PART III

ROBERT ALTMAN

1. There are some notable exceptions: the parody of the Last Supper in *M*A*S*H,* probably cribbed from Buñuel's *Viridiana*; Trapper John and Hawkeye photographed through the flames of a heating pot as they watch Frank Burns being taken away in a straitjacket; a man with a cross on his back climbing the steeple to put the cross in place, at the beginning of *McCabe and Mrs. Miller*; the zoom lens close-up of the dead Sitting Bull, cross prominently displayed, in *Buffalo Bill and the Indians.*

2. "Living in the Present," in *Celebration in Postwar American Fiction,* ed. Richard H. Rupp (Coral Gables, Fla.: Univ. of Miami Press, 1970), 18.

3. Marsha Kinder, "The Art of Dreaming in *Three Women* and *Providence*: Structures of the Self," *Film Quarterly* 31, No. 1 (1977), 14. See Krin Gabbard, "Altman's *Three Women*: Sanctuary in the Dream World," *Literature/Film Quarterly* 8 (1980), 258–64.

4. Doran William Cannon, "Shooting Script," in *On Making a Movie: "Brewster McCloud,"* by C. Kirk McClelland (New York: New American Library, 1971), 213. This fascinating book contains the original screenplay, the shooting script, and a detailed account of the making of the film.

INGMAR BERGMAN

1. Paul Tillich, *Dynamics of Faith* (New York: Harper, 1958), 16.

2. Ingmar Bergman, *Four Screenplays,* trans. Lars Malmstrom and David Kushner (New York: Simon and Schuster, 1960), 150.

3. Paul Tillich, *The Courage To Be* (New Haven: Yale Univ. Press, 1963), 190.

4. Paul Ricouer, "Religion, Atheism and Faith," in *The Religious Significance of Atheism,* ed. Paul Ricouer and Alasdair McIntyre (New York: Columbia Univ. Press, 1969), 98.

LUIS BUÑUEL

1. Both quotations are from Penelope Gilliatt, "Profiles (Luis Buñuel)," *New Yorker,* 5 Dec. 1977, p. 54. As the *New Yorker* has it, the aphorism reads: "I'm not an atheist, thank God." Clearly, it should read: "I'm still an atheist, thank God." Elsewhere, misled by the aphorism, I have referred to Buñuel as an "avowed atheist"; I now stand corrected.

2. Peter P. Schillaci, "Luis Buñuel and the Death of God," In *Three European Directors,* ed. James M. Wall (Grand Rapids, Mich.: William B. Eerdmans, 1973), 119.

3. Gilliatt, "Profiles," 63.

4. Ibid., 57.

5. Schillaci, "Luis Buñuel," 128.

6. Quoted in Jean-André Fieschi, "Luis Buñuel," in *Cinema: A Critical Dictionary, The Major Film-makers,* I, ed. Richard Roud (New York: Viking Press, 1980), 173.

7. Pauline Kael mentions all four versions in her review of *That Obscure Object of Desire* in *New Yorker,* 19 Dec. 1977, pp. 128–29. The titles of the first two are the same as the source novel, one in English, the other in French: *The Woman and the Puppet* (1920), starring Geraldine Farrar; *La Femme et le Pantin* (1929), starring Conchita Montenegro.

CHARLES CHAPLIN

1. E.g., Maurice Pontet writes: "Dans l'errance eternelle de Charlot, a n'en pas douter il y a la composante juive" ("La Signification Humaine de l'Oeuvre de Charlie Chaplin," *Etudes,* Sept. 1954, p. 254). And Jean d'Yvoire: "Le parallele n'est-il pas saissant entre le sort du heros de 'Le Ruée vers l'Or,' et celui du Juif déraciné, errant au milieu des nations qui le méprisent et le rejettent?" ("La Ruée vers l'Or," *Téléciné,* June 1956, p. 5).

2. Roger Manvell, *The Film and the Public* (Hammondsworth, England: Pelican, 1955), 169.

3. James Joyce, *A Portrait of the Artist as a Young Man* (New York: Viking, 1956), 247.

4. Chaplin fought poverty in *City Lights,* greed in *The Gold Rush,* depersonalizing industrialization in *Modern Times,* totalitarianism in *The Great Dictator,* and democratic evils in *A King in New York.*

5. Neil Hurley, *The Reel Revolution: A Film Primer of Liberation,* Ch. 6, "The Liberation Philosophy of Chaplin" (Maryknoll, N.Y.: Orbis Books, 1978), 93–106.

6. Manvell, *The Film and the Public,* 165.

7. Charles Chaplin, *My Autobiography* (New York: Simon and Schuster, 1964), 22–23.

FRANCIS COPPOLA

1. Roger Ebert, "Critic Kael 'Pro-Catholic,'" *Times-Picayune* (New Orleans), 27 April 1975, Section 2, p. 4.

2. See Giles Gunn, "Threading the Eye of the Needle: The Place of the Literary Critic in Religious Studies," *Journal of the American Academy of Religion* 43 (1975), 164–84.

3. Coppola's achievement as a screenwriter extends well beyond the films he has directed and includes co-authorship of *Patton* (1970, Franklin Schaffner), *This Property Is Con-*

demned (1966, Sydney Pollack), and *Is Paris Burning?* (1965, René Clément).

4. William F. Lynch, *Images of Faith: An Exploration of the Ironic Imagination* (Notre Dame: Univ. of Notre Dame Press, 1973), 83.

5. Robert K. Johnson, *Francis Ford Coppola* (Boston: Twayne, 1977), 27.

6. Michael Pye and Lynda Myles, *The Movie Brats: How the Film Generation Took Over Hollywood* (New York: Holt, Rinehart, 1979), 71.

7. Johnson, *Francis Ford Coppola,* 147.

8. It is actually closer to its literary roots than most critics have seemed willing to admit, and an ideal instance of cinematic "adaptation" of literary material. It follows the narrative structure of Conrad's *Heart of Darkness,* if not the literal narrative, but transposes the setting to the present of the Vietnam war and broadens the domain of darkness to suit the tenor of the times. Most significantly, *Apocalypse Now* seems true to the spirit of Conrad, though not to the complex distancing of his narrative device.

9. John Tessitore, "The Literary Roots of *Apocalypse Now,*" *New York Times,* 21 Oct. 1979, Sec. 2, p. 13.

10. Sir James George Frazer, *The Golden Bough: A Study in Magic and Religion,* 1 vol. abr. ed. (New York: Macmillan, 1956), 309; for the full analysis of "The Killing of the Divine King," see pp. 308–30.

FEDERICO FELLINI

1. Andrew Sarris, ed., *Interviews with Film Directors* (New York: Avon Books, 1967), 182–83. In *Film Odyssey: The Art of Film as Search for Meaning* (Paulist Press, 1976), Ernest Ferlita and I treat three of Fellini's films in detail—*La Strada, Fellini Satyricon,* and *La Dolce Vita*—from precisely this perspective. The analyses explore Fellini's use of the image of the road as the visual basis for his preoccupation with quest, in its personal, social, and religious dimensions

CLAUDE JUTRA

1. Pierre Véronneau, "The First Wave of Quebec Feature Films: 1944–1953," in *Self-Portrait: Essays on the Canadian*

and Quebec Cinemas, ed. Pierre Véronneau and Piers Handling (Ottawa: Canadian Film Institute, 1980), 59. In the same collection of essays, see also the "Church and Religiosity" (pp. 162–65), a section of Michel Houle's essay, "Some Ideological and Thematic Aspects of the Quebec Cinema."

2. Ibid., 62–63.

3. Martin Knelman, *This Is Where We Came In: The Career and Character of Canadian Film* (Toronto: McClelland and Stewart, 1977), 60.

4. John Hofsess, *Inner Views: Ten Canadian Film-Makers* (Toronto: McGraw-Hill Ryerson, 1975), 42.

5. Michel Houle, "Some Ideological and Thematic Aspects of Quebec Cinema," in *Self Portrait,* pp. 163–64.

6. Hofsess, *Inner Views,* 45, 47.

7. See, for example, Knelman, *This Is Where We Came In,* 47–48. He notes that "the movie is set just before 'the French-Canadian fact' surfaced as the crucial issue in this country's future. Going back into that era shows why Quebec was ready for the so-called Quiet Revolution when the feudal rule of Maurice Duplessis ended in 1959, and impatient reformers tried to sweep away two centuries of church domination and state paternalism." But he concludes, "For a movie that touches so many political nerves, *Mon Oncle Antoine* is surprisingly, perhaps deceptively, delicate and old-fashioned. The movie doesn't make a big political statement about anything." However, in his article "Claude Jutra's 'Mon Oncle Antoine,'" in *Canadian Film Reader,* ed. Seth Feldman and Joyce Nelson (Toronto: Peter Martin, 1977), 194–99, Bruce Elder discusses at length the political importance of the film.

STANLEY KUBRICK

1. See C.G. Jung, "Concerning Rebirth," in *The Archetypes and the Collective Unconscious,* trans. R.F.C. Hill, Vol. IX of *The Collected Works of C.G. Jung* (Princeton: Princeton Univ. Press, 1969), 113–47.

2. See Gene D. Phillips, *Stanley Kubrick: A Film Odyssey* (New York: Popular Library, 1975), 76.

3. Nabokov received sole credit for the screenplay, but his published version (*Lolita: A Screenplay,* New York: McGraw-Hill, 1974) differs greatly from the released film.

4. See M.-L. von Franz, "The Process of Individuation," in

Man and His Symbols, ed. C.G. Jung (New York: Doubleday, 1964), 179.

5. Speculations abound. See Carolyn Geduld, *Filmguide to "2001: A Space Odyssey"* (Bloomington: Indiana Univ. Press, 1973), 68–70; Jerome Agel, ed., *The Making of Kubrick's "2001"* (New York: New American Library, 1970), 354–56.

6. Agel, *The Making of "2001,"* 330.

7. The version of the novel published in England contains an additional chapter not present in the American version. Alex is now twenty-six and comfortably settled into a dull routine. Apparently, Kubrick was not aware of the chapter when he made his film.

8. von Franz, "Process of Individuation," 171.

SAM PECKINPAH

1. René Wellek and Austin Warren, *Theory of Literature,* 3d ed. (New York: Harcourt, Brace, 1956), 191.

2. "*Playboy* Interview: Sam Peckinpah," *Playboy,* Aug. 1972, p. 70. Peckinpah is here talking about prisoners, but he goes on to apply the same idea to *The Wild Bunch.*

3. M.I. Finley, *The World of Odysseus* (New York: World, 1963), 20.

4. See Philip Young, "The Hero and the Code," *Ernest Hemingway: A Reconsideration* (University Park: Pennsylvania State Univ. Press, 1966), 56–78.

5. See Louis Garner Simmons, "The Cinema of Sam Peckinpah and the American Western, " Diss. Northwestern, 1975, 103.

6. Pauline Kael, *When the Lights Go Down* (New York: Holt, Rinehart, 1980), 116.

KEN RUSSELL

1. Never in film history has the industry so unanimously outlawed one man. Although the causality is by no means clear, the principal film reviews also either damn or ignore most of Russell's work. American critics have been particularly harsh. *Savage Messiah,* for example, is considered "filled with cliches" (Judith Crist in *Film Facts*), "a caricature" (Robert Hughes in *Time*), or nothing but "camp fantasies" (Pauline Kael in *The New Yorker*). In *New York Times,* 19 Oct. 1975,

Peter G. Davis described *Lisztomania* as "unrestrained vulgarity," ignoring the fact that Russell was doing precisely that—examining Liszt's vulgarity; in the same fashion, Richard Eder in the *Times,* 5 April 1976, missed the precise point of *Mahler* by calling it "campy games." But the outlaw has kept his freedom and his temper better than his critics have. Russell's productivity is, accordingly, both a prodigy of cunning and a rebuke to those who sell out.

2. John Baxter, *An Appalling Talent: Ken Russell* (London: Michael Joseph, 1973), 153. The subsequent quotations are all from Baxter, with his warm permission, and are noted in the text.

3. Ibid., 190. See Nureyev's remarks in Alexander Bland, *The Nureyev Valentino* (Toronto: Macmillan, 1977), 34–35.

FRANÇOIS TRUFFAUT

1. André Bazin, *What Is Cinema?*, I, trans. Hugh Gray (Berkeley: Univ. of California Press, 1967), 15.

2. François Truffaut, "A Certain Tendency in French Cinema," in *Movies and Methods: An Anthology,* ed. Bill Nichols (New York: Oxford Univ. Press, 1976), 224–37.

3. See Amédée Ayfre, *Dieu au cinema: Problèmes esthetiques du film religieux* (Paris: Presses universitaires de France, 1953); the chapter on phenomenological film criticism in J. Dudley Andrew, *The Major Film Theories: An Introduction* (New York: Oxford Univ. Press, 1976); and Michael Bird, "Film as Hierophany," in this volume.

4. James Monaco, *The New Wave: Truffaut, Godard, Chabrol, Rohmer, Rivette* (New York: Oxford Univ. Press, 1976), 34–36.

5. Ibid., 29.

LINA WERTMÜLLER

1. Ernest Ferlita and John R. May, *The Parables of Lina Wertmüller* (New York: Paulist Press, 1977), 78–79.

2. Paulo Freire, *Pedagogy of the Oppressed,* trans. Myra B. Ramos (New York: Seabury Press, 1970), 32–33.

A General Bibliography

BOOKS

Andrew, J. Dudley. *The Major Film Theories*. New York: Oxford Univ. Press, 1976.

Bazin, André. *What is Cinema?* 2 vols. Trans. Hugh Gray. Berkeley: Univ. of California Press, 1970.

Braudy, Leo, and Morris Dickstein, eds. *Great Film Directors: A Critical Anthology*. New York: Oxford Univ. Press, 1978.

Cameron, Ian. *The Films of Robert Bresson*. New York: Praeger, 1969.

Cooper, John, and Carl Skrade, eds. *Celluloid and Symbols*. Philadelphia: Fortress Press, 1970.

Durgnat, Raymond. *Eros in the Cinema*. London: Calder and Boyers, 1966.

Ferlita, Ernest, and John R. May. *Film Odyssey: The Art of Film as Search for Meaning*. New York: Paulist Press, 1976.

Getlein, Frank, and Harold C. Gardiner. *Movies, Morals and Art*. New York: Sheed and Ward, 1961.

Hurley, Neil P. *Toward a Film Humanism* (originally *Theology Through Film*, New York: Harper and Row, 1970). Rpt. New York: Dell, 1975.

Jones, G. William. *Sunday Night at the Movies*. Richmond: John Knox, 1967.

Kahle, Roger, and Robert E. Lee. *Popcorn and Parables: A New Look at the Movies*. Minneapolis: Augsburg, 1971.

Kracauer, Siegfried. *Theory of Film*. New York: Oxford Univ. Press, 1960.

Lynch, William F. *The Image Industries*. New York: Sheed and Ward, 1959.

Mellen, Joan. *Women and Their Sexuality in the New Film*. New York: Dell, 1975.

Metz, Christian. *Film Language: A Semiotics of the Cinema*. New York: Oxford Univ. Press, 1974.

Nelson, John Wiley. *Your God Is Alive and Well and Appearing in Popular Culture*. Philadelphia: Westminster Press, 1976.

Paschall, Jeremy, and Clyde Jeavons. *A Pictorial History of Sex in the Movies.* London: Hamlyn, 1975.

Rhode, Eric. *Tower of Babel: Speculations on the Cinema.* Philadelphia: Chilton, 1966.

Richardson, Herbert W. *Toward an American Theology.* New York: Harper and Row, 1967. (See Ch. 3, "The Myth Is the Message," pp. 50–70.)

Samuels, Charles T. *Encountering Directors.* New York: Putnam, 1972.

Sarris, Andrew. *The Confession of a Cultist, 1955–69.* New York: Simon and Schuster, 1970.

Schillaci, Anthony. *Movies and Morals.* Notre Dame: Fides, 1970.

Schrader, Paul. *Transcendental Style in Film.* Berkeley: Univ. of California Press, 1972.

Taylor, John Russell, ed. *Graham Greene on Film.* New York: Simon and Schuster, 1972.

Tyler, Parker. *Magic and Myth in the Movies.* New York: Simon and Schuster, 1970.

Walker, Alexander. *Sex in the Movies.* Baltimore: Penguin, 1969.

Wall, James M. *Church and Cinema: A Way of Viewing Film.* Grand Rapids: Eerdmans, 1971.

Wall, James M., ed. *Three European Directors.* Grand Rapids: Eerdmans, 1973.

ARTICLES

Bazin, André. "*Le Journal d'un Curé de Campagne* and the Stylistics of Robert Bresson." In *What Is Cinema?* Vol. I. Berkeley: Univ. of California Press, 1970, 125–43.

Giles, Dennis. "The Tao in *Woman in the Dunes.*" In *Renaissance of the Film.* Ed. Julius Bellone. Toronto: Macmillan, 1970, 340–48.

Greeley, Andrew M. "When Religion Cast Off Wonder Hollywood Seized It." *New York Times,* 27 Nov. 1977, Sec. 2, pp. 1, 11.

______. "Why Hollywood Never Asks the God Question." *The New York Times,* 18 Jan. 1976, Sec. 2, pp. 1, 13.

Guardini, Romano. "Thoughts on the Problem of the Film." *Cross Currents* 6 (Summer 1956), 189–99.

Ludmann, Rene. "The Cinema as a Means of Evangelization." *Cross Currents* 8 (Spring 1958), 153–71.

May, John R. "American Cinema and the 'God Question.'" *Horizons* 3 (1976), 247–50.

______. "Cinema and Morality." *Horizons* 2 (1975), 91–93.

______. "Con Men and a Conned Society: Religion in Contemporary American Cinema." *Horizons* 4 (1977), 15–26.

Richardson, Herbert W. "Three Myths of Transcendence." In *Transcendence,* ed. Herbert W. Richardson and Donald R. Cutler. Boston: Beacon Press, 1969, 98–113.

Robinson, David. "Thank God I Am Still an Atheist: Luis Buñuel and *Viridiana.*" *Sight and Sound* 32 (Summer 1962), 116–18, 155.

Schillaci, Peter. "Who Will We Get to Play God?" *New Catholic World* 215 (May–June, 1972), 122–28.

______. "Cinematic Sacraments of Our Times." *New Catholic World* 217 (May–June 1974), 114–20.

Sontag, Susan. "Spiritual Style in the Films of Robert Bresson." In *Against Interpretation.* New York: Farrar, Straus, 1966, 177–95.

Wolf, Leonard. "In Horror Movies, Some Things are Sacred." *New York Times,* 4 April 1976, sec. 2, p. 1.

Young, Vernon. "The Moral Cinema." *Film Quarterly* 15 (Fall 1961), 14–22.

Contributors

Michael Bird, a native of Belle Plaine, Iowa, is associate professor of Religious Studies at Renison College, University of Waterloo. His teaching and research interests lie in the area of religion, film, and art. He has written about religious motivations and interpretations of folk art, primitive art, and vernacular art. He is the author of *Ontario Fraktur,* a study of Mennonite calligraphy and decorated texts in nineteenth-century Canada, published in 1977 by M.F. Feheley of Toronto; as well as *A Splendid Harvest: Germanic Folk and Decorative Arts in Canada* (Van Nostrand Reinhold, 1981).

M. Darrol Bryant studied at Harvard Divinity School (S.T.B.) and the Institute of Christian Thought at St. Michael's College, Toronto (M.A., Ph.D.) and is currently associate professor of Religion and Culture at Renison College, University of Waterloo, Waterloo, Ontario. He contributed essays on "America as God's Kingdom" to *Religion and Political Society* and "Faith and History in Grant's Lament" to *George Grant in Process.* His forthcoming study of Jonathan Edwards is entitled *Edwards on God's Kingdom.* He and Michael Bird collaborate on courses in religion and film at Renison College.

Ernest Ferlita, s.j., had his first full-length play, *The Ballad of John Ogilvie,* produced Off-Broadway in 1968 while he was still studying playwriting at the Yale School of Drama. His *Black Medea* was the only American play featured at the first Spoleto Festival USA in 1977; in 1978, it was given a showcase production at the New Federal Theatre in New York. That same year he won first prize in the Christian Theatre Artists Guild's playwriting competition with the *The Mask of Hiroshima,* for which Kevin Waters, S.J., wrote the music. He is the author of *The Theatre of Pilgrimage* and with John R.

May of *Film Odyssey* and *The Parables of Lina Wertmüller.* Father Ferlita is currently chairman of the Department of Drama and Speech at Loyola University in New Orleans.

NEIL P. HURLEY, S.J., has a Ph.D. in Political Science from Fordham University. For twelve years he was an associate of the Jesuit Social Action Center in Chile and professor from time to time at both the Catholic University of Santiago and the National University of Chile. Father Hurley has taught at Notre Dame University, Loyola University (New Orleans), Woodstock Theological Seminary, Florida State University, and Fordham University. He has written over ninety articles on a wide range of subjects, including film, and is the author of *Toward a Film Humanism, Comunicaciones: Teoría e Estrategía* (Universidad de Chile), and *The Reel Revolution: A Film Primer of Liberation.* In addition to preparing a critical study of the films of Frank Capra and Alfred Hitchcock, Father Hurley is currently a member of the Board of Directors of the International Center for Integrative Studies and director of the media institute INSCAPE.

JOHN R. MAY has a doctorate in Theology and Literature from Emory University's Graduate Institute of Liberal Arts. Presently professor of English at Louisiana State University, he is the author of *Toward a New Earth: Apocalypse in the American Novel* and *The Pruning Word: The Parables of Flannery O'Connor,* both published by the University of Notre Dame Press. He has co-authored two books on film and edited a collection of original essays on religion and culture, entitled *The Bent World.* Dr. May was associate editor of *Horizons* and convener of the Religion and Culture Working Session of the College Theology Society from 1976 to 1980.

WILLIAM PARRILL, professor of English at Southeastern Louisiana University, received his Ph.D. from the University of Tennessee in the literature of the English Renaissance. He has published hundreds of reviews of books and films and is the author of *Heroes' Twilight: The Films of Sam Peckinpah.*

TIMOTHY L. SUTTOR, who completed his doctorate at the Australian National University in 1960, is professor of theology and religious studies at the University of Windsor in Ontario. He is the author of *Hierarchy and Democracy in Australia* (Melbourne Univ. Press, 1965), has written numerous articles for major scholarly journals, and is past president of both the Canadian Catholic Historical Association and the Canadian Society of Church History. Dr. Suttor has worked for Australian and Canadian television and organized film festivals on Bergman and Antonioni.

BART TESTA teaches cinema studies at Innis College, University of Toronto. He has taught religion and film at the University of Toronto, the Toronto School of Theology, Laurentian University (Sudbury, Ontario), and the University of Montana. His writing on religion and film has appeared in *New Religions and Mental Health* (New York: Edwin Mellen Press, 1980) as well as several Canadian and American journals.

PAUL TIESSEN, currently associate professor of English at Wilfrid Laurier University, Waterloo, Ontario, received his Ph.D. from the University of Alberta in Edmonton, concentrating on the influence of film on the imagination, style, and technique of a number of twentieth-century novelists. He has contributed essays on literature and film to various journals, including *Canadian Literature* and *Literature/Film Quarterly*. Dr. Tiessen is editor of the *Malcolm Lowry Newsletter* and was guest editor of the special issue on drama and film of *Canadian Drama/L'Art dramatique canadien.*

Index

Religion in Film has been composed into type on a Compugraphic phototypesetter in ten point Times Roman with two points of spacing between the lines. Times Roman Italic was selected for display. The book was designed by Frank O. Williams, composed by Metricomp, Inc., printed offset by Thomson-Shore, Inc., and bound by John H. Dekker & Sons. The paper on which the book is printed bears the watermark of S.D. Warren and is designed for an effective life of at least three hundred years.

THE UNIVERSITY OF TENNESSEE PRESS : KNOXVILLE